Bachelor Nation

Bachelor Nation

INSIDE THE WORLD

of

AMERICA'S

GUILTY PLEASURE

Amy Kaufman

DUTTON

DUTTON

An imprint of Penguin Random House LLC
375 Hudson Street
New York, New York 10014

Sections of chapter 6, "Inside the Bubble," were previously published in the *Los Angeles Times* as "Alcohol, Sex and Consent: Add TV Cameras and the 'Bachelor in Paradise' Party Gets Complicated," June 30, 2017.

DUTTON and the D colophon are registered a trademarks of
Penguin Random House LLC.

LIBRARY OF CONGRESS CATALOGING-IN-PUBLICATION DATA
has been applied for.

ISBN 9781101985908

Printed in the United States of America
1   3   5   7   9   10   8   6   4   2

Set in Minion Pro
Designed by Cassandra Garruzzo

While the author has made every effort to provide accurate telephone numbers, Internet addresses, and other contact information at the time of publication, neither the publisher nor the author assumes any responsibility for errors or for changes that occur after publication. Further, the publisher does not have any control over and does not assume any responsibility for author or third-party websites or their content.

For whomever gets my final rose

Contents

Introduction   1

CHAPTER 1 A Budding Idea   15

Why I'm a Fan: Amy Schumer   33

CHAPTER 2 The Reality of Creating the Fantasy   35

Why I'm a Fan: Allison Williams   53

CHAPTER 3 The Roots of Television Romance   55

Why I'm a Fan: Nikki Glaser   75

CHAPTER 4 The Road to the Mansion   77

Why I'm a Fan: Heidi and Spencer Pratt   94

CHAPTER 5 Drafting a Game Plan   97

Why I'm a Fan: Melanie Lynskey   112

CHAPTER 6 Inside the Bubble   115

Why I'm a Fan: Diablo Cody   140

CHAPTER 7 Method to the Madness   143

Why I'm a Fan: Paul Scheer   168

Contents

CHAPTER 8 Under the Covers   171

Why I'm a Fan: Joshua Malina   183

CHAPTER 9 Falling for the Fairy Tale   185

Why I'm a Fan: Donnie Wahlberg   209

CHAPTER 10 Basking in the Afterglow   211

Why I'm a Fan: Jason Ritter   223

CHAPTER 11 Riding the Coattails   225

Why I'm a Fan: Patti Stanger   245

CHAPTER 12 Intoxicated by Happily Ever After   247

Acknowledgments   267

List of Bachelors and Bachelorettes   271

A Note on Sources   279

Interview List   281

Selected Bibliography   285

Index   295

About the Author   310

Bachelor Nation

Introduction

There was no final rose. I didn't get a chance to say my good-byes. No one even offered to walk me out.

Just like that, I'd been kicked out of Bachelor Nation.

For years, I'd been obsessed with the Bachelor franchise. Even though my beat at the *Los Angeles Times* is film, I enjoyed watching "The Bach" (like batch of cookies, not Johann Sebastian) so much that I willingly opted to spend my Monday nights writing recaps of each new episode.

Because of my coverage, ABC granted me access to a handful of Bachelor-related activities. I attended tapings of the "Women Tell All" specials, interviewing jilted ladies after they'd been left roseless. One season, the Bachelor himself—along with host Chris Harrison and a slew of cameras—even crashed a viewing party at my house.

And then there were the weekly conference calls—probably the least illuminating of the Bachelor press "opportunities." The calls worked like this: Dozens of journalists were given an access code, dialed into an ABC line, and then were allowed to publicly ask the contestant o' the week a question or two. It wasn't soul-searching stuff—it was Bachelor.net.rose.tv.com asking about on-screen smooching.

But suddenly, the e-mails with bland press releases inviting me to participate in the calls stopped showing up in my inbox. I promptly got in touch with an ABC publicist to see if the move had been accidental. "I'm sorry," the rep responded, "we're just so slammed this season that there's no more room on the call." Which, what? How do you run out of room on a conference call?

The situation seemed suspect to me, and my editor at the paper agreed. So he decided to call up ABC's publicity department to get the real story. And what he learned was that, apparently, producers had deemed my coverage "too negative" and no longer wanted me near any show-sponsored events.

I was shocked. Were my recaps snarky? That would be a duh. But who doesn't hate-watch *The Bachelor*? No one takes a show about twenty-five women vying for one man seriously. My editor at the *LA Times* decided we wouldn't write another word about the show until they reinstated my access. Some members of "Bachelor Nation"—that's how ABC refers to us rose lovers—were outraged on my behalf. My Twitter followers sent messages to show producers and network executives complaining that the ruling was unfair. The female-centric blog *Jezebel* even wrote an item about the scuffle:

> *While her coverage hasn't exactly been glowing, it hasn't been wholly horrible either. Perhaps she took one too many stabs at ABC last season . . . So a message to members of the press from* The Bachelor *"family": you're cool, but only when you're doing it the Bachelor-approved way.*

Still, ABC's so-called ban didn't stop me from publicly sharing my thoughts about *The Bachelor*. Even after the paper instituted its "the show is dead to us" policy, I kept watching and tweeting about the show as a fan. And in a way, it was freeing. Without a post-episode recap deadline to meet, I started viewing the series differently—taking in how the Twittersphere reacted to storylines and analyzing how my feelings shifted throughout the course of a season.

I even decided to start an e-mail group, aptly titled "Bach Discush"—I hope you've gotten on the abbreviation train by now—and invited about two dozen smart lady fans I knew to share thoughts about episodes and show-related news on the daily. Whenever a new season was airing, we'd gather in my living room with rosé and SkinnyPop to watch together—something that instantly elevated the viewing experience. Because many of us were entertainment journalists, we'd often cross paths with Bach contestants, and sometimes we could even convince them to come watch themselves on TV with us. Eric Bigger, Ashley Iaconetti, and JJ Lane have all been guests on my couch, and once, Robby Hayes ghosted us after promising to come over and requesting we make him Moscow Mules. I have no use for those copper mugs now, you sockless liar!

While it is, admittedly, fun to make jabs about the drunken contestants with their staged limo entrances, I don't just watch the show because it can be a train wreck. By the finale each season, I find myself rooting for the final two to make it to the altar. I'm weirdly touched by the cheesy proposal—these overwrought declarations of love between two people who've known each other for just a few weeks. In those moments, it's easy to forget that just six couples in the history of the show have wed. (And I think I'm being generous by including the two marriages that came out of *Bachelor in Paradise* in that figure. I refuse to count Marcus and Lacy. Sorry not sorry.)

A part of me—thirty-two years old, single, and Tindering up a storm—wants to believe in the fantasy.

Sometimes, I even daydream about what it would be like if I were on the show. To be clear: Even if I weren't banned, this would be a total pipe dream. I don't even have the kind of hands that an engagement ring would look good on. I still, embarrassingly, bite my nails, and I never get manicures. Plus, my friends often joke that if you were to take a photograph of just my hands, you'd think they belonged to a pudgy five-year-old. When I was in second grade, my uncle, who made his living as a commercial photographer, asked if I wanted to earn $100 by working as a hand model for a toy catalog he was shooting, but when he got a look at my hands, my sister, who was a mere six years old at the time, was given the job over me.

Plus, I wouldn't want one of those gaudy Neil Lane rings, anyway. I want something rare and chic—like a unique crystal with meaning or an antique ring that belonged to someone important. It won't look expensive, per se, but at least I'll know the guy had to go farther than the Kay Jewelers at the mall to pick it out.

Besides, I could never pass the show's stringent yet unspoken body requirements. Even if they generously allowed me to go on as a "plus-size model" or some other bullshit, I'm only five-foot-one, so no one would believe it. I've literally never worn a bikini in my entire life. Not once. I never "lay out." My skin is the color of newly fallen snow. That whole "lounging by the pool" thing? I'll take a book in a blanket-heavy nook, thank you very much.

And have I mentioned I don't drink? As if I wasn't already skeptical enough of the process, the producers would have no chance of loosening me up with alc. Oh, and I'm scared of heights. So helicopters are out. And not in that cute way where it's like, "Tee-hee, I'm so anxious! Please hold me because I'm nervous and not because I desperately want to be near you!" No. I do not want to get on a small aircraft, and if you even take me within ten feet of something with propellers, I will cause you bodily harm.

But honestly? I'd still apply. I WOULD STILL. FUCKING. APPLY. That's pretty dark, right? I mean, seriously: What is wrong with me? Why do I want to be that girl? The bronzed one in a two-piece who bungee-jumps and looks like she was born to have a blinding rock on her slim ring finger. A hollow, spray-tanned shell of extensions and sequins whose personality and intelligence always come second to her looks.

What does it mean to be the chosen one?

It's not a label I've ever known, but it's one I've obsessed over since I was a girl. From an early age, I understood that the most meaningful validation a straight woman could get was from a man. Even before I got my period—on the morning of my bat mitzvah, coincidentally—I was boy crazy. I'd spend hours in my room journaling about the smallest interactions with the opposite sex: *Pete sent me an instant message after school. Nathaniel glanced at me while reading his poem in creative writing. Tyler said he thought I had a good voice in chorus.* If just one of them would choose me—pay me mind for more than a fleeting instant—then I would finally have worth.

"I want a boyfriend. And I'm not just saying that—I feel SO strongly about this," reads one entry from August 2000, when I was all of fourteen. "I just watched *Here on Earth*. SO sad. I am so upset right now. I'm just . . . longing. I know this is dumb, but I'm hoping to meet a sweet guy on vacation. I want to kiss someone that passionately. I want to suck on his lips and breathe him in. I know they say movies are fantasy, but if everyone wants that so badly, it's bound to be somewhere. Maybe I'm wishing for too much too young. I wish I had a mature guy like Chris Klein in that movie . . . wow. I want to find love early on in my life and kindle it always. There are many special people out there—but you have to find them."

How does one kindle love, exactly? Should I be writing *Sixty Shades of Grey* instead of a book about *The Bachelor*? And whatever happened to Chris Klein after those American Pie movies?

I digress. In fact, I actually did have one brief yet emotionally substantive relationship as a teenager with a boy named David. We were both in a singing group together—so hot, amirite?—that had been selected to travel to France to perform as part of an exchange program. At thirteen, I was the youngest one in the group, and David, fifteen, took me under his wing. On the seven-hour plane ride from Boston to Paris, he held my hand as I fell in and out of Dramamine-induced slumber. He sat next to me on all the bus rides and encouraged me to climb to the top of the Eiffel Tower, even though I was trembling with fear.

When we got back to Boston, I rushed to the drugstore to develop my film from the trip, eager to see any pictures of us together. Before I left for summer camp a few days later, he called to say good-bye. My dad answered and handed the phone to me hesitantly, as if he knew how my world was about to change. A boy had never called me before.

At sleepover camp, where I'd stay in Maine for the next two months, David wrote me letters. Every time one arrived, my bunkmates squealed, reading over my shoulder. He sprayed each one with cologne and wrote over and over again how much he loved me. I thumbtacked the notes to the rafter above my cot and spent my rest hours writing back to him in immaculate, bubbly handwriting.

Back at school that fall, though, the budding relationship never came to fruition. I, a lowly eighth grader, was suddenly too uncool for a sophomore. Every time I passed him in the hallway, I ducked into the nearest bathroom to cry in a stall.

It was devastating, but in a way, I reveled in it. I finally had something of my own—real memories, real pain, real letters to tuck away in a secret box under my bed. While my friends were nervously pecking boys on the lips for the first time, I felt like I'd already had my first real heartbreak. And that was romantic.

My dad says that I was always "a dreamy person." As a girl, he tells me, I was constantly caught up in a fantasy world, dreaming about what it would be like to be famous or date a celebrity. My mom has memories like this too. The first day she came to pick me up from preschool, she says she was shocked to find me in the corner wearing a tutu, pearls, and a tiara, pretending to iron in a tiny plastic kitchen. She never outfitted me in frilly dresses and rarely put bows or barrettes in my hair—overalls were the go-to for Baby Amy. Plus, because she was a working mother, a lot of the cooking and cleaning in my house was often done by my babysitter.

"I remember saying to myself: 'My goodness,'" my mom recalled. "'She sees me go to work every day. I certainly don't wear a tiara. Where did she ever get this image?'"

Likewise, my parents' marriage was hardly the stuff of fluffy television romance. Which isn't to say they don't love each other. In fact, they've been married for thirty-three years and often tell me that as they age, they feel their relationship only grows deeper. Still, it was always evident to me that their love was rooted first and foremost in a solid friendship. They met while working together at the same company and only started to fall for each other while teaming up on a project outside of work: They built a replica of a 1938 SS Jaguar 100.

Still, it wasn't common for my parents to engage in mushy public displays of affection. My dad wasn't the type to come home with a big bouquet of flowers for my mom, just because. In fact, he didn't even propose to her—a fact that has always horrified my sister and me. Instead, they jointly decided to wed.

"I don't really recall all of the details, because it was so uneventful," my mom told me recently when I asked her to describe how she and my dad got engaged. "It certainly wasn't the whole romantic, down-on-one-knee proposal, pulling out a big ring. I remember it was around my birthday, and I think he decided to roll the birthday and proposal thing into one and said: 'Well, we could get married. Let's go look for rings,' and that was it."

Reacting to my shock, she insisted that things were different in the 1980s—no one had a flashy ring, women didn't "Say Yes to the Dress," bachelorette parties weren't weekend-long extravaganzas at remote locations—it didn't feel like there was a "big machine" around getting married. Still, she said, she would have liked the memory of a proposal: "When people ask, 'How did you two decide to get married?' I sometimes wish I had one of those dramatic stories to tell."

She does have other stories to share, though, because my dad can be romantic—just in his own unconventional way. Once, he surprised my mom by waking her up at three a.m. and driving to the Berkshires to fly in a hot-air balloon. He loved to spring for sudden weekend getaways to B&Bs on Martha's Vineyard or in New Hampshire. He even tried to get a helicopter to pick him and my mom up after their wedding ceremony, but the venue wouldn't allow it. (Instead, he rented a white 1940s Rolls-Royce to drive them away.)

"I've always wanted to do things on the fringe," he explained to me. "Surprises to make her happy. That element of surprise was a fun thing, and it certainly helped with our connection. We had an experience to share."

OK, so there's definitely some *Bachelor*-esque stuff in there. But on the whole, my model of love and marriage growing up was pretty pragmatic. So how did I get caught up with hoping for red roses and helicopter rides that I wouldn't even go on?

With the promise of free pizza and wine, I lured some of the ladies from my Bach Discush group over to help me get to the bottom of this puzzling question. Surely I couldn't be the only one who secretly dreamed of having a grandiose love story like the ones depicted on *The Bachelor*.

Shocker: I wasn't. But it seemed nearly all of us were embarrassed by this admission. Meredith, a thirty-six-year-old newspaper editor who's been married for four years, recalled how, early on, she was warned by her dad about the harsh realities of romance.

"I remember my father took me aside and gave me really crappy advice," she said with a laugh. "He was like, 'Meredith, if you expect your boyfriend to be showing up at your front door with a rose, you're just going to be disappointed.'"

Even as adult women, this was the mind-set many of us had adopted: Never expect too much from a man. When asked about her ideal date, Sasha—thirty-eight and a television host—joked she'd just be happy if her husband tidied up around the house without being asked: "I come home. The house is clean. There's no pee on the toilet. And I get so wet!"

Tierney, a twenty-eight-year-old TV news editor, also felt like she was typically the more thoughtful one in her relationships, but she quickly countered: "I think it's unrealistic to expect that of someone else. I care a lot more than I thought I ever would about doing special things. And I don't think it's fair to put that same standard on someone else if that's not in their nature."

Still, when pushed, many in my Bach Discush crew admitted

they harbored pretty extravagant fantasies about their love lives. Allison, who works at a talent agency, was surprised that others at the table weren't copping to that "under-the-stars thing we all have in our heads."

"You know, where you're in this beautiful, exotic location and you have a hotel suite to yourselves?" the twenty-eight-year-old continued. "It's got this nice patio and there's a private pool or hot tub and you look up at all the stars."

It quickly became evident we all had somewhat of an "under-the-stars thing" when Sasha and Meredith, the only two married women in the group, relayed their proposal stories to us. As they spoke about the elaborate lengths their spouses had gone to surprise them, we all became silent. Some eyes got googly, while others started to tear.

"See, this is like when I get caught up in the romance of the show," said Katie, a thirty-four-year-old film critic. (Yes, we live in L.A. Can you tell?) "I'm so conflicted about marriage. I do want it, but I'm, like, being told to want it by society. I hate when politicians say 'Mothers and wives and daughters.' If you're not a mother or a wife, you can still be a person. I don't like that having worth as a person means being chosen by someone else."

"We shouldn't all be sent off to an island if we don't get married," Meredith chimed in. "On the show, when they leave and don't get a proposal, it's like it's the end of their life."

I think this is the aspect of the show we all, collectively, had the most trouble relating to. We're all young working women who grew up aspiring to have both careers and families. The idea of meeting a guy, giving up your job for him, and moving to his hometown to support his dreams while living off his salary? It wasn't something we connected with.

"Do you think that's part of the golden ticket that they're selling at *The Bachelor*?" Meredith asked. "Not only do you get a husband, you get luxury. You get a life, and you don't have to worry about it."

"But the guys don't even have aspirational jobs anymore!" Tierney pointed out. "You're gonna get to go on *Marriage Boot Camp* or have Instagram endorsements."

Sure, we'd all thought about how nice it would be to go to yoga in the middle of the day. But after a while, would you start to lose your own identity as a woman? Especially if you devoted your life to raising your kids, and then they ventured off at eighteen to embark on their own journeys?

"I'm empathetic towards the women on the show who think they can't provide for themselves," said Molly, a thirty-three-year-old podcaster. "When I think about a guy going, 'I'll pay for your life, you've done enough,' it's like, 'Do you know what kind of life I think I deserve?' I'll just earn that."

Of course, the Bach Discush gang was coming from a pretty distinct vantage point. We're coastal liberals, most of whom work in the media, and are straight and pretty white. In no way are we an accurate representation of all women in the United States—or even the women who watch *The Bachelor*.

But even the voices in this small sample group made me realize that the way young women think about love, marriage, feminism, and identity in this country is shifting. We're living in an era where Kim Kardashian's nude selfies open up discussions about slut shaming, Lena Dunham refuses to be Photoshopped on magazine covers, and Reese Witherspoon demands reporters #AskHerMore on the red carpet—and yet many of us are still clinging to the traditional notions that we grew up hearing about in Disney fairy tales or sappy romantic comedies.

It's all part of what makes the cultural fascination with *The Bach-elor* so interesting, and it's a big reason why I wanted to write this book. How does a reality show filled with Champagne and tea lights hold such power over us, and how has it affected our expectations of romance?

(Though, let's be real: I also wanted to get to the bottom of what actually goes down in the Fantasy Suite. And we'll get to that. I promise.)

This is not a book, meanwhile, that the people at *The Bachelor* want published. In June 2016, I received a letter from a vice president of legal affairs at Warner Bros. Television, which produces *The Bachelor*. The email said that the company was aware I was "actively soliciting" employees and show participants to speak with me for this book, and wanted to put me on notice that the show's contracts with cast and crew contain a "very clear and unambiguous confidentiality provision" that inhibits them from "disclosing unpublished information acquired in the course of their engagement or participation on the shows." If I engaged in any "conduct intended to induce a former participant to breach this provision," the letter said, I would face liability.

Months later, one of my sources was contacted by a member of the Warner Bros. legal team and asked if he/she had done an interview with me. "We can't stop Amy from asking questions, but we want to know if she is putting anyone in violation of their contract," is essentially what WB told my source. He/she declined to give the show's legal team any information.

As you'll see, plenty of former contestants were willing to speak with me on the record about their experiences on the show. There were, however, a few past participants who asked that I pay them in exchange for an interview—requests I immediately declined. Andrew

Baldwin, the naval officer and doctor who served as the Bachelor in 2007, said if I gave him "a percentage of the book sales," he would "dish all." He then asked me if I was aware of how much money the show had made off him and said he no longer wanted to be a part of such practices. Matt Grant, the Brit who was the Bachelor the year after Baldwin, replied to my inquiry in a similar fashion: "I'm sorry to be blunt," he wrote, "but unless your business opportunity can help my daughter's university fund then I have little interest in getting involved."

And yet, when I reached out to the top brass at *The Bachelor*—including creator Mike Fleiss and executive producer Elan Gale—I received no response. I'm not sure what the folks at *The Bachelor* have to hide. But I'm not here to make friends. I'm here for the right reasons: to tell you how this show is really made and explore why we keep tuning in, season after season.

CHAPTER 1

A Budding Idea

At his family reunions, there was always one person Mike Fleiss gravitated toward: his second cousin Heidi. As teenagers, the two would meet up at the gatherings and hide out behind the garage, sneaking beers and sharing a joint.

Heidi Fleiss, of course, would go on to become known as the notorious "Hollywood Madam," running an illegal prostitution ring that catered to wealthy celebrities like Charlie Sheen—a crime that eventually landed her in prison in her early thirties.

Mike Fleiss, meanwhile, hasn't ended up behind bars. But as the creator of *The Bachelor*, the long-running reality television series on which more than two dozen singles compete for an eligible suitor, he's displayed an understanding of the human desire for love that his cousin was also able to tap into.

Growing up in Fullerton, California, where his mother was a nurse and his father owned a Baskin-Robbins ice-cream shop in nearby La Habra, Fleiss never felt like the guy who could get the girl.

The young ladies at Sunny Hills High School were "unbelievably hot," he once told *Vanity Fair*, but he had a reputation as "the alienated, parking-lot stoner" who had long hair and rode a moped.

Still, he managed to land the interest of class president Alexandra Vorbeck, his high school sweetheart, who would travel with him to study at the University of California–Berkeley. They wed in August 1987 and stayed married for twenty-four years before divorcing in 2012.

At Berkeley, he studied journalism and became the executive editor of the college paper, *The Daily Cal.* His first job out of school was at the now-defunct *Sacramento Union*, where he was paid $323 a week to write about sports. "I thought it was the dream job," he said years later in an interview with the *Contra Costa Times*. "I got tears in my eyes the first time I walked into Arco Arena."

He got laid off in 1989 but quickly found work at the nearby Santa Rosa *Press Democrat*. The job, however, was temporary: The reporter who covered the San Francisco 49ers was out on medical leave, so Fleiss could have the gig for only nine months. It was a prime beat, and he was tasked with writing features and game previews about the team that could stand up against the other Bay Area newspapers.

"He was a very, very good writer," recalled Glen Crevier, the *Democrat*'s executive sports editor and Fleiss's boss at the time. "He definitely improved the quality of writing in the sports section. He found good stories and told them in a way that was entertaining."

So when the 49ers reporter returned from leave, Crevier tried to find a way to keep Fleiss on staff. The only job available in the newsroom, however, was an opening on the copy desk, where the shift ran from four p.m. to midnight.

"That didn't go well for him," Crevier said with a laugh. The job didn't allow for much creativity and required a lot of structure, which Fleiss struggled with. Soon, his colleagues noticed him watching *Married . . . with Children* on the overhead TV when he should have been editing NBA roundups, and Crevier was called in to reprimand him.

"These were professional copyeditors who took pride in what they were doing, and they saw Mike just sort of blowing off the assignments," said the editor. "So I had to take him in a room one day and give him a warning, like, 'Hey, you've got to care more about this job. You've got to really engage in it.'"

But Fleiss only grew more frustrated at the paper. One night after he got home, he turned on the syndicated *Howard Stern Show* and found himself envious of the "complete creative freedom" the program's employees seemed to have. "I was being restricted by the facts all the time!" he said in that 2003 *Vanity Fair* interview. "I felt like I couldn't really do anything creative, because I was always running down what Jose Canseco said."

As Fleiss's behavior in the newsroom continued to deteriorate, Crevier decided he'd have to let Fleiss go. The young sports editor had no writing positions available, and so—for the first time in his career—he fired someone. Fleiss was mad, but it also seemed as if he was resigned to his fate.

"He said, 'You know, that's all right,'" remembered Crevier. "'I had some other things I wanted to do anyway. I want to get involved in the television industry. I'm going to move to L.A.'"

True to his word, Fleiss retreated to the Northern California apartment he shared with his then-pregnant wife, churning out one spec script after another. But no one was biting. After being unemployed, he heard about a low-paying gig at *Totally Hidden Video*, a Fox hidden-camera series where actors pulled pranks on unsuspecting victims. In order to get the job, Fleiss was asked by the show's producers to write five sample stunts; instead, he came up with forty. He found out he'd landed the position just as his wife was going into labor with the couple's first of two children, Aaron, named after TV impresario Aaron Spelling and baseball legend Hank Aaron.

Fleiss was so thrilled that he agreed to take the job, even though it paid $400 a week—less than half of what he'd been making at the *Democrat*. Soon, the family piled into their Jetta and decamped to Los Angeles.

A year later, however, Fleiss was out of another job when *Totally Hidden Video* was canceled in 1992. Fortunately, he now had become acquainted with Bruce Nash, a producer best known for making TV specials filled with outrageous clips. While working for Nash, Fleiss helped put together *World's Deadliest Volcanoes*, *World's Scariest Police Shootouts*, and *Greatest Sports Moments of All Time*.

The biggest hit, though, was 1997's *Breaking the Magician's Code: Magic's Biggest Secrets Finally Revealed*.

Mike Darnell—who served as the president of alternative entertainment at Fox for nineteen years, overseeing hits like *American Idol* and *Family Guy*—decided to buy the magic special after meeting Fleiss. They shared the same vision for the show: an irreverent approach that poked fun at the magicians.

A friendship was born between the two Mikes, and so was a ratings boom. Despite being sued multiple times over exposing trade secrets and for copyright infringement, Fox would go on to air five more of the magic specials.

Darnell proceeded to purchase Fleiss's next big pitch—an idea he was calling *The World's Meanest People Caught on Tape*. The show, Fleiss explained, would feature people doing despicable things—and he already had secured a clip of a bartender stirring a martini with his penis.

"Mike Darnell made that happen for me," he told *Vanity Fair* about the special, which was eventually renamed *Shocking Behavior Caught on Tape*. "Even though it was a sleazy, disgusting little show, with a bartender stirring a drink with his penis, I was proud!"

Clearly, Fleiss excelled at pushing the envelope. He and Darnell almost pulled off crashing a plane in the desert on a special aptly named *Jumbo Jet Crash: The Ultimate Safety Test*, but Fox blinked as production was about to get under way. While many television producers were fixated on creating prestige programming bound for awards glory, Fleiss wasn't ashamed of the fact that many critics considered his shows trashy. On the contrary, he got off on making headlines—and getting ratings—as a result of tapping into a viewer's basest nature.

Darnell, meanwhile, was itching for Fox's next big hit, seething over the success of *Who Wants to Be a Millionaire?* on ABC. While at a wedding in the summer of 1999, he found himself checking the *Millionaire* ratings nonstop. The romantic environment and his jealousy over the ABC hit led him to his next outlandish TV idea: Why not find a single millionaire, introduce him to fifty women, and have him propose to one of them at the end of a two-hour special?

Darnell brought the idea to Dick Clark. But the veteran producer and game-show host was worried the project might tarnish his wholesome reputation.

"Dick said, 'Look, I've been married three times. This is a show that's condemning the institution of marriage, and I don't want to be the guy to do that,'" said John Ferriter, a William Morris agent who represented Clark and Fleiss.

But when it was Fleiss's turn to meet with Darnell, he won over the Fox executive after he said he envisioned the special as a version of a Miss America pageant. He was given ten weeks to put the special together before it aired in February 2000.

In December 1999, the announcement went out wide: "Calling All Brides . . . a Nationwide Search Begins for Potential Brides Willing to Marry a Millionaire Live from Las Vegas on Network Television."

"Are you looking for the man of your dreams?" the press release asked. "Is he tall, is he dark, and is he handsome? Most importantly, is he RICH? . . . During the next month, the search is on for any and all women (over the age of 18) who would be willing to marry a rich man on live television and become 'Mrs. Multi-Millionaire.' A minimum of 50 daring candidates will be selected and flown to Las Vegas for an all-expenses-paid trip to compete for the opportunity to marry Mr. Moneybags during the two-hour television special."

Mr. Moneybags, Fleiss had decided, would be none other than Rick Rockwell, a forty-three-year-old writer and comedian who'd invested the money he made performing in real estate.

"Well, I'm worth about $1.5 . . . [million]," Rockwell said, responding to a November 1999 email from Fleiss.

"It's quite possible he was the only person on the planet who was willing to do it," Fleiss later admitted to *Vanity Fair*. "Our backup millionaire basically wanted me to buy him a Mercedes 500E free and clear."

On television, however, Rockwell delivered. He got down on his knee and proposed to a stranger with a three-carat, $35,000 wedding ring the network had supplied. His new bride was Darva Conger, an emergency room nurse who'd served in the air force for five years. According to their prenuptial agreement, she'd also walk away with an Isuzu Trooper, a pair of diamond earrings, and a $2,500 jewelry spending spree.

Viewers were stunned.

Ferriter, who was in Nashville on business when *Who Wants to Marry a Multi-Millionaire?* aired, stopped into a steakhouse that night to get a sense of the local reaction.

"I walk in and everyone's packed around the bar," he told me when I went to visit him at his office in L. A. "I couldn't get to the maître d' to go grab my table because nobody was working. They were all around the bar. I said, 'What's going on?' And everyone was like, 'These people are getting married on TV and they've never met each other!' So I sidle up to the side of the bar and guys are watching, shaking their heads. Women watching, nodding their heads. I went, 'Oh my God, this is going to be a hit. This is going to be a big hit.'"

Indeed, a whopping 23 million people tuned in to watch Conger and Rockwell get married on TV. To give you a sense of how big of an audience that is, during the 2016–17 television season, the most-watched program was NBC's *Sunday Night Football*, which attracted 19.6 million viewers. On network television, hit shows like *NCIS* and *The Big Bang Theory* average around 14 million viewers these days.

Despite its popularity, however, *Multi-Millionaire* drew harsh reviews from critics. The president of Viewers for Quality Television called the special an "all-time low" in the American public's viewing taste. *Salon*'s Carina Chocano argued it put "moral bankruptcy on parade. And if you're going to put it on parade, put it on parade, enough with the muted grays and wholesome questions. Include a talent show. Have the girls perform a song-and-dance number. Hold a pie-baking race. Make them blow a banana. But try to dress it all up in the cloak of respectability and the air goes out of the balloon and distracts us from what's really important—gawking at people who are very, very ill."

Within days, Fox had much bigger problems on its hands than some nasty reviews. After their hasty nuptials, Rockwell and Conger were immediately sent on a honeymoon cruise to Barbados. It was there, Rockwell later told the press, that Conger revealed she'd only wed him in order to go on the free trip.

Back in the United States, Fleiss was busy putting together a follow-up special—*Who Wants to Marry a Multi-Millionaire: A Television Phenomenon*—that Darnell had ordered to capitalize on the water-cooler chatter. On February 20, the newlyweds flew back to California and filmed an interview for the special with Fox weatherman Mark Thompson—annulling their marriage shortly afterward. Following the interview, Rockwell and Fleiss hopped in a limo together, and that's where all hell broke loose. During the ride, Fleiss got a call from Thompson, who was one of his closest friends. He informed Fleiss that *The Smoking Gun* had published an article called "Millionaire Groom's Dirty Secret," revealing that Rockwell had "slapped and hit" an ex-girlfriend, according to a 1991 restraining order. As a result of the incident, the Los Angeles court had ordered Rockwell to keep at least one hundred yards from his ex.

Fleiss immediately began to lose it. He'd spent the past couple of months talking to Rockwell at least once a day, developing a nine-page questionnaire for Rockwell's potential wives. As Fleiss later told *Vanity Fair*, he turned to Rockwell and began to plead: "That's not true, right? That's not true, right?" Rockwell acknowledged the report's validity but tried to downplay it, insisting he'd never done anything to his ex other than let the air out of her car's tires.

"I was laying down," Fleiss told the magazine. "I was so upset. I said, 'Yeah, Rick is saying that it's true.'"

In the following days, it came to light that there appeared to be other holes in Rockwell's story too. His 1,200-square-foot home had an old toilet in the backyard and hardly appeared to be the lush pad of a wealthy bachelor. It also seemed he'd long aspired to become a famous performer: In 1982, he'd earned a spot in *The Guinness Book of Records* for "longest continuous comedy routine" after telling jokes for thirty hours straight.

"He struck me as totally honest," Fleiss insisted to *The New York Times* as the fiasco was unfolding. "I had no questions about his sincerity. If that was a performance, he should have a couple of Emmy Awards already."

Sandy Grushow, then the chairman of Fox's television entertainment group, immediately pulled the follow-up special, vowing that the network would conduct an internal investigation to figure out how Rockwell had made it on air. In the meantime, Fox had a clear scapegoat: Next Entertainment, Fleiss's production company, which the network said failed to perform adequate background checks on the special's participants. Next issued its own statement, arguing Rockwell had misled the producers.

The news had ripple effects across the industry. In a conference call with reporters, CBS Television president Leslie Moonves said the incident had "made all of us very cautious about what we do. After this happened, I said, 'Go back and do a triple and quadruple check on these people. I want grade-school diplomas.'"

Rockwell, meanwhile, was busy trying to clear his own name, appearing on CNN's *Larry King Live* to argue how sincere his intentions had been in searching for a wife. He told King that he had indeed been subjected to a background check, and he thought his criminal record had been "expunged, or whatever they call that, after seven years, so—I mean, that's not the kind of person I am."

King informed Rockwell that a CNN/USA Today/Gallup Poll

showed 66 percent of the people polled were unsympathetic to Conger, 71 percent were unsympathetic to Rockwell, and 62 percent said the show was harmful to the institution of marriage.

"It was so uncomfortable," Rockwell acknowledged. "I think it did challenge the sanctity of marriage. I think it did make a sham of relationships. I think it did make both genders look bad. I think it was a bad idea gone—worse."

"You wouldn't have seen this twenty years ago on American television, no way," King said, addressing Rockwell and his panel of guests, which included talk-show host Leeza Gibbons, Rabbi Shmuley Boteach, and news anchor Hugh Downs. "I don't want to make a statement. That's a question. Do you think you'd have seen this twenty years ago on American television?

"No, I don't," Gibbons replied. "I mean, I don't—you know, just like twenty years ago we weren't showing navels and people in the same bed. I mean, there's—it is evolving. It is harder to get noticed. There is inherent shock value. I still think there is a basic taste level, though, that if you cross that level, people will reject it."

"I think that this show has longevity," countered Boteach. "Because it caters to all of our fantasies and stereotypes. This was a princess, you know, Cinderella meeting the big prince, and in an age where there is no romance, where guys and girls love each other for the wrong reasons, this thing, beyond the shock value, really bought into that fantasy, and that's why people are so upset to see it unravel."

Of course, well over a decade later, viewers have come to expect far less from our reality-television couples. It's almost a given at this point that couples on *The Bachelor* will break up within a year of their televised engagement, but that hasn't stopped us from tuning in to watch them fall in (temporary) love.

As for Fleiss, he never got in real legal trouble with Fox, because two months after *Multi-Millionaire* wrapped, an outside law firm hired by the network determined that neither Fox nor Next Entertainment had been negligent in casting Rockwell. Fleiss's company, the review said, had hired a private investigator and a national search firm to perform Rockwell's background check.

"We're proud of the work we did on the show, and we're proud of the show," Fleiss told the *Los Angeles Times* in April 2000. "It's become a cultural icon and something the television business will always remember."

Behind closed doors, however, the ordeal was taking an emotional toll on the producer. He called his agent in a panic, fretting that his television career was over.

"Fleiss called and said, 'I'm never going to work. You've got to get rid of all your clients and focus on me,'" Ferriter remembered. The agent said he was still able to book Fleiss some big meetings, getting him in the room with the president of UPN. That apparently wasn't enough for Fleiss, who fired Ferriter within the week and moved over to the Creative Artists Agency.

"He said, 'I want someone who's just going to concentrate on me and nobody else,'" Ferriter said. "I was like, 'Well, I've got fifty clients. If that's the case, I'm not going to be that guy.' He told me he was going to CAA and slammed down the phone. So we split. But I wanted to represent people that were controversial. You want to make a difference. Why be boring? Mike Fleiss was an incredibly creative guy. He was impatient. He was disrespectful. But he was a very creative producer."

Despite the agency swap, Fleiss went into hibernation. Scott Jeffress, who became friends with the producer while they were both working for special king Bruce Nash, went to visit him at his office and found a man dejected. Fleiss was sitting in a huge, empty office where the only furniture was a tiny desk in the corner. He was wearing his sunglasses inside. "It was just the most pathetic thing I've ever seen," Jeffress told me.

"Even though he's tall and burly and thick, he really is a sensitive guy," recalled Ben Hatta, who began working as Fleiss's assistant around this time. "He really got his feelings hurt when Fox put the blame all on him. He was like, 'What the fuck? This is bullshit. Why am I getting all this heat?'"

Fleiss tried to take solace in *Multi-Millionaire*'s commercial success. He tore out a page from *The Hollywood Reporter* touting the special's strong ratings and had it framed. However controversial, he'd created something America couldn't look away from, and the business wouldn't ignore him for long. A few months after the scandal cooled off, Fleiss landed a seven-figure development deal with Warner Bros.' Telepictures Productions.

"That meant a lot to him," said Hatta. "And then he started saying, 'Dude. I got two strangers married in two hours. We can do whatever we want, man.'"

Fleiss set up camp in Burbank, in a building whose bottom floor was occupied by one of those chain restaurants that serves burgers topped with onion rings, and huge slices of cake. He settled on an office that overlooked the Warner Bros. studio lot and had previously been occupied by Tom Selleck. The actor had filled the space with Detroit Tigers memorabilia, and Fleiss was a big baseball fan. It had a shower too, a tidbit he loved to share.

Every day, the six-foot-four Fleiss would wear a version of the same thing to the office: a leather jacket, a black T-shirt, basketball shorts, flip-flops, and sunglasses—even inside. He was a huge fan of the Grateful Dead, Black Sabbath, and Jimi Hendrix. "Mike, be fuckin' wild!" read an autographed album cover signed by Ozzy Osbourne on his wall.

"We'd refer to him as 'The Dude,' because he was just like *The Big Lebowski* in his slippers and his sweats and his leather jacket, smoking and playing the guitar," said Hatta. "He rode around in this old Mercedes. He'd surf in the morning. Sometimes he'd bring his dog to the office. Keeping a conversation with him in his office was a challenge, because he's on the other side playing the guitar, feet up on the desk. He'd start staring off at his things, talking to them—he had all of this Grateful Dead stuff and Chargers jerseys and helmets. You'd have to call him back into reality like, 'Hey, Mike, Mike, what about this?'"

And in the weeks following the announcement of the Telepictures deal, focus was key. Fleiss needed to deliver a strong show pitch and told his team he was looking for big-picture ideas in the vein of CBS's *Big Brother*. But despite endless brainstorming sessions with his staff—followed by sleepless nights—nothing was coming to him. He was so anxious that he came down with a 104-degree temperature, and in some sort of fever dream, the idea for *The Bachelor* emerged.

"A dating show where you watch your relationship evolve," he would tell *Vanity Fair* of the show's genesis. "Within fifteen minutes I had the whole thing in my head: the roses, the house—everything. I swear to God, it all came in like one flash."

His plan was to pull from the elements that had resonated with *Multi-Millionaire* viewers but stretch the idea out over six episodes. He'd class up the premise by adding in romantic touches—hot tubs, sunsets, carriage rides. "He wanted to take the setting of *Multi-Millionaire* and put it on a hillside surrounded by palm trees, roses, a sunset and candlelight," said Hatta. "The viewers for the special were primarily women, so he thought if he upped the romance, he could make it sell."

Of course, Fleiss immediately took the idea to his buddy Darnell over at Fox, but the executive wasn't interested—and was about to have his own reality hit in *Temptation Island*. NBC's Jeff Zucker also turned down the pitch. Even ABC—who eventually bought *The Bachelor*—rejected him at first.

"Nobody was buying it," said Jeffress, Fleiss's old pal who was brought in to help run the show. "It wasn't an immediate sell. Executives were hesitant over the endgame—like, how does the show end? They date and then what happens? Finally, Mike said, 'At the end, the guy drops down on one knee and proposes. And boom! You have that big moment.' And that format worked."

Andrea Wong, ABC's then senior vice president of series and specials, was the one to ultimately buy into the concept. And so *The Bachelor* was born.

Finding the perfect guy to attract twenty-five women, however, would prove difficult. Fleiss's ideal Bachelor was the prototypical manly man—a sporty, smart guy with a good job and some money in the bank. But ABC's Wong was adamant that the Bachelor be able to communicate well with the twenty-five women.

"She'd ask things like 'How will he handle himself? How does he look?'" remembered Jeffress. "You also needed someone who was well spoken and could interview well, speaking in concise sound bites. Somebody who could have multiple conversations and had multiple interests. We wanted him to look sharp in a suit when he showed up. First and foremost, he had to blow these girls away when they got up to the house. When those ladies pulled up in the limo, you wanted to hear: 'Oh my God, he's gorgeous!'"

A casting call for "America's Most Eligible Bachelor" went out nationwide.

"THE SEARCH CONTINUES! THE MANHUNT IS STILL UNDERWAY!" the press release announced. "*The Bachelor*, an original one-hour primetime reality television series, which gives one lucky man the opportunity to meet the woman of his dreams, is hot on the trail of 'America's Most Eligible Bachelor.' The series, which will air during the 2001–02 season on ABC, will give America's most eligible single man a one-of-a-kind opportunity to find his true love, and, hopefully, his bride-to-be. . . . The bachelor will court the candidates, introduce some to family and friends and even take a few of them home to meet Mom! But the big question is: After all of this, when he pops the question, will she accept?"

With reality television still in its infancy, however, there weren't many handsome, financially successful men eager to appear on an untested program. Casting producers scattered across the country, scouring malls, bars, and nascent dating websites. The ideal candidate would be a Caucasian banker or a lawyer with a solid education whose parents were still married.

"It was embarrassing," said Hatta, who was sent to the Third Street Promenade in Santa Monica to recruit potential candidates. "You'd walk up to someone with a clipboard and be like, 'We're doing this reality show that's kind of like *Big Brother* but based on romantic relationships. We're trying to find America's most eligible bachelor, and we're looking for people with careers who like having fun and are really interested in falling in love.'"

After sifting through more than five hundred men, the casting department found Alex Michel. At thirty-one, Michel already had an impressive résumé: He'd graduated with honors from Harvard University, where he majored in history and literature and made both the varsity swimming and water polo teams. He went on to earn his MBA at Stanford University's Graduate School of Business, and then landed a job at Boston Consulting Group.

Michel, who grew up in the affluent suburb of Darien, Connecticut, was about to take a slot on *Survivor: Africa* when he tossed his hat into the *Bachelor* ring. "We really wanted somebody who truly wanted to fall in love, but everyone who goes on TV has an agenda," acknowledged Jeffress. "Alex wanted to travel. He wanted to get into film and television and media."

Fleiss told *The New York Times* that Michel seemed like "the kind of guy you lose a girl to—the guy with the good family and money and the handsome grin." Michel's friends backed up that assertion, describing his "level of charisma" as "Clintonesque." "There isn't a wedding I know of from Harvard or Stanford or any of the derivative feeder schools like St. Paul's that Alex isn't invited to," Michel's college buddy David DiDomenico said in that 2002 *Times* piece.

But even after Michel was locked in, another manhunt continued—this time for the host of *The Bachelor.* The producers wanted a male to take the reins—a guy who was good-looking but not *too* good-looking—someone mature and married and safe. In Jeffress's words: "He couldn't be the guy who was all, 'Hey, baby.'"

Chris Harrison fit the bill. A twenty-nine-year-old Dallas native, he was married and had just had his first son when his agent suggested he take a meeting with Fleiss, who was described to him as "Heidi's cousin."

It was November 2001, and Harrison had yet to become a sought-after host. He'd gotten his start in broadcasting while attending Oklahoma City University, where he played on the school soccer team. In his spare time, the communications major started giving play-by-play commentary of college basketball games on a local cable network. After graduating in 1993, he started working for KWTV, the CBS affiliate in Oklahoma City, working his way up from intern to weekend sports anchor. He stayed there until 1999, when he moved to California with his family to take a job as a lead anchor on TVG, a horseracing network. When he got the call from *The Bachelor*, he was juggling the TVG gig with other freelance work, hosting *Mall Masters*, a game show that filmed at the Mall of America, and *Designers' Challenge*, an HGTV program about designers competing to renovate homes.

You'd think he'd jump at the opportunity to host a major network TV show, but Harrison had reservations about Fleiss—largely because of *Who Wants to Marry a Multi-Millionaire?*, which he thought was a disaster. Still, Harrison agreed to meet the producer, but it was hardly love at first sight between the two men.

"He looked like a guy barfed on by an eight-week-old," Fleiss would later tell *The Dallas Morning News*. "There was just no energy in the room. I couldn't wait for that meeting to end. It was incredibly painful. He was the dullest guy I've ever seen."

Network executives argued that Fleiss had gotten the wrong impression of the potential host and persuaded the men to meet up again three weeks later. This time, things went off without a hitch.

"I guess he got a good night's sleep, or at least a few hours, because he was terrific," Fleiss said in the Dallas paper. "He's articulate, funny, and incredibly gregarious. I couldn't believe it was the same guy."

Slowly, *The Bachelor* was starting to come together. Filming would take place at a Malibu mansion right off the Pacific Coast Highway; the luxurious Spanish Revival–style home so commonly associated with the franchise now wasn't even built then. Each episode would last one hour, and the whole season would be comprised of only six episodes. On the first night, Michel would meet twenty-five women and quickly narrow the pool down to fifteen. By episode two, he'd already be down to eight ladies. Third episode: four women. Fourth episode: three women. Fifth episode: two women. And then the finale.

By comparison, most episodes of *The Bachelor* are now two hours long. There were eleven installments of Nick Viall's season, plus the "Women Tell All" and "After the Final Rose" specials. Viall spent eight weeks shooting; Michel had only six weeks with his ladies. During the first season, each episode cost just $800,000 or so to produce; now, that budget has risen to roughly $2 million.

But *The Bachelor* only really started to take shape after Lisa Levenson was hired as its co-executive producer. Levenson—a thin, beautiful brunette who often toted around a Louis Vuitton bag—came from the melodramatic world of soap operas. And after her arrival at *The Bachelor*, she quickly began to stir up some drama of her own.

Why I'm a Fan

AMY SCHUMER

I STARTED WATCHING DURING TRISTA'S SEASON. I was really into her and Ryan. A firefighter who would write poetry? I was like, "Oh my God, a hot, sensitive guy who will kill a spider? Life is gonna be OK!" He was really sweet, and it was really fun to watch. The vibe wasn't "Let's see what these lab rats will do. We're going to put up mirrors on all the walls."

Because of the reality of the house that I grew up in and my parents' relationship, I'm more of a realist about relationships, and I'm not really interested in the artifice. But it's still fun to see. And we still do hope for that for ourselves. You still do want to be like, "I'm married to my best friend." You want what they're pretending to have. And I do think it's possible. I know it's possible. But I don't like the show because of the possibility of love. It's really just a behavioral study. What will these people do? They cast these women who are very confused and unstable. I like awkward moments. I like *Curb Your Enthusiasm*. I like watching Vince Vaughn in *Swingers*. I like the shows on Bravo. I think it just also makes you feel better. Like: "I'm not crazy, and I'm not delusional."

The producers did talk to me about becoming the Bachelorette. I never really considered it, and there was never a lawyer call or official offer. But I think everyone daydreams about what it would be like to be on there. Because first of all, every girl has the exact same body, and that's weird to me. Why don't they ever mix it up with body type? Just that alone would be really fun to see—if my body type were on that show. The other girls at the pool and me. "Hi! Cellulite! We all deserve love, guys!"

I do think that is problematic. I don't think that's the most problematic thing on that show, but I do think it's up there. I know it's a TV show and whatever, but would it hurt ratings that bad to have a woman whose thighs touch? Would they lose an advertiser? Suck my dick. Some guys don't want to hold onto the thinnest arm that's ever been photographed. "Can't wait to bend that skeleton over!" What if you were afraid of shattering her?

I think the show is bad for women, because it creates gunning for a ring for competitive reasons. You want to get these things not because you'll be happy in life but because you want to show other people you got these things. So you can put it on Facebook. "I got a man and he put a ring on it and you were all wrong and I'm great forever." And I think that's bad for women to see.

The most interesting thing I've seen on the show in a long time was Corinne saying, "Nick listens to me. Guys don't usually listen to me." I remember feeling that way growing up. All through middle school, high school, college—guys weren't like, "I want your thoughts on this." It's like, everyone is drunk and they just want to hook up, and it's so painful that that's all they want from you that you have to trick yourself into thinking that's what you want too. You're just gunning for these moments of intimacy. Some people luck out, and they meet a great person in high school or college. I didn't. I was part of that pattern.

It's kind of awful to watch the show. And it's the thing I most look forward to every week. It's fucked up.

—Amy Schumer, comedian
(Inside Amy Schumer, Trainwreck, Snatched)

CHAPTER 2

The Reality of
Creating the Fantasy

The stretch limousines. The roses. The bubbly.

So many of the key romantic elements we now associate with *The Bachelor* would never have existed had it not been for Lisa Levenson.

"I have to give her credit for a lot of the romance and the magic of it—the fantasy," explained Scott Jeffress, the show's supervising producer. "The limousines, the candles, the Champagne—that's all Lisa Levenson right there."

When Levenson arrived at *The Bachelor*, she came with an impressive résumé. She'd spent five years as a producer on *General Hospital* before moving into the reality-television space, helping to shape CBS's *Big Brother*. Her very first job in the business, however, was on *Jerry Springer*, and it was formative. "You have to produce stuff to happen in two seconds on that show," explained Michael Carroll, who worked as Levenson's assistant on *The Bachelor*.

"She's just a savant," he continued. "She would walk up to the chicks and look very impressive. She's gorgeous, and she wears Prada. She looks the part, so chicks would listen."

If you watch Lifetime's *UnREAL*—the fictional show about a reality dating show that seems a hell of a lot like *The Bachelor*—Constance Zimmer's character, Quinn, is supposedly based on Levenson.

"Lisa's from Scottsdale, Arizona," said Evan Majors, who later took over for Carroll as Levenson's assistant. "I don't know if you've ever been to Scottsdale, Arizona, but they call it a baby Beverly Hills. All the girls there look a certain way. And Lisa just liked nice things. She liked fine wine. She liked nice restaurants. She liked great tequila. She liked to look good, always. I think she was trying to set a precedent and elevate the look and feel of the show."

On-set, she was referred to as the office mom, while Fleiss—who was almost always camped out at his desk with a guitar and a joint— was the low-key dad. Nearly everyone I spoke to who worked on the first season of *The Bachelor* credited Levenson as the brains behind the show's creative direction. (She did not respond to my request for an interview.)

While Jeffress focused on the story elements of *The Bachelor*— How does a guy go about meeting twenty-five women? How will everything be shot and lit?—Levenson focused on what she liked to call the "zhuzh." So if she dictated that every camera shot needed to include candles and flowers, Jeffress figured out how to show off the soft, romantic ambiance through lighting and set dressing. Candles, they both agreed, set the appropriate tone for the show—warming the scene and evoking the intimacy of a dark, romantic dinner.

"But we took it to a level that was way out there. We would have thousands of candles ready to go," said Jeffress. "When it was like, 'OK, candle time!' we'd get everybody on the set—cameras, PAs, me, Lisa—pulling up the layout board to protect the flooring, sweeping and putting candles on the stairs. Lighters would be handed out. And then we'd light them all."

There were so many candles during the first season of *The Bachelorette*, Trista Rehn and Ryan Sutter's proposal scene almost went up in flames. A stage had been built over a pool for the special moment, and there were dozens of candles floating in the water. One of the candles drifted toward a plant that was flowing into the pool, "and the thing started torching," Jeffress said with a laugh. A few fire extinguishers later, everything was back on track.

Besides loading up on roses and tea lights, there was other prep work to be done. Together, the producers identified the two women they thought Michel would take all the way to the finale. ("We were almost always right," Jeffress boasted.) The team would make sure that Michel was prepped with tidbits about certain women, and then made sure to bring those ladies over to him for one-on-one time during the initial cocktail hour. When it came time for him to whittle the group down to fifteen, Michel could eliminate whomever he wanted—save for a couple of women. "We would say, 'We'd like you to keep this one because she's good for TV, and this other one we'd like you to get to know better,'" explained Jeffress. "When it got tough was when it got down to the final five or so. That's when there would be a little bit of back-and-forth. But they'd work with us."

On-set—while the action was still contained to the mansion—Jeffress held court in the control room, a space in the house filled with monitors and an audio mixing setup. Photographs of every contestant were taped above the monitors for reference, and crew members in the field had booklets of those same headshots laminated to loop through a belt. Inside the control room, at least three separate producers were posted at story stations, which were equipped with computers that allowed them to view various camera angles and track numerous conversations. Overhead, audio of whichever conversation Michel was engaged in would be pumped through the speakers to the whole room.

Jeffress, meanwhile, was outfitted with a headset so he could walkie-talkie producers inside the mansion when needed. He urged his team to ask the women certain questions or press harder for juicy follow-ups. If Michel himself needed a push, a house producer pulled him aside—maybe pretending his microphone had malfunctioned—and whispered something into his ear before he reentered the scene with a fresh intention.

To motivate the producing team, Jeffress offered cash incentives. He kept a wad of crisp $100 bills in his pocket and promised one to anyone who delivered strong drama. The first producer to get tears? A hundred bucks! You get Michel to make out with the right girl? A hundred bucks! Catch a chick puking on-camera? A hundred bucks!

"All that shit," Jeffress said. "When you're producing a show, you think in acts. After act one, you need something big to happen so you can cliff-hang. I need to bring people back from commercial."

And if the underlings couldn't get what Jeffress needed, he bought in the big guns: Levenson. Say there's a woman who has just been rejected by Michel. She's doing her exit interview, but she's not that upset—or she's holding in all her emotion. Levenson knew how to crack that veneer.

"She was the most amazing interviewer I've ever seen," Jeffress recalled. "If we needed tears, she would get them. First, she'd walk out there and just give them a big hug. Then she'd give them a shot of tequila. If they wanted a cigarette, they'd smoke a cigarette. Maybe one more shot of tequila. Then they'd start talking, and Lisa would go, 'Oh, honey, I know, I know,' and hug her again. And the girl just breaks. It happened hundreds of times."

So it was all bullshit? Levenson was only doing it for the show—she never truly related at all to these heartbroken women?

"I mean, she's a producer," Jeffress said, shocked by my question. "It was all bullshit. Are you kidding me? She'd come back in and say, 'Are you happy now?'"

Almost everyone who worked with Levenson—who stayed with the franchise until 2007 and is now the senior vice president of alternative programming at Fox Broadcasting—told me they viewed her with a mix of respect and fear. Even Meredith Phillips, who starred as the second-ever Bachelorette, knew it was dangerous to be alone in a room with the co-EP.

One night, Phillips said, her main producer was off-set, so Levenson had to step in to ask the star some questions. It was during that interview that Phillips cried for the first time during her season.

"I ended up crying, and it was an ugly cry," remembered Phillips, who became the leading lady in 2004. "And my producer was so pissed off. He was like, 'What the fuck? I knew it. I knew I should not have taken the night off. I knew she was going to do that to you. That's just the way she is.'

"She was definitely raw and shady," continued Phillips, whom I met with in Portland, Oregon, where she's now a chef. "She'd just get right down to it, and then she'd eventually get what she wanted. So you could never really trust her. I was surprised that I cried, but I think it was mostly because I was exhausted. I was like, 'I want this to be over with, so sure.' And then the tears came. And she was like, 'OK. Done. Got it.' And I thought, 'I don't care. She got it. She got what she fucking wanted.'"

Sometimes, Levenson would even cry herself.

"But then she'd come back into the control room and wipe the tear away and send the next bitch in," said Sandi Johnson, who worked as a producer on the show for the first five seasons. "In another life, she would have been an actress—an A-list movie star who can go in and give emotion, put it on the table, and then just get back to her life."

Back then, Levenson was making roughly $10,000 a week, and she liked to show off her wealth. She was liberal with her spending, often showering her coworkers with gifts. Majors, one of her former assistants, said she sometimes used fancy presents as a way to make up for her moody on-set behavior.

"It was kind of an abusive relationship, because she would get mad at me for something and yell at me, and then she would come in with a $200 robe that she bought me," he explained.

Fleiss worked differently. He never carried a wallet with him, and his wife would often give him a stipend—like an allowance.

"I had to carry his money for him," said Hatta, who assisted Fleiss during season one. "His wife would be like, 'Hey, do you know what happened to that money? I gave him $400 last week.' And I would go in his desk and there was this pile of money in his drawer. He would just hoard it. He was super weird like that."

Once, Hatta said, he and Fleiss went out to dinner, and he watched his boss order $150 worth of barbecue. Suddenly, the producer realized he didn't have his wallet on him. "Yeah, you're gonna have to get that for me, man, and I'll pay you back," Fleiss, who was buying dinner for his family, told Hatta. But he was never paid back by his boss, who was known for parking his luxury car directly in front of the doors of the Bachelor mansion.

He was more generous with his weed. In the early years of *The Bachelor*, Fleiss was constantly stoned.

"If you had to go into his office or you were brought in for a meeting, you were probably going to smoke," said Brad Isenberg, who worked as a production coordinator on *The Bachelor*. "Obviously, you could say no and it would be no big deal. But his office was smoked out like you would not believe. Like, smoke coming out under his door."

Fleiss had no qualms about getting high in front of his colleagues—or even his bosses. While filming Trista and Ryan's wedding special in St. Maarten, Fleiss stood in the corner of a resort conference room smoking a joint during a meeting with ABC brass. "He had no problem blazing in front of network executives," said Hatta, who was in the room. "Nobody said anything about it. It was insane to me."

"Mike's the kind of guy who likes to have fun and sometimes doesn't really care about repercussions because he wasn't going to have any," added Isenberg, who was also on the Caribbean trip. "He had a lot of leeway. And I think for good reason, because he brought a lot of money and ratings to ABC, so they probably let him act the way he wanted to act because he was pretty successful."

Almost from the inception of *The Bachelor*, Fleiss's affinity for partying infiltrated the work environment. During the first couple of seasons, the on-set control room was stocked with a full bar. One of the supervising producers kept a mini-fridge in his office labeled with different strains of pot. Cocktail hour usually kicked off at six p.m., and if you wanted to fit in, you took part in the drinking.

"It was like, everyone was drinking. It was just the norm, and I didn't want to be someone who said no, because you don't want to look like some kind of square," explained Carroll, who started as Levenson's assistant but later became a producer. "I was like, 'Sure. Great. Give me a drink.'"

"We were pretty notorious for what happened on our sets,"

acknowledged Jeffress. "Partying and getting crazy. It was a shit-show. A lot of alcohol. Pot. It was out of control. And it was a blast. We were doing something we loved and making a great show, so we partied. We'd go back to the hotel at three in the morning and drink until five, get up at six, and go again. We had adrenaline for days."

Some of the younger staffers—or employees who lived far from Malibu—just crashed at the "Bachelor pad" when the nights got too late. After a woman was eliminated from the show, her empty mattress was put in a walk-in closet—and that's where the crew sometimes slept. As the season rolled along, the mattresses would pile up, "Princess and the Pea"–style, and producers just climbed on top of the stack to get some shut-eye.

Carroll, who is openly gay, often just slept in the same room as the remaining ladies.

"If it was night six and there were only fifteen chicks left, I'd be like, 'I'm going to sleep in the room with them because there's an empty bed,'" he said. "They'd wake up and I'd be like, 'Hi!' I didn't know any different."

Not everyone was cool with the lax work environment, however. In 2005, a handful of *Bachelor* employees were part of a lawsuit filed against four reality TV production companies (including Fleiss's Next Entertainment) and four TV networks (including ABC) that claimed the employers withheld overtime wages. Eventually, the case became a class-action suit that resulted in a $1.1 million settlement split among more than two dozen plaintiffs.

"It's super dangerous to work with no sleep like that and then get behind the wheel every night and drive home," said a former staffer who participated in the lawsuit. "Yeah, there's a crash room on-site. But the hell I was going to sleep in a crash room. I'm sorry. I have a certain expectation of how people should be treated."

By the time the lawsuit was settled, the raucous work environment had already cooled off. One night, sometime around the fourth season, a drunk crew member was driving down the mansion's windy driveway and hit another car. Some network executives witnessed the accident and put the kibosh on the partying.

But there were other on-set mine fields to navigate: namely, the confusing, often volatile dynamic between Fleiss and Levenson. There were whispers throughout the set that the two producers were in a romantic relationship despite the fact that they were both married.

"You'd catch little things coming around a corner or out of the corner of your eye when they didn't think anybody was in the room or paying attention," said Hatta, who often had to interact with Fleiss's wife as part of his assistant duties. "It was just disheartening. It kind of takes the wind out of you, because I really respected that guy at one point. This just took it down a notch."

Rumors about the executives started circulating when staffers began picking up on puzzling behavior between the two. Levenson's assistant, Evan Majors, frequently fielded calls from her husband in which her spouse had no idea where his wife was. One casting associate noticed Levenson and Fleiss flirting during a rose ceremony, when she sat between his legs, her teeth stained by red wine.

"We could kind of tell that she was overprotective of him," said Erica Rose, who interacted with Levenson as a contestant on *The Bachelor*. "She'd get jealous when people were talking to him. We were like, 'We're not here trying to date *him*.'"

Meanwhile, Phillips—a onetime Bachelorette—observed how the second Fleiss arrived on-set, he and Levenson exited together.

"I even went over to Lisa's house and hung out with her and her husband, and that was awkward," Phillips recalled. "Looking him straight in the face and talking to him like I don't know anything."

Regardless of what happened between Fleiss and Levenson, I've yet to meet one person who worked on *The Bachelor* who doesn't credit her as an integral part of the show's success. She was the one in the trenches, identifying interesting characters, getting juicy morsels, and upping the stakes, employees insist. So when Fleiss was on-set, his interactions with Levenson could become testy—they both had a stubborn streak and bickered openly. But Fleiss actually wasn't around all that much. He had a company to run and was working on developing a slate of reality programming to fulfill his multiyear production deals with ABC and CBS.

And after *The Bachelor* hit, Fleiss was in demand. The show premiered on March 25, 2002, and reviews weren't kind—not that that made a difference in the ratings. On the day of the show's debut, *Variety* published a piece saying the program wouldn't last long, arguing it felt like "a reality series that comes late to the party and just won't leave."

"Besides being insulting to any woman who may not look like a runway model, *The Bachelor*, hosted by Chris Harrison, is just plain boring," the *Variety* critique read. "It's as if the network bankrolled a brothel and positioned cameras to catch the action."

Many critics took issue with the way *The Bachelor* depicted women. Even though Chris Harrison started each rose ceremony by telling the ladies that they could reject Michel's flower if they didn't think he was someone they "might end up marrying or might want to marry," many felt the female contestants were disempowered.

The NOW Foundation, part of the National Organization for Women, gave the show an "F" grade for "sexual exploitation" and "social responsibility." *The New York Times* wrote that the show existed "as a hyperbolic reminder of the pernicious view that man-catching at this point in history has odds analogous to hitting the superfecta." The *Los Angeles Times* said that "arguably the most distasteful aspect of *The Bachelor* is the idea that a large group of beautiful, intelligent women—in this case all under thirty-five—would compete to win the approval of one guy." And *The Washington Post* argued that *The Bachelor* had reduced "courtship and matrimony to a Darwinian TV sport," resembling "nothing so much as a contemporary harem."

The show's creators and stars fired back against the harsh words in the press. "No one is saying 'this is how dating should be,'" reasoned Michel, who said he didn't view any of the women as "desperate." It was just a "weird social experiment," Fleiss explained—nothing more than "something to watch on television." Women were the program's biggest fans, noted Levenson, who suggested ladies responded to the show because "they like seeing that there is a possibility for true love and that they're not the only ones being dumped by their boyfriends."

Not that the audience needed any convincing. Nearly 10 million total viewers tuned in to watch the series premiere of *The Bachelor*, and by season's end, that number had jumped to 18.2 million. Michel, as it turned out, didn't even end up proposing to his final pick, Amanda Marsh, an event planner from Kansas who beat out Trista Rehn.

"I got this ring for you," Michel told Marsh, opening a Harry Winston box. "I'm gonna hold on to it." He went on to tell Marsh that he was falling in love with her and asked if she would move to California, where they could make sure they felt the "same way about each other outside of the fantasy world of mansions and limos." (They broke up less than a year later, after Marsh learned Michel had slept with Rehn during the show.)

Nonetheless, the ratings were so strong that the team got to work on a second season almost immediately. In May 2002, casting director Lacey Pemberton—who still finds the program's eligible suitors today—put out the call in the *New York Post*, saying the show wanted someone "more approachable" than Michel this time around. "I think graduating from an Ivy League school made Alex seem unapproachable to certain people," she said. The second Bachelor, she hoped, would be a guy with a "regular job" who "enjoys sports" and "all sorts of regular activities."

That guy ended up being Aaron Buerge, a twenty-eight-year-old corn-fed Missouri banker. The blond Midwesterner proved to be even more popular than Michel: His season finale—which did end in a proposal—raked in a colossal 26 million viewers.

The Bachelor had become a cultural phenomenon—and that baffled the critical cognoscenti. Just as Buerge's season came to a close, *The New York Times* published two lengthy pieces attempting to get to the bottom of the show's success.

Caryn James, the Gray Lady's chief television critic, said the program's popularity spoke to a deep-held nostalgia: "We're in an age when sexual roles are fluid, and *The Bachelor* offers an escape from ambiguity, a temporary and knowingly false return to an era in which male and female roles were clear—stereotypical, but clear."

Meanwhile, Alessandra Stanley, who became the *Times'* chief TV critic in 2003, argued that the show's appeal was anything but mysterious: "This gauzy ABC dating competition is *Jackass* for women: a reality show that revels in emotional risk taking and rejection in the same way that *Jackass*, the MTV series, celebrates men's foolhardiness and physical pain."

It wasn't long before other networks began attempting to cash in on their own versions of *The Bachelor*. In December 2002, Fox announced its new show *Joe Millionaire*, about twenty women competing for a man they believed was worth $50 million. In fact, lead

Evan Marriott was just a working-class construction guy. The kicker? Mike Darnell—the executive with whom Fleiss had worked on *Who Wants to Marry a Multi-Millionaire?*—was behind it.

"It's a pretty inventive swipe at us," Fleiss admitted to the *Chicago Sun-Times*. "*The Bachelor* show isn't as cynical and I think that's ultimately why it works, because at its heart is romance. I think viewers like to root for real romance and not something that is [as] disturbed as *Joe Millionaire*. . . . I mean, [Fox is] desperate for two things—to try to generate some ratings, obviously, because they are in the toilet, but also to try to damage a great franchise like *The Bachelor*."

Joe Millionaire ended up becoming a huge hit, with more than 34 million viewers tuning in for the finale. Fortunately for Fleiss, the concept really only worked as a onetime stunt. A sequel set in Europe, where there weren't as many people familiar with the original show, tanked.

Anyway, Fleiss was busy running his own production company, which had grown to 300 employees just a year after the debut of *The Bachelor*. Suddenly, he had more shows on prime time than veteran producers like David E. Kelley (*Ally McBeal*) and Steven Bochco (*NYPD Blue*). *Vanity Fair* profiled Fleiss and frenemy Mike Darnell, dubbing them the "Reality Kings." And network executives gushed about him to the press.

"Mike has been a gift," ABC Entertainment president Susan Lyne told the *Orlando Sentinel* in 2003. "He understands the eighteen-to-thirty-four audience and what they're looking for in television."

But though he would go on to produce more than a dozen other reality shows—*High School Reunion, Leave It to Lamas, The Cougar*—Fleiss has yet to replicate the ratings success of the Bachelor franchise.

Which perhaps comes as somewhat of a disappointment to a guy who aspired to have a diverse fifty-year career like Aaron Spelling. (He even named his kid after the *Dynasty* producer, remember?) But maybe not. It's not like he's hurting for cash, anyway. He lives atop the Malibu bluffs in a home worth nearly $14 million with his second wife, former Miss America Laura Kaeppeler, who is twenty-three years his junior, and their two-year-old son. (He filed for divorce from his first wife—his high school sweetheart—in 2012 citing "irreconcilable differences.") He also has two places in Hawaii: a $2.3 million half-acre property in Hanalei and a two-plus-acre home on the North Shore of Kauai that he purchased from Julia Roberts for $16.2 million.

Plus, he's always known his strong suit, and it's wrapped up in the conceit of *The Bachelor*: He's a provocateur.

"I love the excitement that comes when people say, 'You can't do that on TV!' And then we take the dare and respond, 'Oh yes, we can!' I get off on that," he said in a 2003 interview with the *Contra Costa Times*. "If I have any skill at all, it's the ability to come up with ideas that get people talking. With so many choices out there for viewers, you've got to get people talking about your show or you have no chance at all."

In that same interview, he argued there wasn't enough sex appeal on television, complaining that he had to wait three episodes to see Tiffani Thiessen in a bathing suit on the short-lived Fox series *Fastlane*. In that big *Vanity Fair* piece, writer Mark Seal witnessed Fleiss in the edit bay, asking to see more "sexy images" of the female *Bachelor* contestants. When the production team pulled up footage of a drunk woman, Fleiss responded: "I thought we had hilarious shit of her fucked up! . . . I would loop a couple of those barf sounds. Loop the wettest one!"

"Mike would walk by and you would just see the sunglasses over the top of the cubicle, and he'd be like, 'More T-and-A, Sandi. More T-and-A,'" said Johnson, the former story editor. She remembers being impressed by the way Fleiss could "tap into the populist masses," delivering suggestions that were deceptively simple but ultimately had a big impact on the viewing experience. He always encouraged the producers to keep the suspense up, and to repeatedly reemphasize what was at stake: Is there a rose up for grabs? Then we better hear the word "rose" every sixty seconds.

He was also good in a room. When it came time for him to sell a show, he'd trade out his flip-flops and basketball shorts for cowboy boots and black jeans. "He's a great salesman," said Jeffress. "He can walk into a room and pitch like crazy. He's one of the best pitch guys I've ever seen."

But when it came to *The Bachelorette*, Fleiss was the one who needed to be sold. After *The Bachelor* performed so well in the ratings, it wasn't long before viewers—and network executives—wondered what it would be like if the tables were turned. Yet Fleiss wasn't sure that audiences would respond as positively to a woman choosing between twenty-five men.

"Mike was really negative about it. Never did like it," said Jeffress. "And I agreed with him, in a sense. The house with the girls in it hanging out creates a female-driving audience. They're talking about the bachelor, talking about jealousy. Guys in a house together? It's a frat house. It's a big party. Nobody wants to see it. Mike didn't think that was what the show needed to be, but ABC wanted it and said, 'You're doing it.'"

"I was sort of dragging my feet on this one," Fleiss later admitted in a 2003 interview with *Newsday*. "My theory is if it's working, leave it alone. But the network wanted to silence some of our feminist critics, and rightfully so."

Plus, Fleiss and company already had an ideal candidate waiting in the wings: Trista Rehn. After appearing on Alex Michel's season, viewers had fallen in love with the thirty-year-old former Miami Heat cheerleader who spent her days working in pediatric physical therapy. Though she'd been jilted by Michel, the experience helped Rehn realize "more than ever before what kind of person I was looking for and what kind of person I had become," she wrote in her 2013 memoir. As the Bachelorette, she felt she'd be more likely to find the One: "After all, people were being paid to scour the country and find guys who fit my 'type.' I didn't have that kind of time and, buried in student loans, I certainly didn't have that kind of money."

The guys who showed up to woo Rehn had all seen her on television prior to *The Bachelorette* and were eager to date her specifically.

"It wouldn't have worked if we had put up any random girl, and told them they'd have to show up and compete for Girl X," theorized Fleiss in that interview with *Newsday* before the show's premiere. "Guys aren't interested in the notion of getting married, generically speaking. But you dangle some sexy little blonde . . . like Trista . . ."

And the men will be down to compete, apparently. In true Fleiss fashion, of course, nothing about the gender swap was subtle when *The Bachelorette* premiered on January 8, 2003. "For the first time in television history, a woman will be calling the shots!" Chris Harrison announced at the top of the show, before introducing the pilots, firefighters, and professional athletes who would be vying for Rehn's heart.

"Are you ready to fight the same battles the men fight in having the power and the say in the relationship?" the host asked Rehn, completely earnestly.

"I think it's a great thing for a woman to propose," she responded.

Yep, that's right: The Bachelorette was supposed to get down on bended knee and propose to her chosen man at the end of the season. But somewhere along the way—after one guy gifted Rehn with a Tiffany bracelet he'd bought pre-show and another read her a very poorly written love poem—that idea went out the window, sans explanation.

The show never elaborated upon why Ryan Sutter, Rehn's ultimate pick, was the one to give the Bachelorette the Harry Winston sparkler viewers had watched her pick out herself. But Bob Guiney, who vied for Rehn's heart and later went on to become the Bachelor, guessed that being proposed to by a woman would have made Sutter uncomfortable.

"I think that any one of the bachelors would have wanted to propose instead of being proposed to," Guiney wrote in his 2003 memoir. "It probably taps into the same feelings that made me want my wife to take my last name. There are some things that you want to keep if you are traditional, and I'm an old-fashioned guy in a lot of ways, and so were a lot of the other guys there."

Another break with tradition that the *Bachelorette* team was worried about? The possibility that Rehn would sleep with multiple men in the Fantasy Suite. "We were very frightened it would look like Trista's whoring herself up," said Jeffress. "It's changed now, but back then, it would have been, 'Oh my God, she's horrible.'"

Rehn's openness about her sexuality, Jeffress said, helped push viewers past their traditional thinking. "She said, 'Hey, we're grown-ups, and I've gotta know [if we're sexually compatible]. We're feeling it.' Saying that on TV, I think, helped viewers understand that 'Hey, it's OK, these are adults. They're consenting. They're just in a relationship and they may be getting married soon.'"

But critics didn't think the show was as progressive as Jeffress did. The role-reversal was a "profoundly stupid idea," wrote *The New York*

Times' Caryn James, back on the Bach beat. "There's too much sexual stereotyping around, too much of a lingering sense that what makes a man a playboy makes a woman a slut. And *The Bachelorette* is hardly trying to explode those clichés. With its hokey title (a word no one ever uses) and its smarmy attitude (viewers are going to be looking for signs of sluttiness), this gimmicky series plays right into those stereotypes while pretending not to.

"The only stereotype shattered," James concluded, "is that the Bachelorette, who turns thirty during the course of the series, isn't considered over the hill."

A month after that column was published, however, 20.4 million people watched as Rehn and Sutter got engaged. ABC soon green-lit a three-episode wedding special, a lavish affair that the network spent $4 million on; the couple was paid $1 million for their participation. Rehn donned a $70,000 satin Badgley Mischka gown, $50,000 Stuart Weitzman shoes with 282 diamonds on them, and a $1 million Tacori necklace.

The Sutters are still the franchise's longest-lasting couple, and they live together in Colorado with their two children, where Ryan continues to work as a firefighter.

Why I'm a Fan

ALLISON WILLIAMS

I WATCHED THE FIRST FEW SEASONS OF *THE BACHelor,* followed by a hiatus until I graduated from college. My first season "back" was Brad Womack's second season, which I viewed with vigor. I had just moved to L.A., and there was a weekly viewing party at my friend's house. It just so happened that the man who is now my husband also went to that viewing party, so Monday nights were an excellent opportunity for a group-date scenario when he was in town from New York. Thus, it sort of became a staple in our relationship and, eventually, our marriage. We still watch it every single Monday night.

I prefer the seasons of *The Bachelorette*—I'm not going to lie. I obviously love watching a group of dudes fight for the attention of a woman, so there's that. And with time, the suitors are learning to compliment the intellect and personality of the Bachelorettes—not just their looks. I don't exactly love that *The Bachelor* advances and fuels the narrative that women on TV are ... well, the way they're portrayed on *The Bachelor.*

I think that this is a show where you can learn about and engage with your own sense of feminism. I have only ever viewed the series through this lens, but my understanding of the dynamics therein has become more thorough as I've gotten older. I actually think that as the women become more empowered to speak their minds on the series, it provides audiences with more opportunities to learn about feminism. We're even starting to hear that word on the show, which is very exciting to me.

I spent six years on *Girls*, a show that sometimes taught feminism by showing examples of the characters' misguided attempts at feminism—but all of it was told from the point of view of a production staff, writers' room, actors, and director list that was definitely feminist. You can't only absorb the ideals of a feminist world view through shows that espouse them—often, there are more lessons to learn about womanhood on shows where the women (or, more typically, the men) are behaving in ways that proliferate misogyny in one way or another. Especially if you're watching the show with other women—as many people do—there are teaching moments every few minutes.

I find myself wishing the characters would just say, "Let's put a ring on my finger that belongs to Neil Lane, and then we can start dating and see if we actually like each other in the real world." Because it's always too obvious to the audience, once we see the couple reunited "After the Final Rose,"... that the prospect of planning a wedding seems insane to them. They all have this vibe about them that projects: "Give us a minute. We essentially just met."

And increasingly, it feels absurd that they don't know anything about what's happening in the outside world. The fact that the election came and went without hearing any mention of it on this show... feels impossible. I would give *anything* to see a political discussion within this group, but maybe that's just me. Also, that would give them something to talk about on their dates outside of their past relationships, et cetera. What can't you learn about someone's outlook on the world through a healthy debate about health-care policy?

—Allison Williams, actress (*Girls*, *Get Out*)

CHAPTER 3

The Roots of Television
Romance

S ince *The Bachelor* began airing in 2002, dozens of reality television producers have tried to capitalize on the success of the dating-show genre. We've watched people date naked. Date in the dark. Date millionaires. Date pretend millionaires. Date Tila Tequila.

No matter how extreme the gimmick, the Bachelor franchise has spawned the only modern-day dating shows with any serious longevity. Because of the lack of substantial competition in the current TV marketplace, though, it's easy to forget the shows that paved the way for *The Bachelor*'s ascendancy.

The first man to put dating on TV was Chuck Barris, the renowned creator of shows like *The Dating Game* and *The Gong Show*. And in some ways, Barris and Mike Fleiss are cut from the same cloth. Like Fleiss, Barris possessed an innate understanding of what viewers wanted to see—the kind of stuff that critics often deemed morally bankrupt, too provocative, and culturally damaging.

Both men also came up through academia, never intending on going into television. A Philadelphia native, Barris studied industrial management at the Drexel Institute of Technology. After graduating in 1953, however, his career ambitions shifted, and he took a job as a page in NBC's trainee program. Eventually, he moved to ABC, where he was hired to keep an eye on Dick Clark, who was in the midst of the payola scandal. The network moved him from New York to California, and he was named ABC's West Coast director of daytime programming.

But he wasn't long for the gig. After spending so much time observing Clark on-set, Barris came to believe he himself had what it took to create a successful television show of his own. So he quit ABC, borrowed $20,000 from his stepfather, and convinced the network to spend $7,800 on an idea he had for a pilot.

The premise? One eligible young woman would be matched with three male suitors—but she couldn't see her potential dates. The men were hidden behind a partition, and the woman had to decide who she wanted to go out with by asking them questions and judging their answers. (The show also worked in reverse, with one man and three hidden women.) Barris hired a little-known radio disc jockey from San Francisco, Jim Lange, to host the program, which he dubbed *The Dating Game*.

Though Barris felt good about the pilot, ABC initially turned it down. And since they'd funded the test run, he couldn't shop it to other buyers. Fortunately, just a few weeks later, a couple of the network's game shows proved to be ratings failures, and desperate to fill the daytime slots, they gave *The Dating Game* a chance.

"I got a call that said we were going on the air and I was so excited it was pathetic," Barris recalled in a 2010 interview with the Archive of American Television. I tried to interview Barris myself but was told by his wife that he was too ill to speak on the phone; he died shortly after that exchange in March 2017 at age eighty-seven.

When *The Dating Game* debuted in December 1965, there were a handful of game shows already on the air: *Let's Make a Deal*, *Match Game*, *Jeopardy!*, *Password*. But Barris's show was the first on American television to delve into contestants' personal and romantic lives. As he put it in a 2011 conversation with his alma mater: "Television at that time was all question-and-answer shows and stuff like that, and this was spontaneity. That was never, ever in television before. There wasn't a correct answer to a question on *The Dating Game*."

Despite the groovy-looking flower-power daisies that decorated the set walls—and even though it was filmed in Hollywood, which the show dubbed the "dating capital of the world"—*The Dating Game* was relatively tame at first. The show launched during a seminal moment in the cultural landscape. Troops were still embedded in Vietnam, and the antiwar movement was growing rapidly, resulting in protests and civil unrest. Just as men's hair was growing longer, women's skirts were getting shorter—the miniskirt had just come onto the fashion scene from London. The Beatles and the Grateful Dead were topping the music charts, and more than 400,000 people would soon travel to upstate New York to romp scantily clad in the mud at Woodstock.

But it would take a while for *The Dating Game* to reflect the culture. At first, the men came out dressed in stiff blazers and ties and often touted their college credentials. While the women sported flirtier shift dresses with bell sleeves, the questions they asked of their mystery men were rather demure.

- When you feel low down and blue, what do you usually do to get back in the groove?
- If you were a work of art, what would you look like?
- Pretend you are Confucius. Make up a special little proverb for me right now.
- Robert Browning won Elizabeth by poetry. Let me hear some poetry that would win me.
- You've hurt my feelings and I feel really bad and I'm about ready to break out in tears. Would you tell me you're sorry?

Such questions might seem lame now, but television critics of the era were horrified by the show. "Daytime Television Hits All Time Low," a *Chicago Tribune* headline declared. Lange was so rattled by the review that he wondered if he should quit the hosting gig. "In my opinion, a good game show review is the kiss of death," Barris recalled telling the host in his 1993 memoir, *The Game Show King*. "If for some strange reason the critic liked it, the public won't. A really bad review means the show will be on for years."

Indeed, *The Dating Game* would go on to air for decades. While its initial run on ABC came to an end in 1973, the show was revived three more times in syndication. Lange still presided as host on the first revival, from 1978 to 1980. By that time, Barris had already created a handful of other shows, including the hit *The Newlywed Game*, on which three newly married couples competed to prove which pair knew each other best. Barris himself had also begun hosting *The Gong Show*, where amateur performers showed off talents for a trio of celebrity judges—any of whom could strike a massive gong if the act wasn't to their liking. (No, Mike Myers—ahem, Tommy Maitland—was not the original host of *The Gong Show*.)

Barris's wacky personality was key to the success of *The Gong Show*. He came onstage dressed in a tuxedo jacket and bell-bottom jeans that were so loose they looked as if they might slip off at any moment. He sounded so spaced-out that he said viewers often questioned whether he was high. And when he came under fire for his willingness to humiliate Average Joes on television, he insisted his programs were all made in the spirit of good fun.

"The contestants on our shows come because they have a good time," he told Mike Wallace in one particularly testy *60 Minutes* interview. "These people don't take participating on a game show as seriously as you think they do, Mike. It's not a big sociological thing. They just want to have some fun."

Soon, Barris's reputation on *The Gong Show* began to affect his other programs. When *The Dating Game* came back for its first reincarnation in 1978, he told his staff to push the boundaries this time around. No more staid bachelors in suits and ties. Instead, production scouted for single stand-up comedians at the Improv comedy club in Hollywood.

"The '70s version of the show was purposefully out-there, because Chuck was known for *The Gong Show*, so they told us we better be silly," said David Greenfield, who began working as a producer on *The Dating Game* and *The Newlywed Game* in the late '70s. "Whereas *The Dating Game* in the '60s was much more provincial. They'd make a big deal if a couple got married. 'Oh, do you remember John and July? Look at how cute they are!' When I worked on the show, no one got married."

Busy with *The Gong Show*, meanwhile, Barris remained relatively hands-off. He hardly ever visited set, according to Greenfield, but his presence was still felt at the office.

"My very first week at ABC—I'm twenty-three years old—and I

see Chuck riding a motorcycle down the hallway of the office," Greenfield said. "On his birthday, we got him a huge cake, and what did he do with the cake? He jumped in it. That was Chuck. He had to do stuff like that."

As a producer, Greenfield was responsible for prepping the women and helping them come up with questions before walking onstage. Another producer was put in charge of the men, while Greenfield said he landed with the women because he was "cute—then—and tan." During the pre-show briefings, he told the female contestants to "get salacious" and talk about their sex life. There's nothing funny about describing your perfect date, he advised. And then came his most important move.

"Before the first show, the executive producer came up to me and said, 'I don't care how you do it, but when those girls come out onstage, I want their nipples erect.' Now, I don't know if he meant turn the air conditioning up or what. But sometimes they would put a chair in the room, so I would come in, and as sad as this sounds today, I would straddle the girl as I asked her questions."

And how did the female contestants not completely freak out over this? (Slash not file sexual harassment charges against ABC?)

"Freak out?" Greenfield asked incredulously. "It was the '70s. Everybody was doing cocaine. They were smoking dope. There was free sex. It was a totally different time.

"The stuff I got away with, really, is astonishing," he acknowledged. "I couldn't do any of that now. You ask a girl out on a date and they'd fire you."

Greenfield did other things behind the scenes on *The Dating Game* that he's not particularly proud of either. Once, he invited a little person on the show—a guy with a great personality—and put him up against two drips he knew the woman wouldn't find appealing.

"So she picks the little guy and he comes around the partition like, 'Oh—hi,'" said Greenfield, who is sixty-two now. "She cried so much after that show. I apologized so much. It was the worst thing I ever did. The fact that I set her up with a midget, a little person? It's not a nice thing to do. But at twenty-three, twenty-four—to me, it was funny—until after the fact. If anything, I matured and learned from that. Just stick to the program."

Anyway, he knew how others in the business thought of the reality show. *The Dating Game* shared offices with Goodson-Todman, the production company responsible for wholesome programs like *Family Feud* and *Beat the Clock*.

"We'd rib each other in the elevator. It'd be like, 'What are you guys doing, antonyms this week? That's a fascinating show.' And they'd say back, 'Well, what are you doing? Showing girls' you-know-whats this week?'"

But no matter how playful *The Dating Game* got, there was only so much that you could say about a couple of people who'd just been introduced on-camera.

Enter *Love Connection*. In 1983, television producer Eric Lieber debuted the first game show to actually send two singles on real dates.

"*The Dating Game* was terrific, but what happens after the date? That was the genesis of what Eric wanted to do with the show," said coordinating producer Tim Crescenti, who worked on *Love Connection* for eight years. (Lieber died in 2008 at age seventy-one.)

Still, viewers weren't privy to footage from the dates. Instead, the audience was introduced to a man and a woman who had already gone out with each other. One half of the couple—let's say the woman, in this case—walked onto a pink-and-purple set decorated with hearts. She sat down on a couch across from host Chuck

Woolery, whom you may recognize nowadays from late-night TV commercials in which he hawks a digital device that supposedly cures joint pain.

Then Woolery began to ask the woman about the three potential suitors she had to choose from for her date. Clips of each of the men the woman had considered played, and the studio audience then voted on whom they thought was her best match. This was an odd concept, since the date had already occurred, but in any event—the audience results were revealed, and then the woman said whom she'd selected.

This was when we'd finally start to get some good juice about the date. The man whom the woman had chosen—supposedly sitting backstage—would pop up on an overhead screen. The two would relay stories about what happened on their date, and then, if the woman decided she wanted to see the man again, he'd walk out from backstage and they'd smooch and celebrate.

The freedom the daters were given was pretty impressive, considering the intense background checks reality TV producers use these days. First, those auditioning would be rated on what *Love Connection* staff called the PALIO scale: Personality, Appearance, Lifestyle, Intelligence, and Occupation. If your score was high enough—and you were a Southern California resident over the age of twenty-one— you'd be matched up with a stranger and sent on a date without any real screening. After being handed $75 by production, you'd be told to head out on your date, which could take place anywhere except a location that wasn't conducive to conversation: No movies. No concerts. No plays. If you were lucky, sometimes producers would suggest an idea they'd stumbled across in *L.A. Weekly*—a festival, a fair, or a well-reviewed restaurant.

After you'd gone on your date on a Friday, you and your date partner would each receive a call on Monday from a segment producer, who'd grill you both on what went down.

"The producer would call and say, 'Well, Amy, how did your date go with Tim?'" explained Crescenti. "'Oh, we had a nice time. We went to dinner. It was a nice time.' Well, that's not good television. So you call Tim and ask how the date went. 'Oh, she was nice.' 'What did you think of her?' 'I thought she was great.' 'She's OCD about cleanliness. Did that come up?' After Tim talks about that, you call Amy back and say, 'Tim said your apartment was a wreck.' 'He said that? What?' Then all of a sudden you start to get somewhere."

Of course, Crescenti admitted, the goal here was not truly to create lasting relationships.

Of more than 2,000 episodes, he estimated that about two dozen marriages came out of the show. If a contestant came into an audition and started to say how eager they were to find a spouse, they'd be reminded by a producer that "first and foremost, this is an entertainment show. If you're here to find a husband or wife, you're probably in the wrong room."

"There were some people who saw it as a last resort," Crescenti explained. "Like, 'Boy, I've tried everything. Might as well go on this big television show where they know what they're doing.'"

Little did the daters know that if a woman was deciding which of her three options to go out with, she'd often be urged to pick someone she wasn't actually compatible with. "Unknown to you, he has an opinion politically, socially, chauvinistically that's going to trigger something on the date and make great television," Crescenti said. "We might show you a five-minute segment of his video that looks very favorable, but the guy is a chauvinistic jerk and you don't see that on the tape."

After the producer-led debriefing sessions, a few scant details from the date would be relayed to Woolery. And that was the way the host preferred it. He liked to wing it, discovering information in real-time so that he'd have more authentic reactions on-camera. If, however, the couple had slept together on their date, Woolery would be informed via an offstage cue card that read "Boink Date."

"We couldn't even ask outright, 'Did you have sex on the date?'" said Crescenti. "They would have to kind of gingerly walk around that. Chuck would say, 'How did the date end?' The guy would go, 'Well, you know, Chuck, when I woke up the next morning—' and you'd hear the crowd go '*Whoaaaa*.' It was quite a throwback."

By now, though, popular culture had become more sexual: Movies like *Flashdance* and *Octopussy* had women dressed in barely there outfits. Michael Jackson was grabbing his genitals onstage. So to many women, Woolery represented a kind of wholesome everyman. In fact, when asked about the kind of guy they'd like to go out with, many of the women who auditioned for the show said they hoped he'd resemble the host.

"A lot of the ladies found him handsome and charming," Crescenti said, noting that Woolery served as host for twelve years, until the show was rebooted for a season in 1998. "And yet he was an approachable, accessible guy. He was an everyman who wasn't super slick, which was great. I think that was his appeal. He didn't have that 'I'm better than you' attitude. [Creator] Eric Lieber said he was the perfect host because he felt like the host of a cocktail party, or your son-in-law. Likable, safe, and oh, he's handsome."

If *Love Connection* were on the air today, Crescenti believes, "people would think: Snoozeville! They'd want footage from the date, faster cuts, more sex.

"They take people on an epic journey on *The Bachelor*. It's a storybook romance," said the producer. "*Love Connection* wasn't about getting another date. If that does happen, wonderful. But this is not a beautiful love story like *The Bachelor*."

Of course, just a few weeks after Crescenti uttered these words, news broke that Bravo guru Andy Cohen—he of *Watch What Happens Live* and Real Housewives reunion fame—was set to host a Fox reboot of *Love Connection*.

Even better? The show's producer is Mike Fleiss.

"*Love Connection* was always one of my favorite programs," Fleiss said in a press release when the news was announced, a few months before the revival's summer 2017 debut. "Show creator Eric Lieber was a close friend of mine. He taught me a lot about the relationship show format. The first rule—if the cast is good, just stay out of the way."

Indeed, Lieber was the "George Steinbrenner of television shows," according to Crescenti. He demanded the best, and if you didn't play by his rules, you were sent packing. Because he was such a taskmaster, there was always a revolving door at *Love Connection*. Writers were often told their segments weren't up to par, and producers were pushed to mine for juicier information from the daters.

"Each segment had to be tantalizing," Crescenti said. "Eric wanted to make sure things really had a perspective—whether it was lovey-dovey and charming and oozing with affection, or 'Holy shit, I can't believe she said that.' Nothing in between."

Before his death from leukemia, Lieber told the *Chicago Sun-Times* that he most enjoyed "the couples who rag on each other"—though he copped to being depressed when he learned one of the pairs who had wed on the program had since gotten divorced.

"The show succeeds because we believe in honest emotions," he said in the 1992 interview. "And, admit it: We're all a little voyeuristic and enjoy peeking into someone else's life."

Accordingly, the next hit dating show dug even deeper into viewers' voyeuristic tendencies. In 1995, MTV premiered *Singled Out*, hosted by a then little-known *Playboy* model named Jenny McCarthy and a Los Angeles radio DJ, Chris Hardwick.

While *Love Connection* had remained pretty meek—hello, "boink date"—*Singled Out* capitalized on the sex-fueled spring-break culture of the mid-'90s. The show was raunchy, loud, and high-energy, typically starting with a camera pan of fifty young daters screaming their heads off. In an attempt to replicate what it was like to meet someone in a real-life bar setting, the show selected more than three dozen singles and offered them up to one lucky man or woman—or the "picker," as they were known on-set.

The picker—let's use a woman in this scenario—would be seated on an oversized, gaudy heart-shaped throne, hidden from the view of their dating pool. Then Hardwick or McCarthy would ask her a question about her ideal mate that almost always had to do with physical attraction, like "blond or brunette?" If she answered blond, all the brown-haired dudes would immediately walk by her throne and exit the stage. (She did have the option of saving one of the guys as they passed, if she so chose.) She'd then answer another question: "Do you like to be on top or on bottom?" Welp, she's into missionary, so all the dudes who like her on top are goners.

After a few probing questions, there'd be between five to eight guys remaining, and it was on to "Keep 'Em or Dump 'Em." Each man would introduce himself and give a cheesy one-liner—"My name is Chris, and no woman can resist my luscious kiss"—and the woman would decide who sounded best. Her final picks would then attempt to make their way into the "winners' circle" by answering some "deeper" questions and hoping their answers matched those of the picker. "Valentine's Day: a celebration of love or a waste of money?" A true celebration, obviously!

Whoever reached the picker first was subsequently placed back-to-back with her, and then the two were finally allowed to look at each other for the first time. The lovebirds would be offered a complimentary date—perhaps whisked off in a limo to a horseback ride past the Hollywood sign—and that was that.

"I think we were just trying to have fun," Gary Auerbach, one of *Singled Out*'s executive producers, told me. "MTV had a very strong brand at the time, and it was the one place you went to have fun and celebrate. People in their twenties and younger—that was pretty much all they watched."

Like on *Love Connection*, the aim here was not to create long-lasting relationships. Kallissa Miller, another of the show's EPs, said the show tried to own its vapidness, and "most critics got that the entertainment value overrode the shallowness."

Even so, MTV had concerns about how far to push the envelope. After hiring Hardwick as the male host, the network initally wrestled with the idea of bringing on McCarthy as well. "MTV had an issue with her being in *Playboy*," recalled Auerbach, noting that the comely blonde was Playmate of the Year at the time. But after going through the final run-through of the pilot with a different female cohost alongside Hardwick, executives realized they needed McCarthy to make the show work.

"Both men and women liked her because she was sexy but kind of tomboyish," Auerbach said. "She was kind of gross and had fun and didn't get offended by anything."

"She was willing to stick her tongue out and be all silly," added Miller. "Now, that just seems like, 'Oh, yeah, of course. So many girls are willing to do that.' But back then, to have somebody as beautiful as her being like, 'Oh, I'll fart on TV'—that was redeeming."

By the third season of the show, McCarthy had become a ubiquitous pop culture presence. Miller remembered being on a plane and flipping through *Entertainment Weekly*, stumbling upon an article talking about the top ten things the hostess had in her closet.

"Almost every edition had something about Jenny, and I know, because Chris was jealous," said Miller. "He would come to me and be like, 'How come Jenny's getting all the press?'"

Both Hardwick, who has hosted Comedy Central's talk show *@midnight* and NBC's game show *The Wall*, and McCarthy, who has her own Sirius XM radio show, declined my interview requests. But according to Miller, the tension between the two was palpable—though it never veered into spiteful territory.

"I wouldn't say they were BFFs," she acknowledged, "but they had a brother-sister relationship. Like if your sister's getting more attention from your parents, you say, 'How come you're buying her a new car? What about me?' That's how it was for Chris. And his success was linked to her success, so when he saw all these articles in *Entertainment Weekly*—he's a smart guy, and he realized that."

After four seasons, McCarthy decided she was ready to move on to greener pastures anyway, and she landed her own sketch comedy program on MTV, *The Jenny McCarthy Show*. (It debuted in 1997 and was canceled after just one season.) For the final two seasons of *Singled Out*, the network cast Carmen Electra, a model who was best known at the time for—shocker!—posing nude in *Playboy*.

"Jenny is funnier and Carmen is sexier, so I think what ended up happening is [Carmen] took on more of a traditional, almost Vanna White–esque role," said Miller. "That's when Chris shined a bit harder, because there were no longer two comedians vying for the funny role."

As the show gained popularity, MTV began fielding requests from managers seeking to place their clients on *Singled Out*—and a handful of celebrities like Jennifer Love Hewitt and Fergie (then

Stacy Ferguson, just a singer in the pop trio Wild Orchid) ended up as pickers.

Now, a decade on, Miller sees *Singled Out* as a precursor to dating apps like Tinder. The show allowed pickers to flip through dozens of options quickly, making love feel more like a fun game than an overwhelming prospect.

"The idea that you could have fifty guys or girls wanting you is really seductive," she said. "The idea of choice—that massive quantity—had a game element to it that always appealed to everybody."

Singled Out went off the air in 1998 after five seasons. But it wasn't long before *Blind Date* came along to pick up where the MTV juggernaut had left off. When *Blind Date* kicked off in syndication in 1999, viewers were finally able to watch as two people ventured off-set and into the real world, following a man and a woman who'd never met before as they went out on their first date. And we're not just talking coffee or drinks. The couple would meet early in the afternoon and drive themselves to a total of four locations over the course of a day—making the whole thing a ten-hour affair, minimum.

And there was a twist: After the date concluded, witty writers would come up with jokes to fill text bubbles that would pop up throughout the episode. The messages were meant to mirror viewers' own thoughts about the daters or add context to a situation. Like if a guy showed up for his date looking really extreme—bright-orange jumpsuit, scarf tied around his neck, leopard-print fedora—we'd read: "We swear he dressed normal at his audition!" Or maybe a dude made a comment about his attractiveness—he didn't think he was a "10." Suddenly, "That makes two of us!" would pop up over his date's head. You get the idea.

At first, the show wasn't conceived with the pop-up bubbles. Executive producers Jay Renfroe and David Garfinkle—who have since gone on to create the mega-popular survival program *Naked and Afraid*—initially thought they might have enough of a show if they just went out in the field and shot blind dates without any gimmicks.

"But watching two people on a date turned out to be extremely boring," Renfroe recalled, sitting in his office at his production company's Sherman Oaks headquarters. "They don't really say what they mean. So we had the idea to turn it into a human comic strip. We used smart writers to give those characters voices and say what we were all thinking but couldn't say."

But it wasn't all snark. Production actually hired a psychologist to consult on the dates and weigh in on the odds of the couples working out. The shrink would analyze the pair's body language and choice of words so that "we could ground the humor in some sort of reality," Renfroe said. "We would let people dig their own graves first. We never dug the grave for them. So if you saw a guy meet a girl and immediately put her into the category of 'sex only'—and that's what guys do—then the second he did something like that, he was open game."

Soon, ratings were strong enough that production was able to travel outside of Los Angeles to follow daters in cities like Dallas, Phoenix, Las Vegas, and Chicago. Renfroe even got a call from one of David Letterman's staffers on *The Late Show* after one particularly memorable episode in which a woman supposedly passed gas numerous times during her date. "They told me that the writers were taking bets about did this girl really pass gas twenty-seven times during the period of the date," Renfroe said with a laugh.

While the show easily found an audience, it wasn't exactly an incubator for years-long relationships. Of the 1,500 episodes that were filmed over the show's seven-year run, Renfroe could recall only three couples getting married. Auditioning daters for the show, he was surprised to find how few singles seemed to know what they were looking for in a partner.

"We'd ask them who was their type and then try to match people up with exactly the guy or girl that they described," Renfroe said. "But then we'd send them out and they'd hate each other. And if we sent a girl out with a guy who wasn't exactly what she said she was looking for, they'd usually hit it off. Because I don't think people really verbalize what they want. They're not always that truthful about what they really connect to."

There was also little to mask one's true character on the show. From the moment a man arrived on a woman's doorstep, it was evident whether or not they were attracted to each other. And if the pair didn't seem to be a match, things would get awkward fast. There were long car rides filled with uncomfortable silence. But with a cameraman sticking his lens into the back seat, the daters often felt pressure to talk—and not just about their favorite movies or pizza joints. "When you add cameras into the mix and crew who are expecting something, people feel like they need to perform," Renfroe said. "And that forced people to talk about real things. You have to have more honest conversation about things of substance, because you can't be lazy."

There also weren't any lavish, fantastical locations to distract from the one-on-one interaction. Early in the day, there'd usually be an activity—going to the beach, playing basketball, hitting up a comedy club. And then they'd head out to eat. Most of the dates took place at average-looking chain restaurants where the most important feature was the bar. And yes, more often than not, the contestants would get drunk—tequila shots at a Mexican restaurant,

Coronas by the boardwalk, wine at an Italian place. (That's when a taxi would come into play, chauffeuring the pair around for the rest of the evening.)

"We didn't have the *Bachelor* budget," said Renfroe. "And they are selling romance. I think what we provided was reality. We had very relatable dates. I don't know if everyone can relate to being swept away in a private plane to Paris for dinner."

One especially popular *Blind Date* destination was Splash, a now-defunct Los Angeles "spa" equipped with a plethora of *super* sanitary private hot-tub rooms. Producers loved the venue—for one, the show was allowed to film there for free—and it allowed for contestants to show some skin before they, almost always, started hooking up. Splash became so popular that in a later season, during a week of episodes featuring millionaire daters, the owner of the spa was sent on a date of his own. "So many people knew about the place from all the exposure that he'd made so much money," Renfroe said.

So many dates turned out to be total disasters—often in those very hot tubs—that *Blind Date* ended up serving as a cautionary tale for many viewers. Renfroe said he'd often hear from married couples who told him the show had saved their relationships. After watching, some audience members shared, "We'd say to ourselves, 'Whatever problems we have, we can work them out. We just don't want to have to do *that* again.'"

No longer was it considered racy to make out on TV or bare your soul to millions of strangers. By the late nineties, nearly every teen had an AOL account, and some were even starting to find love in online chat rooms. We were beginning to market ourselves—making websites, blogging on LiveJournal—realizing that the Internet and television had the power to make us stand out from the crowd.

Young people now dreamed of being on television, and MTV was there to make that fantasy attainable. Brian Graden, the network's president of production around the millennium, had doubled down on dating shows. Teens would rush home to watch kids like themselves dating with the aid of their parents (*Date My Mom*), lie detectors (*Exposed*), and ultraviolet wands (*Room Raiders*).

One of MTV's most popular dating shows during this period was *Next*, in which a group of singles tried to find love on a bus. Because who among us hasn't dreamed of falling for someone while seated at a table that converts into a bed?

Five guys, for example, would be secluded on an RV—known as the "*Next* bus"—that would roll around to different locations. At each stop, one young man would get off the bus and start a date with a woman at the helm. If at any point she didn't feel like she was connecting with a guy, she could yell, "Next!" and he would have to retreat to the bus. At the next stop, she'd meet her next option.

Like on *The Bachelor*, the bus added a helpful, bubble-esque intensity to *Next*. Contestants had no cell phones, and the windows on the vehicle had been blacked out. All the focus had to remain on the people inside the bus. Sometimes, on episodes with LGBTQ participants, matches started to form before the contestants even met the person they were meant to be fighting for.

"It was always a party on the bus," said Miller, who was an EP on *Next*. "Sometimes the dates would be really stiff, and we'd get on the walkies, like, 'How's the bus going?' And they'd be like, 'Oh, it's a party in here! This one guy just bet another guy to shave his eyebrow off!'

"My favorite shows to produce reveal natural, interesting dynamics between men and women," continued Miller, who—after working on six MTV dating shows—is often called "The Queen of Dating" in the industry. "I see myself as a social anthropologist. And dating is the ultimate way to see how people connect."

Sure, she admits, *Next* may not have led to any great psychological discoveries about the mating habits of young adults. But she still thinks dating shows serve an important purpose.

"You know when you get together with your girlfriend, and you almost want her to have gone on a bad date because the story is infinitely more interesting?" Miller asked. "We all know as women that you have to kiss nine frogs to get one prince. So why not enjoy the process? I meet so many women that are like, 'Oh, I hate dating.' And I'm always sad for women when I hear that—that they just want the end product. I think they're missing out on a lot. I never want women to feel like they're failing when they're having a bad date. Most dates and relationships end. That's just the way it is. But somehow, that's not how it's taught to us. I feel sad about that. It's not embarrassing if you go out on a bad date. No, ladies, it's fantastic. Let's do brunch, and I want to hear every detail."

Why I'm a Fan

NIKKI GLASER

I HONESTLY PROBABLY GOT MY IDEAS OF ROMANCE from Ross and Rachel. A guy needs to pine over a girl for years, and then the forces that be finally bring them together, but it's a long struggle of not being able to say how you feel. And it's all very spontaneous and in the moment.

When *Friends* went away, there was no other romance I really cared about, so I was like, "I'll check [*The Bachelor*] out." You see someone legitimately fall in love, whether it's lust or love or just, you know, getting caught in the moment. I relate to the show a lot. Like, just falling head over heels, in a very unsafe way. "This isn't going to end well, but it's fun to watch."

Because of the nature of the competition on the show, you have to be emotive. It's so interesting to me, because a lot of times the Bachelorettes want to hear from the guys, "I love you and I'm ready for marriage." In regular life, it would be a terrible decision to reveal that stuff—to say "I'm all in, I love you, I want to get married." That's an insane thing to do. In real life, my advice to men would be to play it cool even if you do feel those things. Even though, on paper, I want to hear those things, hearing it would scare me away. I would want the guy who doesn't seem into me.

I'm not proud that I watch *The Bachelor.* I don't think it's a feminist show, but I do think feminists are into it because it's an interesting case study. I don't have guilt about it, because I just like what I like and I'm secure in that. I think we are seeking out these shows that remind us of the '90s and the early 2000s when Britney Spears was the woman to be. It's kind of like a throwback, because it is so vapid and so stuck in the early 2000s. I've watched the Kardashians and when I watched that show, I wasn't one to be like, "I just watch it to make fun of them." It's truly entertaining to me. You shouldn't be ashamed to enjoy reality television, because it's like reading nonfiction. You're just watching people—it's real. I know that they're set-up situations and I suspend disbelief to be able to watch it, but I don't think that there's anything wrong with wanting to watch people be put in a situation that you would never find yourself in.

It's really not a feminist show because the goal is to get married, and I'm just so annoyed by that. Why does everything have to be about getting a ring at the end of this? Why can't they just progress enough to be like, "This is the person you choose to be with in a committed relationship"? It's a sad ending, these two people who barely know each other saying they'll get married. We don't care that much. Just tell us they're going to be together and work on a relationship. That's way more interesting than locking these two into eternity together.

It's all about kids. I think people get married because they want kids. You know virgins who want to have sex but can't until they get married, so they just get married to get this other thing out of the way? It's like that. We need to change the conversation. "OK, so if she wants a family, she still has a family without marrying someone." We don't want to see them getting married. We just want to see them getting proposed to, because the idea of someone wanting to spend the rest of their life with you is better than actually doing it.

—Nikki Glaser, comedian (*Not Safe with Nikki Glaser*)

CHAPTER 4

The Road to the Mansion

I f you are over the age of twenty-one, you are eligible to apply to be a contestant on *The Bachelor*. If you are over the age of twenty-one and have been banned from attending official *Bachelor* events by ABC brass, you are still eligible to apply to be a contestant on *The Bachelor*.

Not that you'll have a shot in hell of making it on *The Bachelor*. But you can still apply!

This was my logic as I scrolled through the casting website the show always advertises during its commercial breaks. *Let's just look at what the application would require. No need to actually press Submit, right?*

As it turns out, if you want to apply to be on *The Bachelor*—or *The Bachelorette*—the online application is your best bet. It doesn't involve much critical thinking—only a few vital biographical details: Height? Weight? Do you have any children? Occupation? What is the nearest big city to you, and how far is it? Have you ever applied to be on the show before? What's your Instagram handle? How about Facebook? Can you send us (the hottest) picture of yourself (in minimal clothing)? Note: parenthetical additions are (obviously) my own.

And, finally: Why do you want to be on the show?

Aha! A deceptively simple question, akin to those horrifically broad "Tell us about yourself" or "Why do you want to go here?" prompts you encounter on college applications. But it was so hard to separate myself from the reality of the situation—you know, the ban, my lack of a bikini body, an overwhelming fear of helicopters/bungee jumping/mean girls—that I found it difficult to pursue the question seriously, even as a thought exercise. *Come on, Amy. Just imagine you look like Margot Robbie. Think about all the fun travel you'll get to do! The potential sex you'll have in a body of water! The Neil Lane ring you'll get to wear for less than a year! The thousands of dollars you'll make from Instagram sponsorships! The lifestyle blog you'll launch! The free plastic surgery you'll get! The subsequent tabloid photo spread! So many gems await you.*

I had nada. So I decided to check out the mail-in application. Perhaps it would necessitate even less effort on my part.

To my horror, this bad boy was loaded with far more probing questions than the online application. This was serious—the kind of thing I imagined the casting crew taking a much harder look at than the online application, which, let's be real, is probably all about the photograph.

If I was going to take this seriously, the mail-in application was the obvious choice. I readjusted my attitude, put on some Brad Paisley—that's what people on *The Bachelor* listen to, right?—and got to typing.

Nickname, age, job, hometown, siblings, yadda, yadda, yadda. No, I've never been arrested or had a restraining order issued against me—but aren't you gonna background check this shit, anyway? I did audition to be on a reality show once, but it was about aspiring journalists who got to work at Rolling Stone, *so I feel like that doesn't even count. I've never been engaged, I don't have kids, I don't drink and will not start on this show.*

OK, now we're getting real: "Are you genuinely looking to get married and why?"

Yes. Because I'm thirty-two and society/your show/my parents make me feel ashamed of being single at this age. Also because I like spooning, watching Netflix, and splitting bills.

"Why would you want to find your spouse on our TV show?"

Truly, how can one answer this honestly without acknowledging one is somewhat of a fame whore? I want a shot with a cute, highly sought-after dude, and if I win, my confidence will skyrocket? I want to go on lavish, over-the-top fantasy dates instead of meeting a guy from OkCupid at a taco truck because "Jonathan Gold gave it a good review"? I want to be engaged but I also would like to make $5,000 by posting a photo with teeth whitener on Instagram?

"Please describe your ideal mate in terms of physical attraction and in terms of personality attraction."

Bearded. Hairy. Not Jake Pavelka.

"How many serious relationships have you been in and how long were they? What happened to end those relationships?"

Ugh, do we really have to go down this road? Fine. Let's say . . . three serious relationships. About two years a pop. I eventually realized: "I don't want to marry you, bye."

"What are your hobbies and interests?"

I am interested in my dog, Riggins, and hanging out with him.

"Do you have any pets?"

See above.

OK, let's zoom through the rest of these. Special talents? Um . . . I'm good at getting people to tell me their secrets. And picking out the perfect gift. Languages? I can speak very poor French that magically gets better when it is being spoken to an attractive Frenchman. And no, I do not have any tattoos. Three surprising adjectives about me: Compassionate. (I'm not as mean as I seem!) Kooky. (I'm pretty weird.) Naturey. (My mom suggested this. It just means I like lying in fields and looking at the moon and stuff.)

Proudest accomplishment? Eek. Maybe moving across the country and setting up a life for myself in L.A.? Is that lame? WHATEVZ I DON'T CARE I'M NOT GETTING ON THIS SHOW ANYWAY!

Oooh, yay, final question! "What have you not found but would like to have in a relationship?"

I guess I've yet to find the appropriate power balance. You know that old wives' tale women often hear, "Marry someone who loves you a little bit more than you love them"? *I've been with guys who I've felt were more into me than I was into them, and it's always been a turn-off. Of course, I've been in the opposite position too, and that sure as hell doesn't feel good. But being with a man who I love and who loves me just sliiiiightly more than I love him? I've never had that. Frankly, I kind of think that whole wives' tale is bullshit, because power dynamics ebb and flow. And if I was on* The Bachelor, *the guy would have all the power in the relationship anyway. So this is probably gonna work out great!*

Now all I have to do is submit anywhere from five to fifteen pictures of myself, making sure to include "good close-up shots" and "full-body pics." I feel like everyone must go with fifteen photos, right? Well, I'm going with zero, since I won't even put a "full-body pic" on Bumble.

Oh, and apparently I should make a video if I want to "ensure"

I'm seen by the casting team and to show off my sparkling personality. The instructions say I should offer up "lots of energy and BIG SMILES!!!" I need to find a well-lit room and make sure I don't stand in front of a window. Instead, I need to find a colorful background that won't make me look "washed out." I shouldn't wear black, white, "intense prints," hats, or sunglasses. I should wear an outfit I'd put on if I were going "to a nice restaurant for dinner."

As far as the content of the video goes, in between my BIG SMILES!!! I am supposed to show off my apartment and my pet. I should talk about my "love story," my ultimate fantasy date, and my favorite actor, Ryan Gosling, whose face is on the tea towels hanging from my oven. I should showcase my freezer filled with Trader Joe's macaroni and cheese, because you want to know "what's for dinner!" I should highlight my couch, because the casting team wants to see my workout "routine." I should end the video by giving both a close-up and a full-body shot of myself. "This is very important!"

Guys. Can you imagine actually doing all of that? Sure, even the most jaded among us have probably fantasized about what it would be like to be on a reality show. But going through all the effort to actually get on one? That's a level of commitment that, frankly, I found difficult to comprehend. I mean, I couldn't even get through the damn application, let alone gin up a fun-and-flirty video and then subject myself to months of in-person interviews.

But let's say, miraculously, I'd sent in the application and video and the producers were so charmed by me that, after a few phone calls, they decided they wanted to meet me in person. And since we're already going out on a limb here, let's say I don't live in L.A.— I'm from Boston. What would have happened next?

Well, I'd be invited to come to L.A. for one of two final audition weekends—all expenses paid—to meet the production team in person. After I agreed to the trip, the show would book my travel, and a couple of weeks later, I'd head to the airport. When I was on the plane, I'd get a text message from my handler instructing me to text them when I landed.

On the runway at Los Angeles International Airport, I'd send the text and hop on a shuttle to the nearby Sheraton Gateway, where the auditions were taking place. Once at the airport hotel, I'd call my handler, who would immediately meet me and rush me to a check-in room in a more discreet part of the building. There, I'd be given a 150-question personality test to bring back to my room and complete there. The test would be filled with multiple choice and true-or-false questions: *Do you have out-of-body experiences? Do you think you can control things with your mind? Have you ever wanted to kill someone?* Some of these questions would be asked several times, reworded differently.

After I handed in the test, I would be told not to leave my room. If, by some chance, a guest spotted me and asked what was going on, I would be told to say I was part of a movie production. I would be given a $50 daily stipend. If I wanted alcohol, I would be instructed to call a specific number, and drinks would be sent to me. I would not interact with any other potential contestants.

This would be the first day of the finals weekend.

The next day, a Saturday, I would wake up around eight a.m. and be picked up by my handler. The handler would proceed to take me to a handful of different stations. First, I'd have a few pictures of myself taken. Then I'd be escorted to a room to have a one-on-one interview with a producer. If I later made it onto the show, I'd come to realize that this room resembled an ITM setup—the kind of space in which contestants give "in-the-moment" interviews, talking about their feelings and experiences. There would likely be candles and mood lighting behind me.

After twenty minutes of speaking with the producer privately, I would be asked: "Hey, do you want to meet some of my friends?" I would be walked to an adjoining room, where I would be greeted by roughly two dozen producers sitting stadium-style. I would quickly become aware that they had watched my entire "private" ITM as it was unfolding on a television screen.

The producers would have me sit down and would start asking me questions, rapid-fire. Had I watched the last season of *The Bachelorette*? Did any of the guys stand out to me? What was I looking for in a man? What was my dream job? If I could have that dream job if I cut off one of my limbs, would I do it? Would I rather have a DDD bra cup or write a cover story for *Vogue*?

Just as the questions started to become more outlandish, the producers would wrap up the session and a handler would take me to meet with the show's therapist. From 2002 through summer 2017, that was psychologist Dr. Catherine Selden.

According to the California Board of Psychology, Selden is a state-licensed psychologist who graduated from Pepperdine University and has no disciplinary actions against her license. She was always made available to contestants throughout the season—she was not a presence on set but emerged any time she was requested—and cast members were supposed to meet with her after they were eliminated.

"I actually really liked Dr. Selden," said Sharleen Joynt, an opera singer who wrestled with leaving Bachelor Juan Pablo Galavis's season but ultimately did so of her own accord. "I felt like she got me. She told me I was the most self-analytical or introspective female contestant they'd ever had on the show. . . . After I exited, they took me to a hotel suite and the doctor was there waiting for me with a room-service menu at, like, three a.m. She's on call 24-7. I had never spoken to a shrink before, but I loved her."

But contestants were first acquainted with Dr. Selden during the casting process. So she would be in possession of the personality test I'd filled out and would spend roughly an hour asking me questions about it. At times, she would get personal: Had I ever cheated on anyone? Did I have a history of mental illness or depression? Did I ever drink too much? Did I ever get into fights when I was drunk?

Next, my handler would bring me to a private investigator. This person would be trained to dig up any skeletons in my closet—partly to use for my storyline but also to get ahead of any tabloid stories that could come to the surface if I was on the show. Had I ever been arrested? Had I ever sent nude photos to anyone? Had I ever made a sex tape? Had I gotten a DUI?

Finally, I would be taken for a medical examination. Samples of my blood and urine would be collected. These samples would be tested for drugs and sexually transmitted diseases. I would fill out my medical history and answer questions about my health. If I were on any medication, I would tell the medical professional, who would want to know whether I would need my pills during production.

Then I would be escorted back to my room and given something called the "fun packet." The questions inside would be light: What's your favorite movie? Who do you look up to? If you could have dinner with anyone dead or alive, who would it be? What's your ideal date? The answers I gave to the questions in the packet would be used in my bio on ABC.com, if I made it on the show.

After I was done with the fun packet, a handler would check on me and walk me out of the hotel. I would be allowed to go out in L.A., as long as I texted the handler when I returned to the Sheraton.

The following morning, a Sunday, I would fly back to Boston and wait to hear if I'd made it past the pool of fifty finalists and onto *The Bachelor*.

In the following weeks, producers would discuss my performance and analyze the materials I'd submitted to determine whether I should be cast. If it turned out I had an STD, I'd be taken out of the running immediately. And apparently, that's the top reason applicants don't make it onto the show.

"I learned a lot about life from those tests," said Ben Hatta, Fleiss's old assistant, who was privy to the casting process. "As soon as the medical tests came back, you'd see that herpes was the biggest thing. And sometimes you'd be the first person to tell a contestant that they had herpes. You'd be like, 'Uh, you should call your doctor.' Why? 'We're not going to be able to have you on our show, but you should call your doctor.' Then they'd realize they'd been denied from *The Bachelor* and now a bunch of people knew they had herpes."

As for the psychological testing, Fleiss likes to say that the Bach has some of the most thorough background checks in the business— a lesson he learned after that whole Rick Rockwell fiasco.

"We're really careful about who we let on the show," he said at the Banff World Media Festival in 2012. "We lose a lot of great potential characters because we're so tough and stringent. . . . Anyone who has any sort of borderline personality disorder or instability or any sort of past involving contemplation of suicide—we just can't take the risk. We just don't."

But according to numerous producers who have worked on *The Bachelor*, the rules aren't always that strict.

"There's psychological tests they have to pass, but there's a window of the pass, do you know what I mean?" insinuated Michael

Carroll, the producer who got so close to contestants that he even crashed in their rooms occasionally. "You'd know there'd be a possibility of [someone] being kind of unhinged—like, she passed, but just barely. You can see it at the casting events during the interviews: 'Oh, this chick is going to go fucking nuts. She's amazing.'"

I asked him to describe the kind of behavior he was talking about. Say, for example, Carroll told a woman to describe her first love. You don't want the girl who says her first boyfriend played lacrosse and went to Harvard. You want the girl who dated a guy who rode a motorcycle and was the bane of her parents' existence. "You want the girl who's like, 'Oh, he was super cool and we would go fuck in his parents' pool,'" Carroll explained. "You get the feeling of who pops on TV and who's coming unhinged and who's gonna go for it."

Rozlyn Papa, an infamous *Bachelor* villain, recalled her session with Dr. Selden being particularly troubling. The psychologist asked Papa if she'd ever struggled with mental illness, and the single mother was candid about her battle with depression. Even though she wasn't feeling low at the time, she was honest about the fact that depression was an ongoing issue in her life.

"If they were really trying to protect you, you'd think that would be sort of a red flag and they would say, 'Well, maybe this is someone who can't handle this kind of pressure,'" said Papa, who ended up getting kicked off Jake Pavelka's season in 2010; much more on that later. "But instead, it was almost like, 'OK, perfect. You're perfect for the show. You're going to cry. You're going to say some really screwed-up stuff.' Looking at it, I can see why I should not have been a candidate."

Frankly, I think you have to be slightly insane to agree to the contract the show makes contestants sign. I've looked at contracts from a few different seasons of the show—the one I'm quoting from here is from 2015—and they barely change from year to year, save for some updates about social media policies. So let's take a walk through the ironclad twenty-seven-page document, shall we?

OK, first off—and this probably seems obvious—you must agree to be filmed up to twenty-four hours a day, seven days a week. But this may also be "by means of hidden cameras and microphones," according to the contract—meaning you're likely going to be caught, at some point, in a less-than-positive light. You should have "no expectation of privacy."

Furthermore, because this is a reality show, you must acknowledge that "elements of surprise" will be included. You must be "prepared for anything," including "twists" and "surprises." "Producer or others connected to the show," the contract reads, "may intentionally or unintentionally make misrepresentations or omissions concerning the Series." Basically: The producers can mislead you, and that's totally kosher.

Here's where we get to an especially important clause, because it's in all-caps:

I UNDERSTAND, ACKNOWLEDGE AND AGREE THAT PRODUCER MAY USE OR REVEAL PERSONAL INFORMATION WHICH MAY BE EMBARRASSING, UNFAVORABLE, SHOCKING, HUMILIATING, DISPARAGING, AND/OR DEROGATORY, MAY SUBJECT ME TO PUBLIC RIDICULE AND/OR CONDEMNATION, AND MAY PORTRAY ME IN A FALSE LIGHT.

In other words: If you get drunk, naked, or just downright bitchy, come off looking terrible, and then lose all your friends and your job? That's on you, babe. Even worse, anything embarrassing that you do on the show—whether you were "clothed, partially clothed, or naked" or "aware or unaware" of being filmed—is owned by the franchise forever.

And you'll probably act a little differently from how you would in your day-to-day life, because you're going to be "separated from [your] family, friends, and [your] regular environment in Los Angeles" until production is finished. Those conditions may expose you to "severe mental stress," and you cannot seek "refuge" anywhere cameras aren't allowed. But if you suffer "emotional and mental distress" as a result of your portrayal on the show, the competition, or the isolation—just remember, you signed off on that.

During production, you might have to engage in "strenuous physical activity" on dates: "hiking, wading, swimming, diving, parasailing, water skiing, other water sports or activities, skydiving, snow skiing, ice-skating, roller blading, and other physical activities yet to be determined." You may have to be a passenger in a watercraft, land vehicle, helicopter, or small plane.

Even though everyone on the show is advised to "refrain from all forms of violence and intimidation," you might be in "close physical proximity" to contestants who could exhibit "physical or verbal aggression." And if you go on the show, you have to be single. You can't be married. You can't be living with someone with whom you have "physical intimacy." You can't even date someone exclusively for more than two months. Once production begins, if you have sex with someone, you need to be aware that you're risking contracting sexually transmitted diseases.

In the year following the finale of your season, you must be available to take part in a "reasonable number" of interviews, photo shoots, and chats for publicity. You also have to agree to take part in any special episodes of the show—like "After the Final Rose" or other reunions—for three years.

And if you make it to the end of the Bach and decide to get married within the two years following the show, the producers own the exclusive rights to your wedding. If they exercise those rights, they're only going to pay you $10,000 per hour of televised programming about your union. As for the ring given to you by Neil Lane? You don't own it—and therefore can't sell it—for two years.

Given all these guidelines, the question remains: Why would anyone agree to go on this damn show? Don't the risks very obviously outweigh the benefits?

There are plenty of former contestants I spoke to who admitted, outright, that they simply didn't read the contract. They wanted to be on TV and figured, "What the hell? How bad could things get?" Others, like Rozlyn Papa, scrutinized the document.

"I read over every word of that contract," she acknowledged. "I spoke about it with my family. We talked about what the repercussions could be and how they may twist things or edit things. But the advice of my family was: 'Just don't give them anything that you wouldn't want to be seen by millions of viewers. As long as you are yourself and you stay away from drama and you don't drink a lot and you don't call anybody names and you respect the other people, then they're not going to have anything bad to show or to say about you.' It's not that I was unaware of the potential ramifications, I just thought that it wouldn't apply to me."

When I'd ask people who have been on the Bach about why they wanted to go on the show, I'd usually get some sort of roundabout answer. "It all started as a joke! My friend submitted me! It's a free vacation! A once-in-a-lifetime opportunity!"

Rarely, it seemed, were past contestants honest about what drew them to be on a reality show—likely because that would mean admitting to being unhappy with the monotony of their off-screen lives.

"Think about it," reasoned Papa. "The majority of girls on that show either don't have a job, or they have a job where they can leave for six weeks. You're looking at women who aren't really in a solid place in life, and probably have issues with identity or love or self-esteem."

She makes a good point. Why apply to go on a reality show if your life is going swimmingly? Even if you're a Real Housewife, a Kardashian, or Tori Spelling, there's something greater at stake—building a brand, getting more followers on Instagram, paying the mortgage.

Being told that you're beautiful and interesting enough to star on television by a reality-show producer? That's a pretty powerful form of validation.

In her 2012 memoir, Melissa Rycroft—yes, the one who was proposed to by Jason Mesnick on *The Bachelor* only to be dumped months later on "After the Final Rose"—admitted outright that she wasn't in a positive mental space when she was cast. She'd just broken up with a boyfriend, and though she was emotionally distraught, she thought *The Bachelor* would give her a fresh start.

"Even though I was still a mess inside, there was something about pretending to be put together that started to make me feel like I *was* that powerful woman I wanted to be, and that made it all easier," Rycroft wrote in her book, *My Reality*. "I wasn't actually going on the show to look for love. I was simply going to move on with my life and find a new, happy place inside of myself. I needed to rediscover me."

For others, the show provides an opportunity to get out of dead-end jobs. Desiree Siegfried—who was Desiree Hartsock before she became the Bachelorette in 2013—was working as a consultant at a

Beverly Hills bridal salon before she went on TV. That may sound like a glamorous gig, but Siegfried said she was actually living paycheck-to-paycheck, just hoping she'd one day be able to save enough to start her own wedding-dress design company. She was so broke that all she did was work and work out. She felt like she was barely getting by in L.A., but even her ticket out of her day job—a spot on Sean Lowe's season of *The Bachelor*—was worrisome.

"Quitting my job was a huge risk," she acknowledged. "And then even paying rent and the bills while I was gone. I didn't have it."

Siegfried took the gamble, but as she made it further along on Lowe's season, she was forced to open up about her money troubles to producers.

"About rent time, I said, 'I won't be able to continue unless you pay my rent,'" she said. "But I was so modest. I should have said, 'Could you pay for my bills too?' I felt so bad. So when I got off, I know I was backed up with all my bills."

And what about the rarer applicant who actually loves their job? Obviously, not every boss is cool with an employee taking an un-specified amount of time off work—especially if that employee's reputation takes a hit during their hiatus.

Harming his image was a major concern for Michael Garofola, who had a prestigious job as a federal prosecutor in Miami when he was cast on Siegfried's season of *The Bachelorette*. He knew there was no way he'd quit his job to go on the show and thought it was highly unlikely that the US Department of Justice would grant him permission for a leave of absence.

"So I go up to meet with the US Attorney, and I was really sur-prised by how well he took it," recalled Garofola. "He was like, 'Well, of course they would want you. You're a great guy and you're a very good catch.'"

Still, Garofola's request had to go through the ethics committee, but ultimately, he received a letter signed by then attorney general Eric Holder saying he could embark on "non-legal, non-paid, outside activity" for eight weeks.

"There were a few people who were against it," Garofola remembered. "But to be honest with you, my sense is that the people who were against it were a little envious. I had a great position as a lawyer and was still able to go have some fun and travel and have this unique experience."

Nick Viall—who, yes, actually did have a real job before becoming a lifetime reality TV star—didn't have to jump through as many hoops to get off work. But when he was nominated by a friend to participate on the 2014 season of *The Bachelorette*, he still wasn't sure it would be beneficial to his career. At the time, he was thirty-three and had just been promoted to account executive at the cloud computing company Salesforce. He didn't want to quit, but everyone in his life thought he should go on the show.

"I kind of became frustrated with my friends," he acknowledged. "I really wanted honest advice. But I equated it to buying a boat. If you go to your friend and are like, 'I'm thinking of buying a boat,' they're going to say, 'You should totally buy a boat. That's an amazing fucking idea.' But boats are a really bad investment. They're a lot of fun, but a lot of work. So everyone just wanted to go on my boat— see me go on TV."

Still, Salesforce was encouraging—promising he could return to the company after he vied for Andi Dorfman's heart. Of course, they had no way of knowing then that he'd end up going on three more nationally televised Bach journeys. Viall did return to Salesforce for a brief moment, but he eventually moved to Los Angeles to pursue a modeling career and do more reality television.

Yes, that's right: After his first stint on *The Bachelorette* with Dorfman, he returned to the show as a surprise mid-season guest in 2015, when Kaitlyn Bristowe was the lady of the hour. As it turned out, Viall had slid into Bristowe's DMs during the off-season, and when she became the Bachelorette, he decided to go on the show to try to date her. He ended up as the runner-up, once again, so then he headed to *Bachelor in Paradise,* the summer franchise spin-off where contestants from various seasons fly to Mexico to drink tequila on the beach and hook up. His turn on *Paradise* was such a hit with viewers that ABC decided to make an unconventional choice, casting him as the Bachelor in 2016. As a result, he finally got engaged—his fiancée was a beautiful special education teacher from Canada, Vanessa Grimaldi. The couple spent their first months together in public on yet another highly visible stage: Immediately after *The Bachelor* went off the air, Viall joined the cast of *Dancing with the Stars.* Not long after that reality show stint, he and Grimaldi broke up.

Keep in mind that when I interviewed Viall for this book in late 2015, he told me he thought his time "finding love on TV" was done.

"I'm Nick from *The Bachelorette,* and I get that," he said at the time. "But I don't want to be recognized for that. I don't want it to be what I'm known for. I'd rather people be like, 'Why do you have so many followers?'"

In that same breath, though, he acknowledged that he got a rush from being recognized. Sometimes, he said, he'd walk into bars and catch himself looking to see if anyone noticed him.

"And you're like, 'What am I doing?' I try to tell myself this isn't going to last. I'm aware of how forgettable we all are."

He may be aware of that fact, but he seems to be doing his darnedest to fight it.

Why I'm a Fan

HEIDI AND SPENCER PRATT

SPENCER: WE BASICALLY ONLY WATCH REALITY TV. The Chrisleys, *Love & Hip Hop,* all the Real Housewives, the Kardashians, *Total Divas, WAGS, Dance Moms.* And *Bachelor* is our only broadcast show, because it's pretty much a cable show on ABC.

Heidi falls in love with the love story, and I'm more about what they're all doing for the camera. I know what's up—they're on the show to get IG followers and #SponCon ads. But the reality is, I went on a TV show just for fame and now I'm married with a kid, so the game is crazy.

Our reoccurring game we play is figuring out what line was re-said in a testimonial that a producer created. Did you really say that, or was that purely for story? There's alcohol involved, so you're pumped up, and the producers are saying, "That was so good, you're so funny. Oh my gosh, people are gonna love you!"

And then there's editing. I have been on multiple phone calls on reality shows where I was talking to one person and they use the footage to make it look like I was talking to somebody else. They bait you in. It's totally a mind game. You're tired, the lights are bright. On *Big Brother,* you'd be in bed completely asleep at three a.m. and they'd call you to the diary room. You will say whatever gets you back into bed because they'll drag it out.

Heidi: With scripted, everything is so regimented and planned out and every character acts a certain way. But with reality TV, you get to see how people really are, which is way more entertaining. Maybe people approve of it less, but it's also more realistic and human.

Spencer: And like scripted is so much better? On *Game of Thrones,* people are getting their heads chopped off and being burned alive and it's like, that's what 20 million people should watch? People being brutally murdered by dragons? That's chill? I would much rather Corinne getting blacked out for America and love than watching people getting murdered for an hour straight. Every hit show isn't a hit show because it's so wholesome and you're learning how to be a better human. People just love hating on other people who get famous for doing nothing. Viewers know people are getting paid and having fun and going to parties.

I used to live-tweet during *The Bachelor,* and I loved it, until it became an unsafe environment. All I did was like a fellow *Bachelor* fan's tweet and she said she wanted to kill herself. It was Anna Kendrick. She wrote something like: "@SpencerPratt just favorited my tweet, looks like I now need to go kill myself."

—Heidi and Spencer Pratt, reality television stars
(*The Hills, Celebrity Big Brother,*
Marriage Boot Camp: Reality Stars)

CHAPTER 5

Drafting a Game Plan

At this point, you're probably wondering: Is anyone here for the right reasons? Does anyone actually go on the Bach hoping to find their soul mate?

If you do, Sean Lowe, for one, thinks you're cray.

"My personal opinion is that if you go on that show and you genuinely think you're going there to fall in love, you're probably a little off," said Lowe, who actually did end up finding his wife, Catherine Giudici, as the Bachelor. "I think normal people do it for the experience. There were a couple girls on my show that came on and from day one they were convinced they were in love with me and I'm thinking, 'No, you're not. You're just a little batty. You're not in love with me. You don't even know me yet.'"

About a month after Emily Maynard sent Lowe packing on *The Bachelorette* in 2012, producers reached out to him to see if he was interested in becoming the next Bachelor. After discussing the idea with his family, Lowe flew from his hometown in Texas to L.A. to meet with executive producer Martin Hilton and top brass from Warner Bros./Horizon and ABC.

"Martin was really protective of the franchise," Lowe remembered. "He was, like, drilling it in my head: 'We want you to stay humble.' . . . I have no aspirations of moving to Hollywood. I would like to think that I'm a pretty humble guy. That wasn't a big concern on my end, but that's what Martin wanted to make sure of. I guess they had painted me as this all-American guy on *The Bachelorette*, and they wanted to make sure that I stayed that way for *The Bachelor*."

As soon as the higher-ups signed off on Lowe, he understood Hilton's concerns. Once he was named the Bachelor, he was given a handler who catered to his every need, constantly running to get him food or drink. Producers started asking him where he wanted to travel on the show and what kind of women he was attracted to. ("I don't discriminate. I said they could be whatever race. I don't really have a type, as long as they're nice and sweet.") Meanwhile, ABC began to market him as America's heartthrob, building him up as a purehearted, religious guy who just wanted to settle down and raise a family.

"They really treat you differently, honestly," he said of the transition from contestant to star. "Like, wait a minute, there's literally almost a hundred people working on this show, you're the lead, and so many people are there to serve you. I can see why that would be one of Martin's concerns, because I think it would be very easy to get a big head."

Every potential star, of course, presents different issues. The producers sent Canadian Bachelorette Jillian Harris to speech therapy in a bid to help her shed her accent but canceled the classes after a few sessions revealed how integral her quirky voice was to her personality. Before Desiree Siegfried was named Bachelorette, meanwhile, producers wanted to make sure she'd present as "emotional" enough. She'd barely cried on Lowe's season and prided herself on her toughness. "They wanted me to be upset when I was talking about how I didn't grow up with money or cry when I was talking to Sean," she said. "I'm like, 'Well, I'm not going to, because I'm not sad about it.'"

If she wanted the lead gig, producers said, she was going to have to show a "diversity of feeling." Siegfried said she assured the team she is, in fact, a sensitive person and would do her best not to "smile through everything."

There are also financial considerations. The star of the show is the only one who gets paid, and the salary is negotiated based on what he/she might make at work during the production time period.

"It's not a lot of money," said Ben Flajnik, the winemaker who was the Bachelor in 2012. "They don't want it to be like you're going on this for the money. It's enough to cover your expenses while you're gone. I think it just depends on where you come from and what your burn rate is."

Jen Schefft, who in 2005 served as the third Bachelorette, regrets how she handled the money talks. She said she didn't have any lawyers look at her contract because she felt like she was at the mercy of ABC and "didn't want to give them any reason to not want to pick me."

"I shouldn't have been such a stupid girl and just wimped out and not stood up for myself," she said, noting she was paid under $100,000. Meredith Phillips, the second Bachelorette, said she only made $10,000, which she was told was the show's flat rate. That figure is exceptionally low when compared to what her successors have made; these days, it would be incredibly rare for someone to make less than six figures as the star of the show.

At least Bachelors and Bachelorettes are given free clothing—something contestants don't get unless they make it to the final rose ceremony. Instead, participants are sent an extremely vague packing list before the show kicks off. Both genders are told to bring clothes for all climates: swimsuits, winter jackets, sweaters, T-shirts, tank tops, casual day clothes, gloves, and warm hats—plus fourteen formal outfits, in case they make it through all of the rose ceremonies. The clothing needs to look good on-camera, so no stripes, baseball caps or sunglasses, small checkered patterns, visible branding, or solid black or white. Oh, and everything needs to fit in two bags.

If you're the Bachelor or Bachelorette, however, ABC hires a personal trainer for you and has you meet with stylist Cary Fetman, who organizes fittings and puts together an entire wardrobe of clothing, gratis. During Emily Maynard's season of *The Bachelorette*, Fetman told *In Touch* magazine that he was given a budget of $350,000 to dress the Southern Belle—and he managed to exceed that figure.

"You get to keep everything, because it's all tailored to fit you, which is amazing—but you also get in the best shape of your life to be on national television, so nothing really fit for too much longer after I came home," admitted Schefft.

Those without professional help prepare for the show differently. Catherine Giudici only learned how to curl her hair the day before she left for the mansion. But Olivia Caridi, a broadcast journalist who knew how important it was to look good on TV, hired a professional makeup artist prior to meeting Bachelor Ben Higgins so that she could learn how to contour her face.

The makeup artist had worked with people on reality TV and figured Caridi wouldn't be getting much sleep. "So she advised on buying a white or a nude eyeliner to put on my eyes to make them look bigger, which I didn't even know was a thing," the contestant told *Allure*.

Ashley Iaconetti, who competed on Chris Soules's season, said she shelled out big time before heading to L.A. She visited a boutique near her apartment in New Jersey and bought four gowns with the aid of her parents.

"I wanted super princessy stuff that I knew I'd never be able to wear again in any other atmosphere," she said. "I was like, 'Let's ham it up right now and play dress-up.'"

The store was willing to discount each dress by roughly $150, but looking back, Iaconetti wishes she'd gotten more of a bargain.

"So many of the girls on the show now get all their dresses for free," said Iaconetti, who had Botox and lash extensions when she was cast. "They're like, 'Hey, I'm going to be on *The Bachelor*. Can I borrow this dress? I'll tag you in a tweet when I'm wearing it in an episode.'"

Instagram sponsorships weren't even possible back when Erica Rose traveled to Italy to meet European prince Lorenzo Borghese in 2006. Instead, the then law student spent most of her time at the gym to prepare for the show. "They did encourage everyone to get into their best shape," said the contestant famous for constantly donning a princess tiara. "They'd say, 'Maybe you want to lose some weight, maybe work out,' whatever. I lost a lot of weight preparing for it—everyone did. They just encourage it. Not to everyone—like if people were already really skinny—but to most of the girls. I was happy I did it because the camera probably does add ten pounds."

In addition to dieting, Rose got hair extensions and went tanning. "The normal stuff," she said with a laugh. She also attempted to learn a few phrases in Italian, though she was disappointed to learn when she arrived on *The Bachelor* that Borghese didn't even speak the language fluently.

Of course, guys stress about getting in shape too. Chris Bukowski—who went on a record five different *Bachelor* shows—first turned up on the franchise during Emily Maynard's season. He was cast only three weeks before production began, so he started going to the gym constantly and eating chicken nonstop, even keeping white meat in his pockets so he could have protein at the ready.

"It was the worst thing ever. I'm not a meathead, and I was slowly turning into one," he recalled. "I would work out before work. I would work out when I got home from work. I'd run, like, six miles before I went to bed. It was ridiculous."

Even Lowe—who worked as a fitness model at one point—cut out pizza and upped his sit-up routine. Which worked out well for him, since he went on to become the most oft-shirtless Bachelor ever.

"I was hoping I wouldn't come across as this really vain, egotistical guy who just has to be seen with his shirt off, because it really wasn't my call," Lowe insisted. "It felt silly, but I'm a gamer. It kind of goes back to being friends with the producers. They're like, 'Come on. We really would like you to take your shirt off.' And it's like, 'All right. I like you, so I'm going to go along with it,' even when sometimes you didn't really want to. 'Whatever, I guess I'll just paint myself as the shirtless Bachelor.'"

Long before the limos roll up to the mansion, producers have already mapped out the roles they're hoping the cast members will fulfill.

"We studied them ad nauseam before they arrived," said former producer Michael Carroll, explaining that a large board with headshots of all the women resided permanently in the office. "You'd pre-categorize everyone and have some shorthand as to who they were. Mom. Southern Belle. The cheerleader. The bitch. We all called them by ridiculous names. The fat one, the hot one, the crier."

And sometimes? The black chick.

Since its inception, the Bachelor franchise has been overwhelmingly white. It took fifteen years for the producers to cast an African American as the lead, with lawyer Rachel Lindsay starring as the Bachelorette in 2017.

Prior to that, however, the show's diversity track record was embarrassing. Of the twenty-five individuals cast each season, there were usually only a couple of people of color in the group. But between 2009 and 2012—when Jason Mesnick, Jake Pavelka, Brad Womack, and Ben Flajnik were Bachelors—there were no black women on the show. And no black men appeared on *The Bachelorette* between 2009 and 2011 when Jillian Harris, Ali Fedotowsky, and Ashley Hebert were its stars.

"We always had to cast a black girl or two. ABC would say that," shared Scott Jeffress, who, to be fair, stopped working on *The Bachelor* in 2005. "It was very obvious to me that it was token. . . . They're afraid of losing the audience. It's absurd. It was very upsetting to me. It would make the show more interesting. When some guy from the South is racist as shit and he becomes bros with some black dude and says stupid shit? That's talking about race, which we need to do today."

Though critics had long made note of the show's diversity problem, it wasn't until a class-action racial discrimination lawsuit was brought against *The Bachelor* in 2012 that the issue started to gain any real traction. In the suit, Nathaniel Claybrooks and Christopher Johnson—two football players who had applied to be on the show—noted that over ten years of the franchise, no person of color had ever been the Bachelor or Bachelorette.

"By only hiring white applicants, Defendants are making the calculation that minorities in lead roles and interracial dating is unappealing to the shows' audiences," the lawsuit argued. "The refusal to hire minority applicants is a conscious attempt to minimize the risk of alienating their majority-white viewership and the advertisers targeting that viewership. Nevertheless, such discrimination is impermissible under federal and state law."

The lawsuit was eventually dismissed in 2012, with US District Judge Aleta Trauger ruling the show's producers had a right to control their creative content and were protected by the First Amendment. Though she said Claybrooks and Johnson had a "laudable" goal, she explained that freedom of speech also gave *The Cosby Show* the right to cast mostly African Americans and *Jersey Shore* to star Italian Americans.

Contrary to the plaintiffs' argument, Mike Fleiss has long said—at least prior to Lindsay's season—that people of color simply don't apply to be on *The Bachelor* or *The Bachelorette*.

"We really tried, but sometimes we feel guilty of tokenism," he told *Entertainment Weekly* in 2011. "'Oh, we have to wedge African American chicks in there!' We always want to cast for ethnic diversity, it's just that for whatever reason, they don't come forward. I wish they would."

Yet while *Bachelor*-esque dating shows on cable networks were filled with people of color—think MTV's *A Shot at Love with Tila Tequila* or VH1's *Flavor of Love*—ABC stuck with its timeworn formula.

"I think it was like, 'If it's not broken, don't fix it,'" said Duan Perrin, who was one of the first black producers to work on *The Bachelor*. "Like, 'VH1 can do that or MTV can do that. They've done it, so we don't need to. We'll keep with tradition.'"

The few women of color who did make it on *The Bachelor* had to fit a certain type. "Pretty, whitewashed, long hair or fake hair," said Evan Majors, Levenson's old assistant, who is also black. Even then, the girl's chances wouldn't be good.

"You just knew that girl wasn't going very far because it never happened, so it became a joke," said Carroll. "We'd actually root for them. Like, 'Come on! Oh, episode two? Man!'"

When Lindsay was named as the Bachelorette in 2017, race was discussed more openly on the show than it ever had been before. Roughly half of the thirty-one contestants who were cast on her season were men of color—far more than had ever appeared on any season of *The Bachelorette*.

But it was hardly smooth sailing for ABC. Right off the bat, Lindsay's season was down roughly a million viewers compared to the previous incarnation of *The Bachelorette* starring JoJo Fletcher. According to *BuzzFeed*, Nielsen ratings said Fletcher's audience was 86 percent white and 7 percent black; Lindsay's was 80 percent white and 12 percent black.

And when racial issues arose, the show didn't do an excellent job of addressing them. Midseason, Twitter users uncovered that one of the white contestants, Lee Garrett, had published a number of racist and misogynistic tweets in 2016 just a few months before he was cast. While ABC publicly denied any knowledge of said tweets, many in Bachelor Nation theorized that production purposely planted a racist in the cast to stir up drama.

And stir up drama Garrett did. The singer-songwriter, who hails from Nashville, immediately began to clash with a few of the black men on the show. His main nemesis was the wrestler Kenny King, whom he repeatedly called "aggressive," playing into a triggering African American stereotype. Garrett appeared to bait King into fights—often within earshot of Lindsay—and their contentious relationship ended up playing out as one of the main storylines of the season.

And even after both men had been sent home, race still featured prominently on the show. Only one of Lindsay's final four suitors was black, leading some African American viewers to criticize her for not supporting "black love."

Eric Bigger, the final black contestant on the season—he was sent home third to last—said he often received words of support from fellow African Americans for making it as far as he did.

"Even last night, I went out and it was like, 'Thanks for holding it down for us,'" he said, just a week after the finale aired in July. "I'm not holding it down for you. I'm holding it down for me."

Bigger, who works as a personal trainer in L.A.—full disclosure: My friend and I did work out with him one day; I almost died—said he'd never seen the show before he went on. He applied to be a cast member before he knew Lindsay was the star and said, prior to dating her, he'd dated exclusively white women for six years.

"When it comes to love, the only pressure you should feel is the pressure you put on yourself," he said. "I'm not going off of what the culture thinks I should do. If I'm supposed to date Amy, I'm dating Amy. If it's Amy and Rachel, but I have the biggest connection with Amy, I'm dating Amy. It's not about the color. It's not fair. It's not even right. It's, like, selfish."

"Think about where we live at," he continued. "There aren't that many African Americans in Los Angeles—at least not the area I'm in. It's not like Baltimore, where I'm from, where I see that every day."

Bigger said he was more worried about discussing class than race with Lindsay, who was open about the fact that she came from a privileged background, attending private school in Dallas, Texas, where her father is a federal judge. Bigger, meanwhile, grew up in inner-city Maryland and couldn't recall seeing his parents in the same room before his hometown date with Lindsay. A number of his relatives spent time in jail, he said, and he was constantly surrounded by crime.

"At one point, I felt like if I really told Rachel where I was from, she wouldn't like me," he admitted to me. "I don't know why, but I was just a little insecure about that. But I said, 'You know what? I'm just going to own it.' I told her I'd come from a challenging environment in a tough city. She comes from a wholesome, grounded, structured family, and I don't come from that. So my thought was that it might make her uncomfortable. But that was a lie that was in my head. It wasn't true. And after I let it out, I felt better."

Ultimately, Lindsay accepted a proposal from chiropractor Bryan Abasolo, leaving runner-up Peter Kraus to become the fan favorite for *The Bachelor*. Even though Bigger was beloved by fans, a few weeks after the show, he said the producers hadn't even approached him about being the Bachelor. In September, it was announced that white racecar driver Arie Luyendyk Jr.—who appeared on Maynard's season of *The Bachelorette* all the way back in 2012—was ABC's unlikely pick.

It all makes me wonder how the producers saw someone like Bigger during the casting process. Was he labeled right off the bat? "Broken family, from the 'hood, overcame adversity?" I'd like to believe that isn't how the show views people—in these stereotypical boxes—but I've seen too much.

During early seasons, at least, notes on each contestant would be circulated among top producers and kept in binders. There was standard biographical information included on all the contenders: name, age, hometown, job, salary, educational background. But certain notes would be highlighted—indicators of personality traits or past traumas for the team to dig into during ITM interviews.

I got my hands on one of the binders filled with annotated bios from Jesse Palmer's season. He was the fifth Bachelor, an NFL quarterback who has since gone on to become a *Good Morning America* contributor. And by the time Palmer was the star of the show in 2004, the producers had this thing down to a science.

Just take a look at some of the notes the producers made about the potential ladies competing for his heart. The remarks—which are verbatim, by the way, though I didn't include every note on every young woman—don't paint the kindest picture of the producers. Instead, they come across as calculating and formulaic—and certainly not sympathetic. I've changed the names of the contestants to protect their identities, since they're pretty much being mocked.

Jamie, 21

- *Seems very young and immature (UCSB sorority chick–ish!)*
- *Wants to find love on TV and have a $4 million wedding.*
- *Get her in the house because she'll drive the other girls crazy—or the other girls will definitely annoy her.*
- *Very produceable—another one who comes with strings.*
- *Could be a star on* The OC *and* Dawson's Creek.
- *She like wants to get like married like—can we stand it??*

Britney, 25

- *Fragile as glass—nervous during interview.*
- *NERVOUS, too SELF-CONSCIOUS, INDECISIVE.*
- *Went to ER . . . had brain hemorrhage . . . had a birth defect . . . could either have surgery or be on medication for the rest of her life.*
- *Whole experience put things in perspective . . . never gets emotional talking about this (but she's crying now). "I don't ever cry about this . . ." "I'm sorry, I'm a wreck."*

- *CRYING IN INTERVIEW regarding her brain surgery.*
- *Challenge living with other girls in one house—other girls won't like her!*

Allie, 26

- *Jewish.*
- *Gets prettier the longer you watch her tape.*
- *First love ended up cheating on her—GET THIS!!*
- *Says she's been through a lot of things in her life (but doesn't say what) . . . GET MORE ABOUT THIS.*

A few days before production begins, the final contestants—and a handful of alternates—are flown back to L.A. This time, they stay at a Sheraton in Agoura Hills, which is closer to the mansion than LAX. Upon arrival at the hotel, each contestant is asked to hand over anything with an on/off switch—cell phone, tablet, laptop—and a handler puts the devices in an envelope.

Over the next couple of days, contestants are confined entirely to their hotel rooms as streams of producers come by to introduce themselves. With nothing to do other than watch TV, the isolation can become maddening—but it also serves to get everyone completely focused on the show. Sans distraction, contestants naturally start fantasizing about the man or woman they're about to meet in a few days.

The participants also start planning how they'll introduce themselves to the Bachelor or Bachelorette after they get out of the limo. Some contestants come in with ideas, though producers always have more far-out gimmicks to suggest.

When Justin Rego turned up on the show with a broken leg, producers suggested he charm Bachelorette Ali Fedotowsky with the line: "Ali, even though I broke my foot, I want you to know I'll never break your heart."

Rego—who went by his wrestling alias "Rated R" on the 2010 season—said he balked at the cheesy idea. Fortunately, when he got out of the limo, Fedotowsky naturally asked what happened to his leg, and he was able to skip the saccharine pickup line.

Not that anyone is forced to show up in a cupcake on wheels. (Ugh, remember that guy?) When Sean Lowe told producers he wanted to "play it straight and be somewhat normal" with Emily Maynard, he didn't receive any pushback. Instead, he was told that he was going to be first out of the limos to meet the single mom—a distinction that goes to anyone the team thinks might really hit it off with the Bachelorette. (Same goes for the person who's last out of the car.)

"If they have high hopes for you or want you to stick around, they don't want you to ruin it on night one by doing something totally off-the-wall and maybe rubbing the Bachelor or Bachelorette the wrong way," Lowe explained.

Once each contestant has an idea of their limo entrance spiel, producers make the rounds to check out everyone's rose-ceremony outfits. Professional hair and makeup is offered on the first night only—you have to apply your own fake lashes for the entirety of the season unless you make it to the final rose ceremony.

After getting all dolled up, crew members put microphones on each contestant. Everyone waits anxiously in their room for a few hours, hair falling flatter by the minute. Finally, groups of five are called downstairs and sent into limos. This is where the cameras greet everyone for the first time. It's only a 4.6-mile drive from the hotel to the mansion, which takes roughly eight minutes. On the way, there's usually a Champagne toast or a few shots of Fireball tossed back to loosen the nerves.

At the mansion, the limo idles in front of the driveway gates. There are some makeshift tents set up, where contestants are able to get out to have their hair and makeup touched up or take a quick pee. Everyone is told the order in which to exit the limo when it pulls up in front of the house.

Then it's time for the car to actually roll down the driveway. When the mansion comes into view, it's impressive, surrounded by massive lights and cranes that make the production look like a movie set. When the chauffeur is ready to open the limo door, everyone is instructed not to thank or look at the driver.

"Take your surroundings in," a producer advises, "enjoy it, and have fun."

Why I'm a Fan

MELANIE LYNSKEY

THE THING I ALWAYS HAVE LIKED ABOUT REALITY television—and especially dating shows—is the human interaction in them. People try to present a particular image, but then they can't help themselves, and they're just themselves at a certain point. I like observing the differences and the behavior of how the Bachelor is with each of the women. It feels really voyeuristic.

I've always been very impulsive when it comes to love. By the time I was twenty-one, I think I was engaged, like, five times. I was kind of crazy. I'd get into these romances and suddenly I'd be engaged to somebody and then I'd break it off. I'd live with people after a week. So watching *The Bachelor*, I'd think, "These people are nuts if they think it can happen so quickly!" And then I was like, "Wait a minute. I got engaged to someone I'd known for ten days. And he proposed to me with the top of a Champagne bottle."

I always had the idea that there are a lot of people who are right for us. When I was a teenager, I imagined that I would have, like, six husbands or I'd have children from five different men. That seemed so bohemian and romantic to me, and I felt like there were so many amazing people in the world. But as I got older, I started realizing stability was nice—just being with one person who you can trust.

So, no: I did not have the princess dream at all. And I don't know why the show is stuck on that particular narrative. I don't know if it's a way that they're trying to class the show up a little bit, by saying it's about love and marriage, but it just seems so unrealistic to me. I mean, I get that part of the fun of watching the show is seeing the ring and the proposal. And my crazy side is like, "Go for it! How wonderful!"

But it's easy to make promises and say, "I'm here to protect you, I'm going to do anything you want, I'll move to your hometown and everything will be great!" Then, when they watch the show together and have to witness everything it took to get to that point—I just don't think that most people have what it takes to recover from that. So in the back of my mind, when they're making these promises on the finale, I'm like, "Oh, well, just wait and see."

I think there are a lot of old-fashioned concepts that the show is trying to keep alive, but all these women have made the choice to do it. . . . And if you're in a place in your life where you're making super healthy decisions and being positive and responsible, you're probably not going to make the choice to be on *The Bachelor* or *The Bachelorette*.

But I feel protective of the contestants. I think the producers have a responsibility to be good people. I understand that these people are signing contracts, but they always think, "I'm not going to look ridiculous, because I'm not ridiculous." And then they do.

—Melanie Lynskey, actress (*Heavenly Creatures,*
**   *Two and a Half Men, Togetherness*)**

CHAPTER 6

Inside the Bubble

Villa de la Vina—or the Bachelor mansion, as it's now known to millions of viewers—is hidden off a canyon road just a few exits on the Ventura Freeway past the Kardashians. The Tuscan estate, situated on about nine acres of land north of Malibu in the Santa Monica Mountains, was built in 2005—but production only moved there in 2007, during Brad Womack's first season.

ABC doesn't own the 7,590-square-foot Agoura Hills home, however; the man who built it does: real estate developer Marshall Haraden. He and his family live in the six-bedroom, nine-bathroom house roughly ten months out of the year and decamp to a nearby hotel when production is under way. (Production pays for the hotel stay as part of the lease agreement.)

The show takes up residence at the mansion twice a year, for forty-two days each time. When they come in, all of Haraden's furniture comes out: "Everything leaves—everything that's not tied down, that's not part of the home," he told *Us Weekly*. "Curtains, TVs, pots and pans—clothes—everything in one day goes out."

I would have talked to Haraden myself, by the way, but he backed out of our interview a day before it was supposed to happen. I was all set to drive out to the mansion and have the owner give me a personal tour, but then he called to let me know that ABC had advised him not to talk to me. "I just want to maintain a good relationship with my clients," he told me.

Fortunately, Haraden has talked to just about everyone else about the mansh, and a handful of my friends have been there for press events, so I have a pretty good sense of what it's like there. It's also been up for sale a few times—first in 2008 for just under $13 million, and then in 2009 for $6.8 million.

Not surprisingly, it's also become a tourist destination: "People think that when the show's on TV, it's happening at the house," Haraden said in an interview with *People*. "Sometimes when we come home from dinner at nine or ten at night, there's people outside the gate climbing over the fence or on top of their cars trying to take pictures."

Despite the lookie-loos, Fleiss has said he laments not buying the house before it became so pricey. (In 2017, Trulia estimated it was worth $7.4 million.) "I wish I had bought this place years ago," he told the *Toronto Sun* in 2013. "But I wasn't sure if we would get canceled every year and we kept getting picked up."

Since production has to start from scratch every time they come in, it takes about two weeks to set everything up. Villa de la Vina was built to resemble a rustic mansion in Italy, though it was constructed with materials from a variety of countries: Morocco, Mexico, India, and China. So the production designers tend to go with rich, deep colors—always painting the walls with a new coat of dark paint before each season. There are also certain props that tend to look good on-camera: big lanterns, stone sculptures, and oversized candlesticks.

Angelic Rutherford, who has been leading the art department on the show since 2003, tries to switch up the feel of the decor depending on who's living there. When girls are bunking up for *The Bachelor*, she wants the mansion to "feel feminine and colorful," she told *Elle Decor* in 2016. "The fabrics have to be really versatile—it's not like you can cover the couches in velvet, because the girls are wearing their bathing suits on the couch during the day, and when it's a rose night, it needs to be dressy and reflect that night."

Story producers set up in the room to the right of the front door, tracking the house action on monitors. The control room is farther away, in the garage, and there's a smaller stand-alone building on the property that production uses to shoot ITMs.

After contestants have their meet-cutes in the driveway, they're led directly into the mansion's family room—referred to by the crew as the "Mixer Room." The foyer that leads to the Mixer Room is where Chris Harrison tells the cast it's time for a rose ceremony—and that area is called the "Tink-Tink Spot." Get it? Because that's the noise the glass makes when the host taps it to get everyone's attention? The actual rose-ceremony room usually is the living room, but the furniture is pulled out to fit all the hopefuls. This is also where contestants head when they want a drink, since the room houses a huge bar—but it's covered up during the ceremony.

Upstairs, there are three bedrooms, but the accommodations are cramped. Contestants sometimes sleep twelve to a room in bunk beds, and everyone's living out of a suitcase, so luggage is usually scattered across the floor. Each contestant is also gifted an additional piece of luggage with some freebies inside: beauty products, padded bikinis, jewelry, or jeans to wear throughout the season.

Everyone has to do their own laundry and cook for themselves too, though the kitchen is well stocked. If you have a dietary restriction—say you're vegan, or gluten-free—the staff will cater to your needs. Run out of face wash or nail-polish remover? The production assistants will head to CVS for you too, as long as you make a shopping list. In other words, you're not allowed to go anywhere—sometimes, if you're really lucky, production will let you spend thirty minutes at a local gym, nail salon, or beach. But that's rare.

And inside the mansion, there are hardly any outside distractions. Some contestants are allowed to keep journals or Bibles. But electronics—phones, computers, televisions—are obvious no-nos. You can't listen to music or catch up on the news. Reading material, like books or magazines, isn't allowed. There isn't even any gym equipment.

It's all part of a well-designed producer strategy called "The Bubble." Inside the bubble, all that matters is the show. Everyone around you—fellow contestants, producers—is talking about the Bachelor or Bachelorette, so that's all you start to think about too. In a budding relationship in the outside world, you have your friends to gossip about a new paramour with. But at the mansion, you can only confide in producers—who have a vested interest in you falling for the Bachelor or Bachelorette—or fellow contestants, who are after the star too.

So sure, maybe you're bored sometimes, or start to feel a little stir-crazy. But you don't have to work, you're getting free food and drinks and lying out by the pool. You're part of an elite group that has been chosen to be on national television—and to many people, that's far more alluring than a nine-to-five, even with some bizarre strings attached.

"For some people, this is the princess dream they've thought about," said assistant-turned-producer Ben Hatta. "They're in a mansion on a hillside in California with people making them food and bringing them drinks and wearing gowns. Even if they're not into the guy, there's competition for the rose, because they want to see what will happen next. When the mansion door closes, you're like, 'Are they having fun in there? My life at home isn't as exciting as hair and makeup and wardrobe and limos.' Those kinds of things really play into the psyche and basically [mimic] the feeling of love."

When Clare Crawley—yes, "sex"-in-the-ocean Clare—turned up at the mansion on Juan Pablo Galavis's season, she was shocked by how quickly she felt herself falling for the Venezuelan single dad.

"But you have nothing to think about," she emphasized. "Not even tying your shoes. Not even what food you're going to order. You don't have to think about a single thing other than him. Imagine that: For three months, that's all you focus on. That's all you think about. All you talk about. So it's almost sped up really fast."

Behavior she might typically second-guess? She didn't have a night to sleep on it during *The Bachelor*. "You don't really know what to do, so you just kind of go with it," she said. "But the producers know that. They control every moment of it."

Just ask them.

"The cast is told what to do all of the time," said Brad Isenberg, a former *Bachelor* production coordinator. "You're on a schedule: our schedule, not your schedule. Even if there's nothing happening, it's scheduled. It's a part of being controlled."

Though each season takes eight weeks to shoot, only about a third of that time is spent at Villa de la Vina before the show takes off to travel. But the early weeks inside the mansion are instrumental in laying the groundwork for the rest of the season. Not only is this the period of time with the least outside distraction, but it's also when the cast learns how to act on-camera. Everyone is asked to participate in a couple of "man chats" or "girl chats" a day—staged conversations that producers set up between different participants where the topic of discussion is predetermined.

Say you're sitting in the Mixer Room, talking casually with a few ladies about Farrah, the woman in the house you all can't stand. A producer—who has a headset on at all times—suddenly comes over and formalizes the discussion by asking you to participate in a girl chat. Maybe you're asked to continue talking about Farrah and elaborate on why you hate her so much—or maybe the producer wants you to change tack and speculate about the date the Bachelor is currently on.

"A producer walks around and asks, 'Who wants to be in a girl chat?' And the girls who want air time are like, 'Ooh, me! Me!'" explained Sharleen Joynt, a participant on Galavis's season who loathed girl chats. "I said no every single time. But as the cast dwindled down, you had to participate. So you sit there and a producer's like, 'So, what do you think they're doing on the date right now? Are you surprised that so-and-so got a rose? Can you believe girls are going home this week? Are you nervous?'"

During the early years of the show, such chats weren't a requirement. But a few seasons in, producers realized that all that time cast members were spending by the pool or lounging on the couch could be used more wisely. The chats could also be used as a bartering tool: "If you talk shit about Amy on the date, we'll turn on music and you guys can watch a movie or something," producer Michael Carroll recalled of one bribe.

The girl chats bothered Joynt so much that many of her journal entries—some of which she graciously read to me over Skype one night from her New York apartment—focused on her disdain for them.

"I'm already feeling ready to crack. Give up. Maybe I am even more introverted than I suspected," she wrote on her third day in the mansion in 2013. "The most painful, draining part of any day are the staged conversations. . . . The smaller conversations with cameras where the girls speculate about dates or recount theirs are nothing short of torture for me. Watching certain girls' faces contort beyond what seems natural. Splitting into two white grins—every word, every action—because a camera is on them when moments before they seemed relatively normal."

Of course, the deepest revelations typically occur during ITMs. Sometimes, participants can be asked to sit for up to five ITMs a day, answering questions about their state of mind and digging into their emotions. I'll get into the psychology of these sessions in a bit, but a big part of what helps contestants to open up is—ding, ding, ding! You guessed it: alcohol.

Before discussing the on-set alc, I want to make one thing clear: No one on *The Bachelor* is forced to drink. There's no requirement that one must throw back shots or do keg stands to procure a rose.

But there's always alcohol on-set. Every kind, and lots of it. It's a constant, and it is frequently being offered, free of charge. Oftentimes, producers will drink with cast members to make the whole endeavor feel more socially acceptable.

One field producer told me he still believes he got a job on the franchise only because he was open about his affinity for partying.

"I think one of the reasons they trusted me with that position is because—I don't want to say I'm good at drinking, but I hold my alcohol well and I don't really lose my focus," said the "party producer," whom I met for coffee—not drinks. "So it's like, if I want to have a shot with a contestant, he'll take a shot with me—or five. You have to build a rapport. Basically, it's like, 'Hey, man. We should talk. How are you feeling? You seem a little tense. Let's take a shot.' People just keep pushing it and pushing it and pushing it and before you know it, things happen."

In the mansion, especially, many contestants told me they drank because they were bored. It's not like you wake up with the intention of getting wasted, but then it's two p.m., you decide to have a beer by the pool, and if that continues at a steady rate until two a.m., you find yourself drunk.

"There's nothing to fucking do," agreed Carroll, the producer. "If I don't have a book or TV or a movie to watch and there's a fridge full of white wine and Champagne and beer and a bar, I'm going to sit by the pool and drink. Duh. And when you go on a date, I'm going to give you a box of Champagne in the limo. Of course! That shit? It makes everything different."

Liquor also quells the social anxiety. Imagine being in a new environment with gorgeous people who make you feel insecure, and there are dozens of cameras tracking your every move. Plus, everyone else is drinking. So you feel like you need a glass in your hand to fit in.

"You're standing in a room where everyone's drinking, and there's definitely not any filtered water there for you to drink," said Jesse Csincsak, the snowboard instructor who was (briefly) engaged to Bachelorette DeAnna Pappas. "They put something in your hand, it allows you to relax. So are they telling you, 'Oh, you have to drink'? No, but I can promise you that if you're acting tense, they're going to soothe your pain with a couple of shots."

It's not something that most of the producers have ethical misgivings about either. These contestants are adults of legal drinking age.

"I'm willing to let them do anything any twenty-five- to twenty-eight-year-old would do at a party with mixed company. And look, if things get unsafe, then you step in," said Scott Jeffress. "One thing that will never happen on my set is, like, a rape or something. I would never allow some guy to walk into the room of some girl who's passed out. Everyone has to be cognizant of what they're doing—even when two people get really drunk and want to have sex, if they're too gone, it's like, 'No. Put them to bed.'"

But after years of only loosely monitoring the on-set drinking, alcohol consumption on the franchise finally spun out of control in the summer of 2017. It happened on *Bachelor in Paradise*, which had served as the perfect frothy summer filler for ABC when it premiered in 2014. From its inception, the show was more about a good time than fairy-tale romance. It has a tongue-in-cheek tone, even using the love theme from *Footloose*, Mike Reno and Ann Wilson's "Almost Paradise," over the corny opening credits.

And the show, which typically airs in August, has proved to be a solid ratings draw during an otherwise slow television period. In 2016, the third season's finale drew roughly 5.6 million viewers— just a tad less than the 5.7 million who tuned in for the season premiere of *The Bachelorette* the following May.

But the spin-off's fate came into question just a few days after filming began on *Paradise*'s fourth season at the Playa Escondida resort on June 4, 2017. The precipitating event? Corinne Olympios and DeMario Jackson—two contestants who had previously been labeled franchise villains—got drunk and hooked up. According to a source who was on-set, the two quickly got naked in the water and proceeded to engage in what looked like "soft-core porn." At one point, the source told me, Jackson briefly performed oral sex on Olympios; the two did not have penetrative sex.

At first, the incident seemed par for the course in *Paradise*. Contestants regularly get frisky in the open and have sex in bedrooms without doors—though the footage rarely shows anything that raunchy.

A couple of days later, though, the two contestants were pulled aside and told that two producers had filed third-party complaints with Warner Bros., the production company that produces the ABC show, related to the pool encounter. The entire cast was flown back to the United States. On June 11, Warner Bros. released a statement announcing production had been suspended while it investigated claims of alleged misconduct.

Olympios hired a high-profile Hollywood lawyer, Marty Singer—who has represented John Travolta and Charlie Sheen—and issued her own statement. "Although I have little memory of that night," the twenty-four-year-old said, "something bad obviously took place." Jackson, thirty, retained his own counsel and did a sit-down with *E! News* claiming the hook-up was consensual.

On June 20, Warner Bros. announced that its internal investigation did not "support any charge of misconduct" or show that the "safety of any cast member was ever in jeopardy." Production resumed, but a slew of new rules were instituted: Contestants had to adhere to a two-drink-per-hour maximum, and before initiating sex, they had to check with a producer tasked with making sure both parties were able to give consent.

Though the show eventually went on to premiere that August—to 5 million viewers, no less—the incident in Mexico disturbed many critics and viewers, raising larger questions about the overall Bachelor franchise, where alcohol has always flowed freely and served as a lubricant for obtaining juicy sound bites and drama.

"For many years, the Bachelor shows have implemented alcohol as a tool of manipulation to elicit whatever responses they want from contestants," Jennifer Pozner, a media critic who researched *The Bachelor* for her 2010 book, *Reality Bites Back: The Troubling Truth about Guilty Pleasure TV*, told me. "There's an ever-present need for drama, which is defined on the show as women crying, men fighting, women having catfights, women saying they're going to die alone. Those conditions they seek are not conducive to the protection of cast members' safety."

Indeed, plenty of contestants have become so intoxicated that they only see the extent of their drunken behavior when it eventually airs on national television. Chad Johnson learned that the hard way during the third season of *Paradise*, when he began drinking before the cameras even starting rolling on day one. He wasn't tipsy; he was hammered. By the time production on *Bachelor in Paradise* kicked off at eleven a.m., he'd already taken seven shots of Jack Daniel's whiskey and downed a whole bottle of wine.

Because, he figured: Why not? He'd agreed to go on *Paradise* because it seemed like a paid vacation, replete with bikini-clad women, a private beach, and an open bar. Also, alcohol loosened him up—he wanted to be liked by his new castmates, and when he drank, he felt like he was instantly funnier.

"Plus, when you're filming the show, you have this adrenaline pump of being on TV, so you can drink more and are still capable of walking and talking," Johnson, age twenty-nine, explained. "There are points of time on the show where you're still conscious, where in the real world, you would have been asleep somewhere ten hours earlier."

But no one on the production team put Johnson to bed. Instead, he passed out on the sand as crabs crawled over his face. The next morning, he learned he engaged in an aggressive make-out session with one female cast member and hurled insults at another who was born with only one full arm. He was also told he'd soiled himself during his sleep.

Johnson's behavior that night had consequences: Within hours, Chris Harrison was dispatched to tell him he was no longer welcome on the show. He was asked to pack his bags and return to the States.

The move came after Sarah Herron—the contestant Johnson insulted for her disability—gave an ultimatum to production: Either he goes or I go.

"I ran to the producers and said, morally, I can't be here and I don't think we're setting a good example by keeping him in the house," Herron recalled. "I thought it was poor form for the franchise to keep someone around that was jeopardizing our safety for ratings' sake. And producers took it really seriously, because the next morning, Chad was sent home. It felt like a true testament to the fact that they do have our backs."

Chris Bukowski doesn't share that sentiment. When he last turned up on *Paradise* in 2015, like Johnson, he got blackout drunk—starting off with four vodka sodas before eleven a.m. Though he said he does not remember the experience, he was later told he'd stepped into a fire pit, gotten into a shouting match with a producer, and told a fellow contestant he would hook up with his mom.

"The day after, not only is the hangover bad, but the consequences—that this is gonna be on TV—are even worse," he said. "I still take a lot of the blame for the way I was, but I think producers hold responsibility too. They're the ones supplying the alcohol and the place I'm sleeping and what I'm eating. It's almost like going to a bar—at the right time, the bar owner is going to cut you off and put you in a cab. And the producers should also cut you off instead of continuing to feed you the juice."

Alcohol also helps to fuel the kind of ballsy behavior often needed to catch the eye of the Bachelor or Bachelorette. From the instant contestants walk into the mansion, the competition is under way. Everyone is sizing one another up. Even if you're considered good-looking in your small Iowa hometown, you're now surrounded by two dozen other people who are also great catches.

"It sounds weird for me to say this about other guys, but I'd never seen anyone who looked like these dudes. I was intimidated," said Brooks Forester, a handsome but decidedly less muscular guy who competed on Desiree Siegfried's season of *The Bachelorette*. "I didn't have a ton of time to get in the greatest shape, so I just kind of went how I tend to carry myself every day. And that wasn't the case for those guys. One guy took his shirt off and we were like, 'Jesus! Put your shirt back on!' There wasn't a muscle in his body that wasn't completely shredded."

So OK, maybe you're one of the bros who's jacked. But you're a bartender or a "freaking insurance salesman," like Sean Lowe. And you're up against racecar drivers, high-powered attorneys, and Ivy League grads.

"A lot of these guys had some really impressive statistics, and I didn't have all that much, in my mind," said Lowe. "I think the competition can play with people's minds. You just have to really sit by yourself and think, 'OK, what are my intentions here? Do I want to beat the other guys, or is there something here [with the Bachelorette]?"

It can be hard to figure out your feelings for the person at the center of the game—er, show—when the competition begins before you've even spent five minutes with them. Take night one. You walk out of the limo and meet this eligible Bachelor—an encounter meant to suss out little more than physical attraction. Then, if you're lucky, you corner him for a couple more minutes in a poolside cabana before another lady steals him for a second. Based on those interactions, the Bachelor will hand out a "first-impression rose" to the woman he's most taken with.

And scoring that rose is a game-changer. When Nick Viall received the special bloom from Andi Dorfman on *The Bachelorette*, he instantly decided he was in it to win it.

"I went from 'What the fuck am I doing here? This is ridiculous' to being the one guy where she's like, 'You know what? I like you the best so far,'" he said. "In that little world, it seems silly, but you're like, 'Fuck yeah!' It's a perfect little prop they have, because whoever gets it, it's very dangerous."

And if you don't get the first-impression rose, you need to get one at the rose ceremony a few minutes later. Bob Guiney, who went from contestant to Bachelor, does a good job of describing how disorienting this can be in his 2003 book: "I didn't even know how I felt about being there, or whether I even wanted a rose, until the moment I thought I wasn't going to get one," he writes. "Then I knew for sure that I wanted one. It was just that simple principle that something becomes so much more attractive when you suddenly fear you can't have it."

And when the dates come into play? The stakes get even higher. Sure, the outings on the Bach are famously extravagant, featuring horse-drawn carriages, Rodeo Drive shopping sprees, and Broadway-show cameos. But they're also just a chance for the contestants to get out of the mansion.

"I think when you are sort of trapped like that, you look forward to even getting out of the house," said Rozlyn Papa, the villain from Jake Pavelka's season. "It wasn't just about Jake. It was about getting to do something exciting. [The producers] come in and announce names and it's like playing Bingo. We're like, 'Those are my numbers! Yay! I'm the winner.'"

Entire teams are devoted to crafting the dates on *The Bachelor*. You can't just go to dinner and then go out dancing. You need to "take a real date and put it on crack," explained one segment producer who helped shape the franchise's romantic rendezvous for years. Dinner? Let's have it on top of a bridge in San Francisco that's accessible only via helicopter. And when you descend, there's your favorite country singer putting on a private concert just for you to dance to.

"If you're Amy from Oklahoma, here's what happens," Michael Carroll posited. "Amy from Oklahoma comes on the show and she's one of twenty-five chicks. In her head, there's some weird kismet thing that happens where she feels already—prior to ever showing up—that this guy must be for her. 'I mean, out of all the women in America, I'm one of twenty-five! I'm Amy from Oklahoma! He must be my man.' So she's already in it.

"And then you take her on a date where she flies in a helicopter over the Hollywood Bowl and fucking whoever plays," he continued. "Then you take her to a rooftop and give her a rose and give her a necklace and 'ahh.' It's a panty dropper."

Dozens of date ideas are pitched to executive producers in the weeks leading up to each season—and no date gets approved until the network signs off on it. The team tries to create dates that at least somewhat incorporate the Bachelor's interests. But the main requirement? That the date's budget is $0.00.

That's right: nada. Yes, there's a budget allotted for dates—only $20,000 or so for each one—but segment producers often aren't even told what it is. Instead, their aim is to get everything for free through trade-outs—a sort of barter agreement through which a company offers its goods or services in exchange for the advertising power of *The Bachelor*.

To pitch this kind of arrangement, producers reach out to different hotels, airlines, and restaurants and tout the value of having their business appear on ABC prime time. I obtained one letter that a field producer emailed the director of sales and marketing at a Lake Tahoe resort in 2003 in the hopes of filming Jesse Palmer's season at the hotel. In the note, the producer states her request to shoot a segment for Palmer's season at the Resort at Squaw Creek, explaining that eight cast members and "incredibly minimal documentary-style camera crews" would be on hand. She outlines how the show's goal is to put a spotlight on how "luxurious" the resort is, as the premise of *The Bachelor* is "opulence, luxury, and exclusivity." "We create and showcase an untouchable ideal man and his lifestyle," the producer writes. "He lives in a mansion in Southern California and offers the women on the show incredible experiences the average American can only dream about."

So why should the mountainside resort agree to be on the show? The producer says that, in 2003, *The Bachelor* often earned higher ratings than NBC's *The West Wing* and attracted more viewers than the World Series. On average, she says, about 20 million viewers watched per week, putting *Bachelor* advertising spots at a value of $250,000 per 30 seconds. If the Resort at Squaw Creek were to be featured, she says, the segment would be worth more than $750,000 in advertising dollars.

Then she gets into detailing the free stuff she actually wants. In exchange for all this advertising, the resort should host *The Bachelor* without any fees. Air travel—via private jet and commercial airliner—should be provided for two dozen cast and crew members. There needs to be lunch and dinner—alcohol included—for eight cast members, though a "simple hot meal" will suffice for the twelve crew members. The four executives, however, "will need a nice meal."

All cast activities, like dog-sledding, snow tubing, or ice skating, should be free. Ground transportation to the resort will be needed. And when the show is in production, entrances and exits must be closed to other guests.

In exchange, the producer promises, *The Bachelor* will do at least one of three things: 1) Feature a chyron "at the lower one-third of the screen" identifying the resort when the cast arrives there during the episode. 2) Include an "in-story" mention in the episode—meaning a cast member will talk about how much fun they had at Squaw Creek. 3) A sign featuring the name of the resort will be shown during the episode.

There's no way the resort would agree to all that, right? Wrong. Usually, producers manage to get what they want, especially when traveling to foreign countries where the tourism board is eager to lure Americans on vacation. And if a *Bachelor* staffer can't get the majority of a date provided for free, that date idea is typically just scrapped.

Once the trade-out is secured, segment producers complete a full pitch that explains the highlights of the date and the beats that the crew is aiming to hit during the episode. So when *The Bachelor* ended up heading to the Resort at Squaw Creek, this was the plan:

(Jack, by the way, is Jesse Palmer—the Dianes are the women he's dating. Production often employs cutesy code names like this to keep things under wraps during filming—Sonny and the Chers, Lois and the Clarks, etc.)

Date Pitch:

Meets them at their pad: Our handsome prince picks up his princesses and drives them onto the airport tarmac; he stands there, studly, next to his hundred tons of steel, as the ladies board the aircraft. . . .

The kids arrive to a winter wonderland: It is the ultimate play day and the ultimate ice-breaker (ba-dump bump).

Snow Tubing: The kids walk over the base of the mountain, where 8 snow tubes and 8 outfits await them. Jack and the Dianes begin the date tubin' the bunny slopes; the laughter is infectious as we see our gals and guy slippin' and slidin' down the side of the mountain. Who will get a ride with Jack????? Who will Jack pull aside for a hot cocoa? There will be a bench, blankets, and a bar set at this location.

Next, Jack and the Dianes move over to a gigantic heated swimming pool. The main aim in this segment, it seems, is to show some skin, as the date pitch notes that the girls will "look like they just hopped out of a Smirnoff ad as they bare all (almost all)." Sipping Cristal, they get steamy in the hot tub and then come inside to warm up by the fire. The group cheers to a great day, the pitch reads, literally counting their lucky stars as they gaze up at the sky.

Pretty standard Bach date. There's an element that brings a wow factor—private plane. Anybody can rent a fancy car. But a "hundred tons of steel" feels unattainable—and it keeps the date moving, because traffic isn't an issue.

A five-course meal does scream luxury, except that ain't nobody gonna eat it. It doesn't look cute, and chewing doesn't sound fantastic on a live mic. Plus, the cast is always able to get a private meal before or after the date if they want to avoid chowing down on-camera.

Which is a shame, really, because these couples are often being offered high-end cuisine. Oftentimes, renowned chefs will walk out to the table to describe the dishes they have prepared for the lovebirds—dishes that some production assistant typically just digs into later, cold.

Often, the dates on the show fit into a specific category. There are cultural dates, which almost always take place when the show is traveling. You're in Ireland? Well, you're probably going to go drinking at a local pub. Finland? Yep, you'll be meeting Santa Claus—because that's where all letters to the magical man are postmarked.

Then there are charity dates, which, oddly, tend to be the raciest outings. Because any proceeds raised on these dates go to a good cause, producers have more leeway to ask cast members to behave in a way they otherwise might not. Remember that Models and Mutts date from Juan Pablo Galavis's season, where the ladies posed in revealing outfits alongside rescue dogs? That was for charity.

Then there are adrenaline dates. These are the kinds of dates that no one actually wants to go on because of the fear factor—but also the ones that usually bring a fledgling couple closer together. Maybe you rappel down the side of a skyscraper or go on a parabolic flight and float in zero gravity.

"You release so many endorphins in those situations that when you're in them with somebody you're sexually attracted to, there's this instant bond," said a former segment producer. "You're like, 'We survived this!'"

And the people who are sent on the adrenaline dates? Bingo! They're exactly the ones who are most afraid of them. The crew scours the questionnaires that are filled out during the finals weekend to figure out which cast member is scared of what. "If you do an adrenaline date, you don't want to send someone that loves heights and is an adrenaline junkie," the producer continued. "You want someone who's scared. And the reason they all go through with it is because they're there to take chances. They say that over hours and hours of interviews, and now they're being put to the test. That's why they never crap out."

There's some research to back this theory up, by the way. In 1974, psychologists Donald Dutton and Arthur Aron published a paper in the *Journal of Personality and Social Psychology* titled "Some Evidence for Heightened Sexual Attraction Under Conditions of High Anxiety." In it, they detailed what has since been dubbed the "Suspension Bridge Experiment." The researchers sent eighty-five men, ages eighteen to thirty-five, across two different bridges. One bridge—let's call this the scary bridge—was 5 feet wide and 450 feet long, made of wooden boards, and had "a tendency to tilt, sway and wobble" with low handrails that created "the impression that one is about to fall over the side." The other, safer bridge, was built with sturdier materials, "did not tilt or sway," and rested just ten feet above a rivulet.

After crossing each of the bridges, the men were stopped by a young woman who explained she was working on a project for her psychology class. The men on the scary bridge filled out the woman's survey using more sexual imagery than the men on the safe bridge did. The men on the scary bridge were also more likely to call the woman later. (She had given all the men her phone number.)

"They proved that people in a more precarious position were more susceptible to romantic love," explained Dr. Helen Fisher, who serves as the chief scientific advisor to Match.com and has written six books on love and marriage. "And, I would add, that is most likely because the precarious is the novel position—it's going to drive up the dopamine system, so you're primed. You're ready to fall in love."

As a biological anthropologist, Fisher studies love for a living—what our brains look like when we're falling for someone. So if you were on *The Bachelor* and started to feel butterflies in your stomach? There'd actually be a lot going on in your noggin. Because when

Fisher put people who were madly in love into a brain scanner, she found a lot of activity in a factory near the base of the brain called the ventral tegmental area. That's where we produce dopamine—a natural stimulant that gives us motivation, energy, and focus.

When you're in love, that system goes into overdrive: You have the motivation to find a spouse, you're filled with so much energy that you're totally elated, and your focus on your new paramour borders on obsession. "Somebody's now camping in your head," Fisher explained.

"People who are on the show have been primed," Fisher continued. "Any kind of novel situation drives up the dopamine system in the brain. And reality TV is a state of real novelty. You're suddenly in a house that you don't know, with an awful lot of people you don't know. You're really fighting to win life's greatest prize—a mating partner—and it's going to happen rapidly."

Which invites the question: When you have that much dopamine pumping through your system, how are you supposed to differentiate between lust and love? Lust, as Fisher describes it, is our sex drive—the craving for sexual gratification that isn't focused on a particular person. Love, however, creates a sort of euphoria. If you're falling in love with someone, that person takes on a special meaning.

"You don't think obsessively about somebody when you just want to have sex with them," Fisher said. "But any stimulation of the genitals can drive up the dopamine system and push you over that threshold into falling in love. When you're on one of these shows, presumably they're going to give you an array of the opposite sex who have the characteristics you're looking for in a partner. And the timing is right. Everybody knows that you're looking for a lover, a sweetheart. Proximity is right in front of you. There's all these people milling about who want to go out with you. And the dopamine levels are going to be driving up because of the novelty, so it's almost a perfect situation for people to trigger that brain circuitry for romantic love and be off to the races."

What can we take away from this, dear readers? If you go on *The Bachelor*, you're fucked. In other words, even if you don't think you're susceptible to producer manipulation, even if you swear you're just not attracted to that guy and his cheesy suits—you're probably going to feel like you're falling for him. Your brain is working against you.

I've heard it from countless former contestants—otherwise rational people who felt like they had an out-of-body experience while they were on *The Bachelor*. In this vein, let's examine one particularly disturbing incident that Clare Crawley had while dating Juan Pablo Galavis. For those of you who watched Juan Pabs's season, you'll probably recall that he wasn't exactly the most beloved Bachelor. He didn't propose to the woman he chose at the end of his season, Nikki Ferrell, and never told her he loved her either. He often dismissed the concerns of his would-be wifeys by repeating "*ees okay*" (it's OK) over and over again in a condescending tone.

And then there was what he did to Crawley. On her final date with Galavis, she was taken on a helicopter ride, because duh. At some point during the ride, astonishingly, the couple found themselves alone. As in, no cameras around. Crawley was shocked and took the opportunity to ask her quasi-boyfriend how he was feeling about the impending finale. (At this point, she and Ferrell were the only two women left standing.)

"I was like, 'It's coming up! How are you feeling?'" Crawley told me. "And he goes, 'I don't know. I liked fucking you.'"

I. Liked. Fucking. You.

I mean, are you dead? I am six feet under.

"But, girl, hear me out on this, OK?" Crawley said, sensing what must have been my very obvious disgust over the telephone line. "If you're in a relationship with a guy and you love each other and he leaned over to you, like, 'Babe, I love fucking you,' you're going to be like, 'Fuck yeah! You better!'"

Which, I guess? But he didn't even say he *loved* fucking her. He said he *liked* fucking her. AND THEN HE SENT HER HOME THE NEXT DAY! How could she let this stand?

"My gauge was so off and so skewed at that point," she said. "You have the producers going, 'Yeah, but I really do think he likes you, Clare. You should stick around.' I'd just been in a crappy relationship before the show and didn't have a strong sense of self, so I didn't know. 'Is this right? Is this wrong? Should he be saying that?' In any other situation, I'd be like, 'No. I need to talk to him for, like, five hours and figure this shit out.' But you don't get that opportunity. You kind of go into robot mode."

Even Sharleen Joynt—who left of her own volition a few episodes before Crawley got the boot—found herself falling under the show's romantic spell. After her one-on-one date with Galavis on a private yacht, she wrote this in her journal:

> Everything is just so designed for romance, I can see how if you were single, didn't necessarily know what you were looking for, couldn't tell a deep connection from a superficial [one], and were somewhat naïve, hopelessly naïve and not very cautious, you could fall in love. The focus is so on *it* all the time. You're constantly prompted to talk about him, what you two share, how it makes you feel, how seeing him with the other girls makes you feel. There's no escape.

Of course, she was able to escape, ultimately telling Galavis that the idea of a proposal seemed impossible to her. Others, like Craw-ley, had less of a grip over their emotions. Chris Bukowski told me that when he was on Maynard's season—the first of his many Bach stints—he started preparing himself to propose to the Bachelorette even though he hardly felt ready.

Before his hometown date, he was able to sneak into a hotel business center and get on the Internet. He immediately Googled his name, because he was on *The Bachelorette* and that's the kind of thing these people do. When the results of his search popped up, he was surprised to learn that many fans were predicting he'd win the show.

"And I'm like, 'Holy crap. Am I going to have to propose to this girl?'" Bukowski said. "Before that, I didn't think I was going to make it that far, so I wasn't really preparing for that. But then I started freaking out, like, 'I could totally marry her. I'm just going to have to figure out how it's going to work.'

"I was totally going to propose, for sure. One hundred percent," he acknowledged. "That's all you know, and that's all you're fighting for that whole time, and if you get to the end—I feel like that's the whole reason you're there."

Fortunately, Maynard let him go before he had to get down on one knee. But as we learned from Fisher, when you fall madly in love with someone—or feel like you are, anyway—you can overlook anything. The part of the brain that is associated with decision-making—the prefrontal cortex—actually begins to shut down when you're crazy in love.

"It's called positive delusions," said Fisher. "So you'll say, 'Well, of course my parents will like her. She comes from a different race that my mother hates, but my mother will get over it.' But when you fall madly in love with someone, it is an addiction. It's not insanity, but you can do pretty stupid things."

I think this helps to explain why so many cast members drop the L-bomb early on. And why the Bachelor or Bachelorette often seems slightly weirded-out to be hearing those three little words after, you know, two weeks.

All of the attention felt unwarranted to Jen Schefft, anyway. "All these guys are coming on strong and telling me how great I am and I just—I was like, 'I don't believe you,'" said Schefft, who was chosen by Andrew Firestone before she ended up in the power position. "'You don't know me. You've never met me. Never talked to me. You're just saying this for show purposes.' I thought it would be so fun, but it was actually really uncomfortable and intimidating."

And yet, just a few months before with Firestone, she herself was in that very mind-set. She felt like the wealthy tire heir was the only guy in the world. She wanted his time and attention. She wanted to look her best, say the funniest thing, stand out in the crowd.

"You just," she said, "you just lose total perspective."

The perspective that leads you to question what's happening inside your mind and your body—which steers you away from rational thought about life outside of the bubble.

Why I'm a Fan

I DIDN'T START WATCHING THE BACH UNTIL CHRIS Soules's season. I've only been watching for about three years. I was totally cognizant of the phenomenon before that, but I was a very casual viewer, and I didn't get hard-core until a few years ago when I officially stopped leaving the house and had to start entertaining myself in the evenings. And then I got addicted so fast. I was always more of a dirty Bravo reality-show girl, and it didn't occur to me that something this juicy could be on ABC.

There's a psychological illness that seems to feed these women. It's not like, "I'm going to come on this show and see if this guy is right for me." They show up convinced that they have feelings for this person. I assumed that there would be contestants that left the show because they weren't attracted to the Bachelor, and I've never seen that happen. You're like, "Oh no, this is like a cult. These women are totally fucking obsessed with this guy and with winning." And I think it's because of masterful producing. There's, like, manufactured Stockholm syndrome. It's amazing.

The women on the show are very aware of the rules of the show—these arbitrary rules created by a team of producers have become intertwined with their own reality. Like, I heard a woman on Nick's season say, "If he sleeps with someone before the Fantasy Suite, I'm going to be hurt." I was like, "Oh my gosh, she's letting the production schedule dictate when it's appropriate for him to have sex with someone." Like, if it's Fantasy Suite, that's OK with her. If it's not Fantasy Suite, it hurts her feelings. That is so bizarre to me.

The show has made me feel really ugly, because I assume that the women they cast are based on their perception of what a man would want—and all the women look the same to me on the show. They always have the same kind of long barrel curls and they're all skinny. There's no one that looks like me.

And honestly, I think the reason a lot of us enjoy watching it is because it makes us feel superior. I feel bad admitting that, but it is fun to sit on my lofty perch and be like, "Oh my God, look at this blonde babbling about how she loves kids." I sometimes watch it because it's fun to watch stupid people mate. I feel real bad about that. And I also feel bad about the fact that I have found myself laughing at people's pain so many times. I remember on Kaitlyn's season, there was a guy everyone called Cupcake. She dumped him and there was this long, lingering shot of him sobbing hysterically on a hill. I laughed so hard.

—Diablo Cody, screenwriter (*Juno, Young Adult*)

CHAPTER 7

Method to the Madness

I can make you say some fucked-up shit."

I was sitting across the table from Michael Carroll at a restaurant a few blocks from his house in northeast L.A. when he suddenly threw out that tease. I'd been asking him about how ITMs worked. If you're on the Bach, you have to do as many as five ITMs a day—at the mansion, in the middle of a date, from the back seat of a limo. . . .

"In-the-moment" interviews, conducted by producers, are key to the show's narrative. They provide running commentary for viewers throughout each episode, giving us insight into house dynamics or just how head-over-heels a contestant is for the Bachelor. So the sound bites need to be succinct, revealing, and emotional.

Which brings me back to Carroll. He was trained in the art of upping the ante and thought he could trick me into making some out-of-character remarks, just as he did as a producer on the show. So we decided to role-play, pretending I was on an imaginary date with the Bachelor and Carroll had pulled me aside for a quick ITM.

"Oh my God, so are you guys having an amazing time?" Carroll began.

"It's OK," I responded, shrugging.

"What do you mean?" he asked.

"I mean, like, it's fine. It's just a fine date."

"You're on a one-on-one right now," he said, his voice growing more stern. "Do you know all the girls back there want to be on a one-on-one right now? Like, what is it about him that you're not jiving with?"

"I don't know," I answered. "It's hard for me to open up."

"Do you want to go home?" he said, as if it was a threat.

I shook my head. "No."

"Then fucking *why* are you really into him?"

"Do you think he's going to send me home?" I asked, ignoring his question.

"Well, he might if you don't really try or show him you're interested," he said.

"What do you mean 'try'? What should I do?"

"Try to be *fun*," he said, disgusted. "Try to be interesting! I was watching you from the control room and you look like you couldn't give a fuck. Do you want him to think you couldn't give a fuck? *Really?* That's how you want to do it?"

I was silent.

"Watching you and him is like watching fucking paint dry," he continued. "I want to kill myself. You are boring me to death, and I know you're way more fun. If you're not into it, you can go home tomorrow if you want. You don't have to be here. Do you want to go home? *No?* Well, great. Why don't you show us that you're having a good time?"

Well, damn. That was aggressive. Suddenly, it was easy for me to imagine how you might say some "fucked-up shit" on the show, no matter how sober, equanimeous, or impenetrable you'd thought yourself to be. The power of suggestion is real, especially when someone is berating you and making you feel like a disappointment.

And, ladies, just imagine that in that moment, you were also on your period. That's right, the producers have been known to keep track of when the women in the house are menstruating—which often occurs simultaneously, because that's what happens when women live together—so that they can schedule ITMs accordingly.

"When women cycled together in the house, it created a completely different vibe," producer Ben Hatta told me. "The more dominant woman would basically set it off, and then another would come and say, 'I had my period three days before I came in the house and now I'm having it again, what the fuck is wrong with me?'

"So a girl's now crying mid-interview about nothing, or being reactionary to things that are super small," he continued. "It helped the producers, because now you've got someone who is emotional—and all you want is emotion. If a girl's feeling the butterflies for a guy already, when she gets into that state, her feelings just become more powerful, so she's probably more willing to tell that guy she loves him. And maybe one of the producers knew she was in that emotional state and was like, 'You know what? Now's a better time than ever. You should do it, you should do it, you should do it!'"

In other words, when you see a contestant bawling on *The Bachelor*, they're often upset about something other than the Bachelor. Hatta explained it this way: Say he was talking to a girl about how she hasn't been on a date in two years. She starts reflecting on her love life, wondering if there's something wrong with her. Now she's tearing up. So then he would pivot the conversation toward the Bachelor, getting her talking about how much falling in love would mean to her after so many years of singledom.

"And all of a sudden," he said, "she's the desperate woman."

It's a tactic that bothered many former contestants I spoke to, including Brooks Forester, who referred to the practice as "emotional leveraging." "They'd try to get me to talk about something from my childhood, for example, or something really personal about a family member," he recalled. "Evoke this emotion out of you and then try to attach that to what's happening to the world of *The Bachelor*."

In many ways, cast members ultimately fall in love not in a helicopter or Fantasy Suite but in the interview rooms. Think about it this way. You've come on a show hoping to fall in love—well, maybe hoping for $1,000 a week from SugarBearHair, but let's keep the intentions pure for the sake of this example. You're opening up about your hopes and dreams, describing your ultimate marriage partner. And there's this producer, telling you that the Bachelor embodies all the characteristics you're seeking in a man. That very producer is also starting to become someone you consider a close friend. Sure, they're there to do a job, but it really seems like they understand what you're going through.

Relatability is one of the key attributes successful *Bachelor* producers possess. I spoke to one former segment producer who'd gotten married young, when she was just twenty-one. By the time she started working on the show, she'd had a husband for years— meaning she embodied so much of what the young women on the show aspired to.

"So I would allow them to talk, but I would make sure that I mentioned my husband in some way," she told me. "I would take something that was their problem and put it on myself. There would be twenty minutes of me talking about myself—all unusable stuff—but then all of a sudden I'd go, 'I just want that for you, because I know how special you are, and I know you deserve this.'"

The endgame, she said, is getting a contestant to open up. To do that, the contestant must feel like they can trust you. And they're more likely to trust you if you're open with them about your own life—even though the details of your life, as a producer, will never be broadcast on national television.

Not that every contestant bonds with their producer. On the contrary, things can often get testy between the two parties—especially when a producer is looking for a sound bite that a contestant is unwilling to give. During ITMs, producers will ask a question—let's say, "How important was this day for you?"—and a contestant is supposed to answer by using the question in a complete sentence: "This day was really important for me because it was the first day I could really see the Bachelor being my husband."

"But sometimes you don't want to complete the question they're asking," explained Forester. "So I'd be like, 'What are you trying to get at?' They tell me, and I say, 'Cool, this is my own version of that sentiment.' They'd always just continue to ask the same question formatted different ways, and it's like, 'I just told you I don't want to say that. You just reshaped the sentence and moved words around.'"

Sharleen Joynt, from Juan Pablo Galavis's season, became so resistant to what she felt were leading, obvious questions that a handful of producers were brought in to try to work with her. After her first one-on-one date in Seoul, she sat down for an ITM that should have lasted twenty minutes but ended up taking an hour. The problem?

The producers wanted her to say she was falling in love with Galavis, and she wasn't biting.

"The producer was asking 'Have you ever felt this way so soon?' and I was like, 'Yeah,'" she said with a shrug. "I pretty much didn't give the answer they wanted at every turn, and the gist was definitely that I was not effusive enough. It became a big issue. . . . Eventually I was like, 'I don't know what you want me to say. It was a nice date. It was fine. I'm interested. It's been one real date. I'm not falling in love with him.' I pretty much shut it down."

In Seoul, she still had some fight left in her. But down the line, Joynt said, she found herself so tired of the long ITMs that sometimes she'd kowtow to the producers' requests just so she could get out of the interview room. Chris Bukowski did the same thing.

"I was saying lines verbatim from producers because I'd been sitting in a stupid room for an hour and just wanted to go," said the five-time franchise vet. "You would say something you totally didn't even believe or want to say, but they just keep asking you and asking you and asking you—just like you're being interrogated. You see people who go to prison because the interrogation is so good that they're finally like, 'All right. I fucking did it.' I mean, they put you in a room with no air conditioning, nothing to drink, and just ask you the same questions over and over. By the end of the day you're like, 'Shit. Maybe I did do it.' And then you're in prison for the rest of your life."

Which, yes, sounds like hyperbole. But after thinking about it for a while—and maybe watching a little too much of Netflix's *Making a Murderer*—I realized Bukowski was on to something. So I went out and bought *Police Interrogation and American Justice*, the 2008 book by Richard A. Leo that explains the tried-and-true methods officers use to obtain confessions from potential criminals. And what I found, frankly, was kind of disturbing, because the similarities between a police interrogation and a *Bachelor* interview are rather striking.

Let's start here:

"Before any accusation or confrontation, police seek to increase the suspect's anxiety by removing him from any social setting in which others could provide psychological support," Leo writes.

Check. *Bachelor* contestants are always sequestered during their ITMs.

"Or," he continues, "interrogators may try to make the suspect perceive that the interrogation will go on much longer, if not indefinitely, if he does not comply with their wishes."

Sound familiar? *If you don't say you're falling for Juan Pablo, Sharleen, you might have to stay in this damn room all night.*

"For suspects who are already sleep deprived, fatigued, distressed, or suffering from physical discomfort," Leo writes, "interrogation exacerbates these conditions. . . . The need to escape may become so overwhelming that it overpowers any rational considerations about the effects of confessing."

Yep. *Bachelor* contestants are often coming into ITMs already tired, intoxicated, or upset. So why not just say what the producer wants and end the interview already?

"Interrogators may also alternate displays of sympathy with displays of hostility, positively reinforcing the suspect with friendliness when he says what they want to hear but negatively reinforcing him with anger when he does not," the book says.

This also rings true. Yes, producers sometimes go the tough love route, à la Carroll, but on other nights they're telling you how much they care about you and want you to find a husband just like they did when they were twenty-one.

And yet despite all I'd heard about the captivating powers of *Bachelor* producers, it wasn't until I met Elan Gale that I saw it firsthand.

Gale, the show's thirty-four-year-old executive producer, is somewhat of a celebrity in Bachelor Nation—and even outside of it. He has more than 200,000 followers on Twitter, thanks largely to a comedic hoax he orchestrated called "Diane in 7A." On Thanksgiving in 2013—back when he had only 30,000 followers—he started tweeting angrily about a woman on his flight who was supposedly being rude to a flight attendant. Fed up with her behavior, he sent alcohol and a stream of notes over to her row, one of which advised her: "Eat my dick." He also tweeted photographic evidence of the notes the two passed back-and-forth.

The stunt went viral, but days later—just as a rumor began to surface on Storify that Diane in 7A had stage-4 small cell lung cancer—Gale admitted there was no Diane.

No matter: He had already become an Internet celebrity. Since then, he's befriended a handful of stars, including Chloë Grace Moretz, Kelly Oxford, and director James Gunn, who even gave him a tiny cameo in *Guardians of the Galaxy Vol. 2*. He dated *Bachelor* contestant Casey Shteamer after she was eliminated from Ben Flajnik's season, and his current girlfriend—a decade his junior—is former *Castle* actress Molly Quinn.

He also has an eccentric look. His huge, curly fro is reminiscent of Sideshow Bob from *The Simpsons*. He rarely seems to cut his bushy beard. And he loves jewelry, often sporting chunky rings on every finger, beaded bracelets, silver chain necklaces, and tiny hoop earrings.

And sometimes, it seems like there's nothing he won't share online—save, of course, for his secrets from the Bachelor franchise, which has employed him since 2009. He's documented a recent weight-loss journey with shirtless selfies and photos from his scale. He stopped drinking in 2013 and often posts intimate blog posts about sobriety.

"Why did I drink so much?" he mused on his Tumblr, *All the Hate Mail!*, in 2015. "Because I wanted to feel everything and when I was drunk there was no barrier between me and my highs and lows. There was no filter. I was a corked bottle of emotion . . . crying for no reason and laughing for no reason and raging at the empty sky. Feeling all of it."

My first interaction with Gale occurred in 2011—not surprisingly, on Twitter. He must have stumbled upon the Bach recaps I was writing for the paper, because he suddenly posted this note: "There's usually something endearing about 'Bachelorette' recaps from @amykinla."

From there, we struck up a playful rapport. I'd hang out with him at *Bachelor* events in between interviewing contestants, and he even got Ben Flajnik and Chris Harrison to crash one of my viewing parties, cameras and all. Sure, he'd rib me about my critiques of the show—"You don't need to be so snarky, you're smarter than that"—but it always felt like he respected my opinion.

That changed during Flajnik's season in 2012, when ABC publicity invited me to attend the "Women Tell All" taping. Along with a group of reporters, I sat on a cavernous sound stage watching the production—which was taking place a room over—on a monitor. (No media were allowed to be in the studio audience.)

Flajnik's season was a rather contentious one, because he ended up proposing to the woman who had been cast as the villain, Courtney Robertson. As the season unfolded, however, it became clear that Flajnik was unaware of just how unkind Robertson had been to the other women competing for his affection. All the negative press about Robertson's conniving ways was starting to give Flajnik second thoughts about his wife-to-be, and in a last-ditch effort to save the relationship, Robertson showed up at the "Women Tell All" to apologize for her behavior.

During the "Women Tell All," Robertson was very emotional, crying and asserting how she really is a good person. Then Chris Harrison had to cut to a commercial break. Some other reporters got up to grab some grub from craft services, but I stayed in my seat by the monitor. That's when I realized that the microphones onstage had accidentally been left on—and that I was now privy to what was meant to be private conversation.

Here's where Gale came in. He walked over to Robertson, who was dabbing her eyes with a tissue.

"I didn't play with my hair once. Aren't you proud?" she asked him.

"Yes," he replied. "That was good."

She said she wished she could take a cigarette break, and they started discussing the brand she smokes—American Spirits, apparently. After a few minutes of this kind of banter, her tears had dried.

"I'm not feeling very emotional anymore," she told Gale. "You made me feel better. I appreciate it. But I don't know if I can show that emotion again."

"You have to," Gale urged. "This is for you. This is for you and Ben."

Needless to say, after I published what I'd seen—Gale basically coaching Robertson to cry—he was none too pleased. Our relationship was never the same after that, and not long after, I found myself banned from *Bachelor* events—though I have no idea if Gale was behind that or not.

In the short time I spent with him, however, I was able to get a tiny glimpse of the power he holds over the contestants who go on this show. Multiple cast members I approached said they would be willing to speak to me but were worried about saying anything negative about Gale for fear of losing his friendship.

Flajnik was one of them. He told me how much Gale had helped him move past his grief over losing his father—a struggle he spoke about openly during his season.

"Elan was really instrumental in my life and talking through my feelings—whether it was for TV or not," said Flajnik, who called from his home in San Francisco. "I looked at Elan as a therapist, almost. I enjoyed sitting down for multiple hours at a time with someone who would listen.

"I still genuinely value the time that we had together in talking about our lives and helping each other. Really," he insisted. "I think that's why we've maintained a friendship that's more than just surface level and skin deep."

Even Sharleen Joynt—who seemed well aware of Gale's role in toying with her emotions during Galavis's season—had mixed feelings about him. While she struggled to find common ground with many producers, he was the only one she really connected with. She relied heavily on Gale's guidance when she decided to leave the show prematurely, following his advice about how to make a smooth exit. In her journal, Joynt wrote that Gale often told her she was his friend, "one of his favorites," and reluctantly admitted that he'd become her "personal coach, therapist, and bodyguard." "He's nothing short of brilliant," she wrote.

"I didn't know how I was going to leave, and I was stressed out about it," she said of planning her exit. "I was like, 'America's gonna hate me.' And he said, 'If you listen to what I say, America will love you.' There was one time where I was crying and asked him to give me a tissue and he said, 'No.' I was like, 'You're just gonna let me cry like this?' And he said, 'Yes. America will love it.' And he wasn't wrong. Viewers love tears."

While Joynt still harbors affection for Gale, Chris Bukowski has a harder time reconciling the producer's actions. As you know by now, Bukowski has been on the show five times—so clearly, he's somewhat of a glutton for punishment. He went on both *Bachelor in Paradise* and its now-defunct predecessor, *Bachelor Pad*, on which former contestants moved into the mansion to drink, hook up, and compete for a $250,000 prize.

The first time Bukowski went on *Bachelor in Paradise*, he suffered a knee injury and had to leave the show early. Even though he'd only been dating a girl he'd met on the Mexico set for a few days—Elise Mosca—he nonetheless asked her to leave the show and travel back to Chicago with him.

She obliged, and soon the couple was on a first-class flight back to Chi Town. Once they arrived, Bukowski quickly began fielding calls from Gale, who wanted to know how things were going between the lovebirds. The producer asked the couple to send him home videos of themselves "doing everyday things," Bukowski said.

"Elan would call at midnight and be like, 'How are you feeling about her? Do you think you would propose to her?'" Bukowski said. "I'm like, 'Elan, I don't know, man.'"

Despite Bukowski's ambivalence about the new romance, Gale offered to fly him and Mosca back to Mexico. There, production would put them up in a local hotel suite until the final day of filming. That's when Bukowski would propose to Mosca with a Neil Lane ring.

Bukowski didn't feel great about the plan, but he didn't know what else to do. After so many seasons on reality television, he'd badly tarnished his reputation—particularly on *Bachelor Pad*, where he hooked up with numerous women and seemed to have little regard for their feelings. If he proposed to Mosca, he reasoned, he'd look like a stand-up guy.

Back in Mexico, Bukowski had daily meetings with Gale in which the producer would urge him to seal the deal with a ring.

"All right, listen. Are you going to propose?" Bukowski said Gale would ask. "I flew out two rings. If you don't do it, someone else is going to. Are you going to do it? You've got to do it. This is going to fix your image so much. America's going to fall in love with you guys."

Bukowski met with Neil Lane, who offered him a diamond to propose with. He took it back to his room for a night to mull over the plan, sleeping next to the ring box and a bottle of tequila.

"I'm thinking, 'Holy crap, I've got to propose to this girl,'" he remembered. "So I called my mom. I'm like, 'Mom, I don't know. Should I propose to her? I don't, like, love her or anything.' She's like, 'Oh, son, do whatever you want. You have my support either way.' At this point, she was probably just so tired of all this shit."

It wasn't the answer he was looking for, and his dad was no help either, advising him to just listen to his mother. Confounded, he told Gale he was ready to go through with the proposal.

"I knew, one hundred percent, there was no way I could be with this girl," he admitted. "I couldn't even stand her at one point. It was just so bad. But I honestly thought that me proposing to her and getting engaged on national TV was going to get people to forgive me for the way I acted in the past."

The night before he was supposed to get down on one knee, Bukowski didn't sleep a wink. Mosca—who was totally in the dark at this point—kept asking him what was wrong. When it was finally time to get up, he thought he was having a heart attack. And just when he thought he might vomit, he ran over to Gale and said he couldn't go through with the plan.

The producer sat down with Bukowski for an hour, trying to get him to change his mind, telling him how close he was to the finish line. If he got engaged to Mosca, the happy couple could return to *Bachelor in Paradise* the following summer to show off their success story.

"I'm like, 'Elan, I won't be with her by next season,'" Bukowski replied. "I'd made up my mind. He could have fed me twenty drinks at that point. There was no way I was going to propose to her."

As you might imagine, Bukowski doesn't pop up on Gale's Instagram feed these days. But plenty of other *Bachelor* contestants do, where the producer waxes poetic about the very same people he's convinced to cry on-camera. He posts photos of himself hugging, carrying, and snuggling various cast members, some of whom he refers to as his "children."

"I love everyone in this photo and if you say something mean about them I will kick you," he captioned one 2016 snap of him and five ladies from Ben Higgins's season.

You can see how this all gets confusing. Does Gale really count cast members as his friends, or is he just doing his job? Can both simultaneously be true?

"You have to draw this weird line where you're kind of their friend, but you're not their friend," explained Hatta. "You do care for them, in a sense, because you're learning all these things about them, and they're human. But at the end of the day, you are making television. So if you know a guy's going to break a girl's heart, you can't tell her. You have to build her up to where she's like, 'I'm gonna go on this date and tell him I love him!' Telling her she has to give her all when you know he's gonna let her go and you have to let it play out."

And getting too close to a producer can prove dangerous. No one knows that better than Craig Robinson, whose romantic relationship with a *Bachelor* staffer cost him a reality TV career and her a job on the show.

After he was booted from Ali Fedotowsky's season of *The Bachelorette*, Robinson—who worked as a lawyer in Philadelphia—began negotiations to appear on *Bachelor Pad*. That's when he started talking to Karri-Leigh Mastrangelo, an executive producer who'd been with the Bach since its inception in 2002.

Mastrangelo was involved with casting Robinson on the second season of *Bachelor Pad* in 2011. During the casting process, he said, she began calling him every day, and the two started a flirtatious relationship. According to Robinson, Mastrangelo—who was married at the time—told him that he was the first cast member she'd ever been "interested in" and that she wanted to help him win the show.

"She was like, 'You're a lot smarter than these other people,'" he recalled. "I just kept thinking, 'If I can go on the show and have her in my corner the whole time, I could definitely win this thing.'"

After completing the requisite drug and STD testing, Robinson was set to appear on the show. About a month before filming was slated to begin, he planned a trip to Los Angeles to visit a college friend. When Mastrangelo found out he would be in town, Robinson said, she offered to pick him up from the airport. On the flight from Philadelphia to L.A., Robinson was so anxious that he "drank a ton," and when he got off the plane, he immediately spotted the producer in baggage claim.

"She walks up to me and starts making out with me in the middle of baggage claim at LAX," he told me. "I was like, 'Oh my God, what the fuck is going on?' And then she just basically didn't go home the whole weekend."

Mastrangelo did not respond to my repeated requests for comment. But according to Robinson, over the next three days, the two spent all their time together. Things got intimate, but they never consummated their relationship. And on his final night in town, Robinson and Mastrangelo decided to meet up with Elan Gale at a karaoke bar in the San Fernando Valley. The trio began drinking, and at one point, when Gale went to the bathroom, Robinson and Mastrangelo took the opportunity to kiss a bit. The make-out session lasted a little too long, though, because Gale returned and witnessed the two mid-lip-lock.

"So Elan looks at me and says, 'What the fuck was that?'" Robinson remembered. "He's like, 'I've got to go home, because what I just saw was not right. We'll talk about this tomorrow.'"

The following day, Robinson got a call from Gale, who told the contestant he was going to have to report the hook-up to Mike Fleiss. Mastrangelo was fired from the show, and Robinson was told he would no longer be a part of *Bachelor Pad*. He eventually returned to his law practice, and she has gone on to find other work in the television industry, working on programs like *Celebrity Wife Swap*. The two kept in touch for a while, Robinson said, but have not spoken in about three years.

At least the two suffered ramifications of an *actual* romantic relationship. Just a year before Robinson and Mastrangelo's affair, Rozlyn Papa—a contestant on Jake Pavelka's season of *The Bachelor*—was accused of having an inappropriate relationship with a producer that she still claims never even took place.

It all began when Papa, who worked both as a model and a makeup artist, was filming introductory footage for the season. A producer named Ryan Callahan flew to Virginia to help production put together day-in-the-life footage of Papa and her son. Callahan was nice, Papa remembered, trying to ease her concerns about going on the show and telling her how great of a guy Pavelka was. She said this was the only time she ever spent alone with the producer.

Cut to the second week in the house. Papa said she wasn't that into Pavelka, but otherwise, things in the mansion were par for the course. Then, just before a rose ceremony, Harrison pulled her outside to have a private conversation.

"This is something we've never had to deal with in the history of the show," the host told her. "I am very sorry that we have to have this conversation. Rozlyn, you entered into an inappropriate relationship with one of our—with one of our staffers."

Papa, looking flummoxed, remained silent.

"That staffer is no longer working with us," Harrison continued. "Because of what happened, we feel it's now impossible [for you] to then now form a meaningful relationship with Jake. Out of respect for everybody here, the girls, Jake, yourself. This is something that we take incredibly serious for everyone on the show. And we feel that there was a line that was crossed with our staffer."

"I'm not gonna say anything," Papa replied. "That puts me in a bad position."

"The bottom line is this," Harrison said. "We feel, because of what has happened, it's impossible for you to continue on the show. And we feel that you need to leave tonight. Go pack your stuff and then there's a van waiting for you."

Reflecting on the exchange now, Papa said she was blindsided.

She couldn't process what she was being accused of. "It was like he was speaking Portuguese," she said.

She was so embarrassed that she'd been asked to leave that she didn't want to defend herself or beg to stay. Instead, she rushed to gather her things and exit as quickly as she could.

In the hours following her departure, her mind began to clear, and she became increasingly angry. She was taken aback that the production had fired Callahan, whom she'd viewed as a sort of confidant on-set. No one from the show ever clarified what was "inappropriate" about their relationship, which she still insists was never sexual.

That's not what Harrison says, though. In numerous interviews as the season aired, he defined the relationship as "physical," saying other girls on the show "saw it" and that Callahan "confessed more than once and to more than one person."

As for Papa, the only odd moment she recalls between herself and Callahan happened after she received the first-impression rose on night one. Because the producer had encouraged her to pursue Pavelka—whom she wasn't excited about initially—she was eager to show him the rose.

"I thought he would be really proud of me, so I took out the rose, like, 'Look what I got!'" she said. "And he just scowled at me, turned, and walked away. I think my heart just sort of dropped at that point, because I couldn't figure out why he was acting that way. Was he angry? Was he jealous? I think that there was definitely an interest on his end that hadn't been expressed before—and it was not something that I thought much of."

After she was sent home, Papa got in touch with Callahan. She said she was confused by what had happened, particularly because neither of them had given production any reason to think they were more than friends.

"And he said, 'Well, that's not true,'" Papa recalled. "'I did talk to them, because they could just see it on my face that I really cared for you in a way that I didn't care for the other contestants. And so I told them how I felt about you.'"

Callahan did not respond to my request for an interview. To this day, Papa is still upset that he never stood up for her, but she thinks he probably remained quiet in the hopes of saving his television career.

"You go on that show and you are meat for the grinder," Papa said with a sigh. "One way or another, they're going to make you good TV."

The editing process, of course, is essential to shaping a narrative like this. And that takes place far from the mansion, done by staffers who never have any interaction with cast members.

It all starts with loggers—employees who watch raw *Bachelor* footage and transcribe it all, replete with time codes. Those transcripts are given to story producers, who give the editors a sense of what they're looking for in an episode. The story producers break down each episode into acts. An act—which can be anything from a rose ceremony to an argument at the mansion—takes place between two commercial breaks.

Even when that outline is in place, editors are still able to access the raw footage—usually as much as 2,000 hours worth of it. And that can be crucial when it comes to "Frankenbiting"—one of the main techniques editors employ to create certain narratives. A "Frankenbite" is a sound bite that has been re-cut so that it has a different meaning. Let's say the Bachelor says, "I do not want to go on a date with Trish." If an editor took out the words "do not"—making the sentence "I want to go on a date with Trish"—that would be a Frankenbite.

"With editing, everything is malleable," said one editor who worked on the show for three seasons. "You can make it whatever you want. You think, 'Oh, she's going to say something bitchy and we'll use that.' No, no, no. You make whatever she does bitchy."

Even without Frankenbiting, there are ways to recontextualize scenes. Imagine that a story producer hands over footage from a one-on-one date between a woman and the Bachelor. The date went pretty well, but the editor is told by a story producer to make it seem like the couple went on the worst date in history.

The date lasted three hours. Sure, the Bachelor and his lady had plenty of conversations, but the editor isn't going to showcase any of those. Instead, he's going to take the shots where they're both sitting in silence. Maybe he'll throw in one where the woman takes a pro- longed sip of wine from her glass. Even though the Bachelor told his date, "We really have a lot to talk about," the editor will Frankenbite the clip, turning it into "We don't really have a lot to talk about." And then that edited sound bite will be layered over footage in which you don't need to see the Bachelor's mouth moving—a shot of the ocean view, perhaps, or the tiramisu no one has touched.

And voilà! Instead of a three-hour gabfest, the date has trans- formed into twenty seconds of total awkwardness.

"I'm thinking, 'This is what I want to happen.' Then I make the footage tell that story," the editor told me. "I don't care what [actu- ally] happens. It's like I'm handed a big bucket of Legos and think, 'What do I want to build today?'

"There's no allegiance to what happened in reality," he said. "The only things that are definitely happening are the rose ceremonies. The only other goal is entertainment, and that's why the show is suc- cessful."

Clare Crawley learned that the hard way. When she was on *Bach- elor in Paradise*, editors made her the butt of a joke by making it seem like she was confiding in a raccoon. Yes, you read that correctly. After some house drama, Crawley went outside to cry and vent to someone—a fellow castmate, perhaps even a producer—but editing made it appear as if she were talking to a wild animal. Though the bit was clearly meant to be comedic, Crawley said she's encountered many viewers who took the gag seriously.

"People message me and say, 'You're so psycho. I can't believe you talk to raccoons,'" she said. "I'm like, 'I'm the psycho one? Me, or the person who actually thinks that I talk to raccoons?' People are clueless to editing."

Though she long felt that the editors on the show were like "the man behind the curtain in *The Wizard of Oz*," she actually met the man responsible for the raccoon cut at a wrap party for *Paradise*.

"He was like, 'Just so you know, I'm the one who put the raccoon stuff in there,'" she said. "I was literally like, 'Really? You're owning up to that? Do you know how much grief you caused in my life from people actually thinking I was talking to raccoons?'"

Which, yes. It's probably not fun to have people thinking your BFF is a raccoon. But *Bachelor* edits have had far more serious repercussions. Flajnik, for one, still blames the editors on his season for the demise of his relationship with the so-called villainous Robertson. While he came off looking fine—"They're never gonna make the main person look bad, right? You're the knight in shining armor"—he feels the show went to extreme lengths to make his onetime-fiancée appear evil.

"You do all this work for everyone for so long and it's like, '*This* is the end product you decided to display to the entire world?'" said Flajnik. "I felt super emasculated. It was like, 'God, that's not really how I remember it, but that's how everyone else is gonna see it, and that sucks, because that's not who I really am.'

"I'm not saying I want to be in a relationship with Courtney," he clarified, "but I blame the higher-ups in production for the way they handled and portrayed our relationship. And that's why Mike Fleiss and all of them don't reach out to me. They know I don't want anything to do with the franchise."

Robertson declined my interview request, but in her 2014 book, *I Didn't Come Here to Make Friends: Confessions of a Reality Show Villain*, she talks about how producers relished her over-the-top antics. A few weeks into filming, she wrote, the team already recognized she was a "loose cannon, especially after a glass of wine."

"As time went on, and as it became clear that Ben liked me and I'd be sticking around for a while, I got pulled into confessionals and found myself trying to be a comedian on-camera, doling out increasingly outrageous insults," she wrote.

That's the interesting thing about contestants who end up fulfilling specific *Bachelor* character types—the villain, the drunk, the virgin, the Southern Belle, the aspiring musician—a lot of them cop to their part in the creation of those roles.

Remember Erica Rose, the tiara-wearing wannabe princess whose daddy was a plastic surgeon? Even though she knew she'd come off looking like a spoiled brat by wearing tiara headbands, she decided that going along with the producers' costume suggestion was a better idea than ignoring it.

"If you don't go along with them, they're going to portray you that way anyways, so essentially, I just allowed it," she said with a shrug. "When we were moving into the mansion, they told me to go up to Chris Harrison and complain about the fact that there weren't any maids. At first I didn't want to, but then I realized it would be funny. I feel like I was in on everything, so I didn't feel exploited in any way."

Same thing for Justin "Rated R" Rego, the former wrestler who left Ali Fedotowsky's season after it came to light he was making phone calls to an ex back in Canada. (No surprise here: He was a villain.) Even though Rego hadn't wrestled professionally for more than two years when he applied to be on *The Bachelorette*—in fact, he was the assistant manager at a fitness club—he still threw his alter ego's name on the form to spice up the otherwise "vanilla" application.

On his first night in the mansion, Rego said, producers asked if he'd put his "Rated R" T-shirt on under his dress shirt. As soon as he exposed it to Fedotowsky, he became enemy number one in the house—the guy who looked like he was just on the show to advance his career. So later that evening, when Harrison asked the cast to vote for the contestant who was "here for the wrong reasons," Rego won out.

"That's when I realized, 'Oh, I'm *that* guy this season,'" he said. "I was blown away that everything was going to come down on me. So it was like, 'If this is how the storyline is going to be, I'm going to make this a damn good storyline. Let's do it.'"

So in ITMs, when producers would ask him to answer a question as if he were his bombastic Rated R character, he went with it. One day, he said, Gale asked if he'd be interested in spending a little extra time with Fedotowsky: "Let's say we let you leave the house and you walk to her house. Is that something you'd be open to?" Even though he was on crutches at the time—which would obviously make walking a challenge—Rego responded that it would be "dope" to see more of the Bachelorette. So Gale revealed his plan.

While Fedotowsky's residence was just up the street, Rego was driven forty-five minutes away to a curvy, cliffside road. There, he was told to get out and hobble down the street on his crutches as the cameras rolled. The scene would later be used to make it look like Rego had gone to extreme lengths to see his love interest. But in fact, he was just chauffeured over to her place later in the day.

"I know the importance of a storyline," he said, explaining why he went along with the scheme. "There were some nice, great human beings on that show. You, the viewer, never saw them. If I'm going to be on a show like that and get that once-in-a-lifetime opportunity, I'm going to make the best of it.

"With the producers, you can either cooperate with them and stay on the show and have all these great things happen and have these stories sixty years later to tell my kids," he said, "or you can not cooperate and be like, 'No, I don't want to say that. I don't want to do this.' And then it's like, 'OK, we're not going to film you, and you're going to get eliminated.'"

The most brusque producers will admit as much too. They don't follow a handbook of moral guidelines. As far as they're concerned, once a cast member signs on the dotted line, anything is fair game.

"Look, I don't want to see anybody get hurt," said Scott Jeffress. "But I do want to make good television, and if somebody's feelings are hurt, I'm sorry. You signed up for it. I'm very adamant about having cast embrace the show that is shown on television. In other words: Look, you may have said this a little differently than what it appears to be in the cut, but that's what the viewer heard, so embrace it. Own it. This is you. I don't put up with a lot of cast members saying producers made me do this or that. I'll get on the phone, call them up and say, 'They didn't make you say anything. We asked a question and you answered it, OK?'"

Jeffress, who now works as an EP on MTV's dating show *Are You the One?*, says everyone in the reality television industry is constantly trying to push the boundaries. And with every year that passes, contestants become more willing to expose their minds and bodies.

"I mean, look where we are. I've got people having sex on-camera. I can't show it, but they're having it," he said. "If it was legal to put electrocutions on TV, they'd be doing it if it garnered ratings and if advertisers would sponsor it. That's really where the moral standard lies—with the advertisers. They'll pull sponsorship from a show that they think goes too far. But advertisers are flocking to *The Bachelor*."

Why I'm a Fan

PAUL SCHEER

I'M A LATECOMER TO THE *BACHELOR* GAME. I
would say Ben Flajnik was kind of my entry-point season, when I
began loving the show, because he was a terrible Bachelor. I used
to think with guys like Andrew Firestone: "Oh, yeah. That guy
looks cool." And now it seems like they're like, "Fuck it! Let's just
have fun with these dummies!" No offense to anybody, but one of
the Bachelors lived at home with his parents. That's not the prize
you want to put on TV. None of these people are prime husband
material anymore.

There's a voyeuristic quality to the show that is so fun. You go,
"Oh my gosh, what would it be like if I was in that situation? Why
are they reacting like that? Why are they doing this?" You're constantly putting yourself in their position, which makes it, in a weird
way, aspirational. We have all dated. It's the only thing that we can
all do equally—that we're all experts in. I'm not an expert on how to
build a fire or a hut on *Survivor*. I can't sing or tell you if someone is
off-pitch. But I can tell you, "Oh, that girl's going to be trouble," or
"That guy's a dick."

I think that there's always a turned-up nose at the franchise because if you haven't watched it, you have an assumption of what it
is. On Howard Stern's show, they give him so much crap for being a
fan. The listeners call about it and they complain about it. But
whenever someone makes fun of people watching *The Bachelor*,

I'm like, "Well, you haven't watched it, then, because I used to feel the same exact way." I've been with my wife now for thirteen years, so I'm so far out of the dating pool it's ridiculous. And it's funny to see the current dating world vicariously and talk about it together. We argue about who the best person on the show is—she'll shoot down who I like, and vice versa. And then it's like, "Well, wait. If you don't like that person on the show, why do you like me?"

You can't just dip your toe in. It will take me like six months to get through an hour-long drama that I have all lined up, but I can watch a Sunday-to-Monday night of *The Bachelor* and it's like cotton candy. You eat it. It's delicious. It disappears. Where did that go? I can't believe I watched four hours of it.

I think it's the best-produced reality show on television, hands down. They've been doing the same thing over and over again, essentially, for [thirty-five] seasons. But you're always invested. It may get predictable, but that predictability doesn't make it boring.

—Paul Scheer, comedian (*The League, Veep*)

CHAPTER 8

Under the Covers

After Clare Crawley's father died, she started to feel anxious all the time. She didn't feel comfortable leaving her house. The thought of driving on the freeway made her jittery. And getting on a plane? She wouldn't even consider it.

So signing up for *The Bachelor* represented more than just taking a shot at love. Going on the show meant she was trying to conquer her anxiety, ridding herself of her fears by facing them head on.

Still, before she flew from Sacramento down to Los Angeles to meet Juan Pablo Galavis, her sister gave her one Xanax pill, folded up in a tissue. "Keep this in your pocket, and if you ever get in a situation where you start to panic, you'll be OK," Crawley's sibling advised.

But she never ended up swallowing the pill.

Because once she got on the show, her nerves started to dissipate. By the time production traveled to Vietnam, Crawley was astounded at how far she'd come. "I started sobbing, because I was like, 'I wish

171

my dad could see me here. I wish he could see me without anxiety and know what I'm feeling—the most free feeling in the entire world.'"

To commemorate the moment, she decided to ask the producers if she could go for a late-night swim in the ocean. It was well after midnight, and she wasn't supposed to leave her hotel room.

"Absolutely," she said they responded, "but Juan Pablo's the reason that you're here, so do you want to share that moment with him?"

She liked the idea, so she and a camera crew wandered over to the Bachelor's room around four a.m. Despite the hour, he was game for an adventure. The two ran down to the beach and hopped in the water. Crawley said she was crying, and he hugged her, saying how happy he was to be able to share the moment with her. Then they went to bed, separately.

But when the ocean encounter played out on television, it appeared far more scandalous. There was lots of kissing, and it looked as if the couple potentially had sex in the water.

"I felt like I was kicked in the stomach, because that had been one of the best, greatest feelings in my entire life—feeling that sense of relief from anxiety," Crawley said of watching the episode. "I felt so betrayed by the producers. You put [in] slow motion, sexy music, muffled sound, and it seems like, 'Oh my God, what's happening?' Nobody gives two shits about somebody overcoming anxiety. I think that's so much more relatable, but of course they have to make it look like drama."

Things only got worse from there. Shortly after the late-night swim, Galavis confessed to Crawley that he felt guilty about their ocean dip. "That was good, but at the same time, it was kind of a little weird for me," he told her in his thick Venezuelan accent. "To me, it's hard, this whole situation, because I have a daughter. I don't want her to see what happened. If she sees it, I don't think it will be that nice."

Taken aback, Crawley started crying, saying she hadn't intended to "disrespect" his daughter. Not only, according to her, had nothing sexual occurred between her and the Bachelor—but Galavis hadn't hesitated to go to the beach with her. And now, after the fact, he was trying to make it seem like she'd lured him into some scandalous trap?

"In any other position, I would have looked at him and been like, 'First of all, there was nothing wrong with what happened,'" she said. "I was trying to look at it from his perspective, like, 'OK, maybe he did feel bad.' But now I look back on it and I'm going, 'Hey, bro, you could have said no.' I was so crushed, because he had essentially taken that moment away from me."

The incident marked a watershed moment on *The Bachelor*—one of the first times two cast members appeared to have sex prior to the Fantasy Suite. Since the program's origin, sex has typically been reserved for the Fantasy Suite—rose-laden luxury hotel rooms that the final three contestants get to spend the night in—separately—if they so choose. The special evenings take place after hometown dates but before anyone gets down on a knee, therefore becoming the last opportunity for the finalists to sleep together before getting engaged.

The Fantasy Suite dates don't actually occur over three consecutive nights—there's a day filled with interviews in between each romantic night. But in theory, the Bachelor or Bachelorette could still be having sex with three different people in the span of a week. A situation that wouldn't fly with most fledgling couples outside of the Bach.

"I was like, 'Uh, could I have set something up like this in college where I could date twenty-seven girls and they're all cool with it?'" said Lorenzo Borghese, the Italian prince who was the ninth Bachelor. "It's kind of like watching boxing, where you see a guy getting beaten in the head but you're cheering. If the guy were out here on the street, you'd try to break it up. But when it's treated like, 'Hey, this is the game,' you accept it."

Early on, however, producers weren't sure how accepting contestants would be of the Fantasy Suites. Women in particular struggled to compartmentalize the idea that the Bachelor had just been intimate with another woman, said Scott Jeffress.

"Women really felt like it was creepy and weird," the producer recalled. "So you just have to say, 'Look, this is just the way the show works. It's not his fault. Are you feeling it? Do you feel like you're ready to go to that level yet? Because now's your chance—just saying.' And once they get on the date with him, it all goes away. It's their world and there's no one else there."

"There was more resistance in the beginning, and then it lessened," agreed Michael Carroll. "Girls just got more understanding of what it is. If you come and you're final three and you want to lock it down, there you go."

Of course, there are no explicit rules forbidding anyone from sleeping together earlier in the season. But if you have sex before the designated time and outside of the designated place, there's a good chance you'll be treated like Crawley was.

"If Clare had bided her time and waited however many episodes until Juan Pablo invited her into his Fantasy Suite," wrote *Slate*'s television critic Willa Paskin, "she would have been celebrated as a woman willing to make herself vulnerable for love. Instead, she got the easy-woman edit and a scolding about sexual propriety from a guy proudly wearing multiple women's spit. It may be hard out here for a pimp, but it's way harder for a bachelorette."

That was especially evident when Kaitlyn Bristowe had her turn as the leading lady in 2015. Early on, Bristowe made it clear she was a rule-breaker when she let Nick Viall join the cast of men competing for her affection. Viall had just come off Andi Dorfman's

Bachelorette, and after he was sent home as the runner-up, he and Bristowe struck up a flirty friendship. They exchanged messages online and spoke on the phone, and when Bristowe was selected as the Bachelorette, Viall decided to throw caution to the wind and turn up on the show again—and she allowed him to stay.

Viall's late arrival instantly stirred up controversy. The other men were displeased that someone Bristowe had a prior relationship with had been allowed on the show at the last minute. And to make matters worse, she seemed insanely attracted to him.

"We'd spent five weeks doing nothing but talking to each other beforehand," Viall later explained to me. "The physical part was playing catch-up to the emotional. . . . There's a reason why we looked like we wanted to rip each other's clothes off: because we fucking did."

Which explains why, after a one-on-one date in Dublin that consisted almost entirely of making out, Bristowe asked Viall to spend the night at her hotel. Though viewers only saw a closed bedroom door, revealing subtitles (Viall: "I want to know every part of you" #shudder), and heard moaning, which made it obvious what was going down.

But the next day, instead of celebrating her sexual escapade, Bristowe looked forlorn. She still had half a dozen men left in the competition, and she felt things "went too far with Nick."

"And it's not about me feeling bad that I was intimate with him," she insisted in an ITM. "I feel bad that I have relationships with these other guys that are so great and mean so much to me."

Later, during a heart-to-heart with Chris Harrison, she confessed she'd had sex with Viall.

"To be honest, I was kind of disappointed in myself," she told the host. "After my one-on-one, we went back to my hotel, and I just really regret it."

"Well, that's good," Harrison replied, insinuating that her behavior was, in fact, regrettable. "We all screw up. And the way I feel is: Where do you go from there? That's a sign of good character."

Eventually, she told Shawn Booth—the man she'd end up engaged to at the end of the season—about her relations with Viall. Though he had a difficult time accepting the news, obviously Booth was able to move past the admission. America, however, couldn't seem to look past Bristowe's pre–Fantasy Suite rendezvous.

When Bristowe sat down with Harrison during the "Men Tell All" episode after the season wrapped, she revealed that she was being bullied online by those who disagreed with the way she'd conducted herself on *The Bachelorette*. The host proceeded to read some of the mean stuff that had been directed toward Bristowe, including a tweet calling her a "whore" and an email that said she had "no morals" and "should just crawl in a hole and die. I hope the fans break her spirit so that our kids can see that whoring behavior isn't rewarded."

Andi Zeisler, co-founder of the nonprofit feminist organization Bitch Media, believes the vitriol stemmed from the discomfort many viewers still have with the idea that women have the capacity to date and have sex without emotional attachment.

"People are very threatened by the idea that that is actually something that occurs and has become a pretty standard part of contemporary dating life," said Zeisler, also the author of *We Were Feminists Once*. "And the show made the entire storyline that season about the fact that she had slept with one of the suitors 'too soon.' It became such a central storyline in a way that it never had and never would on *The Bachelor*."

Conversely, if a contestant makes it clear they won't be having sex due to religious or moral beliefs, that also garners a lot of attention.

Sean Lowe was dubbed "The VIRGIN Bachelor" on the cover of *Us Weekly* after he declared he didn't plan on sleeping with anyone on the show. He wasn't technically even a virgin; he had recommitted himself to Christ after a few premarital encounters and vowed to remain celibate until he walked down the aisle.

Nonetheless, the idea that a twentysomething Bachelor would pass up the opportunity to hop into bed with a handful of ladies proved to be juicy tabloid fodder. "The girls are stunned to learn Sean's saving himself for marriage," *Us Weekly*'s 2013 headline continued, promising to explain how "awkward" the Fantasy Suite dates were and how "the winner copes with her sexless engagement."

While he may have made headlines, unlike Bristowe, Lowe was embraced by Bachelor Nation because of his beliefs.

"I think a lot of people found it refreshing," he said. "Like 'Wow, OK. So this show doesn't necessarily have to be on the scandalous side. Here's a guy that believes what I believe and he's kind of a stand-up guy. He's not ashamed to say that he's not handling the Fantasy Suites the way that most people do.'"

Heading into the show, Lowe said he knew he wanted to make his intentions clear to both the women on the show and *Bachelor* fans. Whether he liked it or not, he said, he knew people would be looking up to him, and he wanted to represent himself and his faith accurately.

Desiree Siegfried, who is also a practicing Christian, felt the same way when she was Bachelorette.

"I would never go have sex with three different guys. I actually wouldn't condone it," she said. "I love girls like Andi and Kaitlyn, because they are like 'girl power' and whatever. But you are on TV, so regardless of if you want to be a role model or you don't—you are one. Ten-year-olds are going to watch you. We shouldn't just give in to so many guys—we need to be empowered in the way of, 'Yeah, the guy is going to pursue me, but I don't need to give it up.'"

Regardless of your gender, Lowe argued, having sex on all your Fantasy Suite dates is "unhealthy." And it can cause trouble down the line. "Even if you end up with the fantasy proposal that everybody wants at the end," he said, "then you're left answering questions with your new fiancée about why you did those things. Maybe that's my personal convictions, but sleeping with three people in three days can't be good for you."

And yet if you watch the Bach, you're probably under the impression that most finalists have sex in the Fantasy Suite. Of course, plenty do—often because they're so worked up after weeks of unresolved sexual tension.

"People underestimate how horny you get," one *Bachelor* contestant told me. "What I cannot believe is that more people did not bring vibrators. You're in these constant situations where there's a lot of buildup. There's a lot of making out, and then you're pulled away from each other. After a while, I just wanted to fuck him so bad."

When contestants finally make it to the Fantasy Suite, what happens there doesn't necessarily remain a secret. Producers almost always know what goes down behind closed doors because oftentimes, they sleep in the same two-room villa as the special couple—just a wall over, where they can literally hear what's going on. But most cast members aren't that tight-lipped about the overnights anyway. It's that whole "if a tree falls in the forest" thing—plus, by that point in the competition, contestants have been primed to spill every detail in ITMs.

Of course, it's also easy to employ smoke and mirrors, making it look as if two people had a racy night together when, in fact, they kept their clothes on. Maybe you film a shot of the lights in the bedroom switching off before the cast members even get there. Or exclude the moment when someone leaves the suite after a few hours of late-night conversation.

"There were a lot of girls that would go into the suite with him and then puss out and be like, 'I'm going. Make sure you show me leaving,'" said Carroll. "And of course, we may or may not show her leaving."

Once you're inside the Fantasy Suite, the suggestion that you're supposed to be having sex isn't exactly subtle. In addition to the rose petals, plush bed, and soaker tubs, producers will leave a handheld camera and bowls of condoms everywhere. "It was like, 'Oh, *OK*, so we can be safe if we want to be,'" said former Bachelorette Jen Schefft. "But honestly? We don't need a bowlful."

Schefft, for one, said she was so tired by her third Fantasy Suite date that the idea she'd stay up all night having some crazy sex romp was laughable. By the time she got back to the room, she said, it was four a.m., and she had to be up in four hours to resume filming. So she passed out instead.

Crawley also remembers feeling exhausted. "I was so worn out from having to be 'on' the whole time that I just wanted to sleep so bad," she said. And while she was awake, she was busy enjoying seeing how Galavis acted without the cameras on him. At one point in the evening, she recalled, he disappeared into the bathroom. When she crept in to see what he was up to, she was surprised to see him dancing alone in front of the mirror.

"He was literally doing a body roll, watching himself body roll in the mirror to this music," she said with a laugh. "I was like, 'Is this for real? Is this really fucking happening?'"

Because there are no producers physically around, it can feel like "Mom and Dad are gone," as Lowe put it. Contestants begin to unveil their truly authentic selves, finally given the opportunity to ask all the questions they've been holding in. Sometimes, the inquiries are mundane: "What do you do all day? Where the hell do they keep you?" Or they're the kind of thing you wouldn't want to ask in front of a producer: "Why did you get that tattoo? Do you really want five kids?"

"Oh, and are you sure you really want to have sex with me on national television?"

"You may not be here next week, so are you gonna fucking hate me forever if we do this?" Flajnik said he asked the women he brought on his Fantasy Suite dates. "I very much left the ball in their court, because I totally understood the position they were in."

After all, you don't want to be faced with a scorned lover when that reunion taping rolls around a few months later. That's what happened to Andi Dorfman after she slept with, and subsequently rejected, Nick Viall.

When the Bachelorette had to talk to her ex during the "Men Tell All" episode, a bitter Viall asked: "If you weren't in love with me, I'm just not sure why, like, why you made love with me."

Dorfman didn't take to the question well. She said it was "below the belt" to reveal they'd had sex and that the moment "should have been kept private." And the reveal would later send Dorfman's then fiancé, Josh Murray, into such a rage that she thinks it ultimately led to the demise of their relationship.

For his part, Viall said he regrets what he said to Dorfman—even though he doesn't feel he was slut-shaming her.

"I'm not trying to defend it—it wasn't the platform," he acknowledged. "But I also wasn't trying to shame her. If sex isn't shameful, then you can't shame someone for saying they've had sex. The truth is, if a girl had done that, all the feminists in the world would have been like, 'You go, girl! Way to call him out!'"

Slut-shaming became a big topic of discussion again in the wake of the *Bachelor in Paradise* scandal in the summer of 2017. After news broke that Corinne Olympios was the one involved in the alleged misconduct, many stories recalled her sexual behavior on Viall's season. During her stint on *The Bachelor*, she took off her bikini top on a group date and later snuck out of her hotel room late one night to try to have sex with Viall pre–Fantasy Suite.

Even though she said she did not recall the *Bachelor in Paradise* incident—she was too drunk, she said—she publicly described herself as a victim. Was she in control of her actions that night? Did DeMario Jackson cross a line by hooking up with her? Did production watch misconduct unfold before their very eyes?

The controversial encounter began a discussion about consent on reality television, and when the cast returned to Mexico—sans Olympios or Jackson—the show did attempt to create a teachable moment, with Chris Harrison leading a discussion on the meaning of consent.

"How do you know when someone has given consent when you are getting intimate with somebody?" Harrison asked the group. What about if somebody is passed out or unresponsive? What if they're drunk?

"Verbal consent is the best way to know that someone's giving consent," replied cast member Taylor Nolan. "People can give you nonverbal cues with their body language that they are consenting, but I think it's also really important to get that verbal consent to make sure."

"Just because somebody gives consent in the beginning doesn't mean that they can't have the right to say no at any point," added contestant Ben Zorn. "So consent needs to be throughout everything."

The discussion was surprisingly well handled, but it still left many feeling icky given the fact that the show was milking the Olympios/ Jackson drama over a two-night premiere. And anyway, did the chat—or the new rules implemented by Warner Bros.—actually lead to more mindful drinking or sexual activity on the show?

According to Vinny Ventiera, who was in *Paradise* both before and after the season-four shutdown, Wells Adams—who served as the bartender—kept a log to make sure no contestant had more than two drinks per hour. But because the cast knew they were restricted to two drinks per hour, "people made sure they were getting two drinks every hour consistently," Ventiera, who works as a DJ, said. In other words, the new rule might have actually resulted in the cast getting *more* drunk than before the rule was instituted.

And by the time Canadian Daniel Maguire arrived in Mexico—he missed all of the Olympios/Jackson drama—the rules were even more lax.

"There was a gray area too," Maguire told me. "Like, they weren't super strict on it when I was there. There was no log. If people really wanted to drink, they would find a drink somewhere."

The other new rule, however—the one about asking for producer permission before having sex—was followed strictly. If two contestants wanted to spend the night together, Ventiera explained, each would separately go to their respective producer to express that desire in a filmed declaration.

But even behind so-called closed doors, the contestants are well aware they're being filmed. On the third season of *Paradise*, Ventiera said he once placed a flower vase over a security night-vision camera he spotted on a table so that it wouldn't catch him getting intimate. "This year," he said, "they put that camera on the ceiling so nobody could touch it."

Why I'm a Fan

JOSHUA MALINA

I DON'T KNOW IF I CAN CLAIM TO HAVE SEEN EVERY episode, but I think I've seen almost every season. That's probably something I should be whispering to you, or not admitting in an interview altogether, but I believe I've watched almost the entire series in its entirety.

As an actor, I'm supposed to say reality TV is anathema to me because every reality show is replacing a show that I could be on. There was always this concern that reality TV was going to put actors out of work. I even remember a time when the mega-success of *Who Wants to Be a Millionaire?* seemed to be threatening the continued airing of *Sports Night*. That was the first time I thought, "Well, maybe I am feeding this thing that is out to kill me and my ilk."

As a genre, there are some super-duper low-end reality TV shows that are not the best of our culture or high art, but even those can be fun to watch at the end of the day as you plunk down onto the couch. They generally ask very little of you and there's something to be said for that kind of TV as well. I like my BBC, *Downton Abbey, The Wire*—but there are often times when I want to dial down the brain to about 3 percent and watch something else.

I spend a lot of time saying to my kids, "Don't do that or that," while we watch *The Bachelor*. It's kind of an object lesson in how not to comport yourself. "Don't go on group dates. That's not a thing. This is not normal. Don't make out with eight people in one night. You don't have to make out with somebody the first time you meet them at all.

And if you do, maybe explore your relationship with that person for the entire rest of the day. As romantic as it might sound to arrange for a private concert with your date, it's really not romantic and it's very horrible and awkward. So if you're ever tempted to pay for a tertiary-level pop star to serenade your date, don't do it." So rather than banning my children from watching it, it's like: Let's see what we can learn from this.

The show lies right on this delicate line between feeding my cynical side, which is major—being snarky and laughing at people and seeing ridiculous people do ridiculous things in order to get dates and supposedly win love. But like most cynics, my cynicism is born out of disappointment in things not being the ideal that I would prefer. The show can be savored on two levels—the laughing and pointing at people putting themselves in absurd situations on television for my entertainment, but underneath it, what I'm hoping for is to see romance and real connection.

I mean, I will watch a video of a woman who raised a lion for twenty-five years, and then five years later she comes back to see the lion and he recognizes her and runs over to her. And I love it. I'm spending most of my time on Twitter snarking on people and then I'm like: "Wait a minute. Lion reunion!" There's just something life- and soul-affirming to see true love. It may not be there in abundance, but it is there occasionally on *The Bachelor*.

And I did not go, but I got invited to Jade and Tanner's wedding. It was a very brief conversation with my wife, who looked at me like, *Honey, we watch the show, and that's where it ends.* She was looking at me like, *Am I going to lose you to Bachelor Nation?* I would have liked to tell the story.

—Joshua Malina, actor (*Scandal*, *The West Wing*)

CHAPTER 9

Falling for the Fairy Tale

J ade," the note read, "your presence is requested at a royal ball tomorrow evening from 8 pm until the last stroke of midnight. Shhhh, it's a secret—the prince doesn't know you are coming."

Jade Roper drew her hand to her mouth and gasped. The women who had gathered around her on the couch, waiting to hear who had been selected to go on a one-on-one date with the Bachelor, immediately became envious. "It's like Cinderella!" one cooed. "I'm so jelly," another lamented.

Soon, a glam squad descended upon the mansion. "We have to get you ready for your ball tonight!" a pink-haired stylist told Roper, taking her by the hand. "We are going to transform you!"

The lucky contestant was brought to a room that had been outfitted with dozens of gowns, designer heels, and diamond jewelry. "Like, everything a princess can imagine," Roper described in a subsequent ITM.

She tried on numerous dresses and a pair of Christian Louboutin shoes that were meant to resemble glass slippers. "If you like them," the stylist teased, "you can keep them." The twenty-eight-year-old former *Playboy* model was also gifted a pair of diamond earrings from Neil Lane.

After she was all dolled up, Roper walked down a red carpet and got into the old-school Rolls-Royce that would chauffeur her to the royal ball. There, Bachelor Chris Soules was waiting, nervously rehearsing the waltz in his tuxedo.

"I have never been to a royal ball before. I mean, I live in northeast Iowa, and I farm," he told the camera. "Tonight, I'm a prince, and I'm looking for my Cinderella. . . . I hope this is the beginning of my fairy tale. And I hope that at the end of all this, my fairy tale comes true."

Once Roper arrived, the two enjoyed an intimate dinner. Then Soules took her to a nearby ballroom, where a full orchestra was waiting. He escorted her up to a platform in the center of the room, and they danced in the shadow of a movie screen playing a clip from *Cinderella*, the 2015 Disney live-action remake of the classic animated film. The movie was set to hit theaters just a few weeks after the fairy tale–themed episode of *The Bachelor* aired on ABC, which is owned by The Walt Disney Company.

"This is what you deserve," Soules told his date. "The princess thing works well for you."

Back at the mansion, many of the other women were seething with envy. But no one was as upset about missing out on the date as Ashley Iaconetti. Before filming began, she'd gone to a boutique with her parents, who spent roughly $1,600 on four glitzy dresses for her to wear on the show. Determined not to let the money go to waste, she put on one of the gowns while Soules and Roper were at their ball and walked around the house, sulking.

On the episode, this behavior made Iaconetti come off as a tad unhinged. She complained about how she was a hopeless romantic, such a fan of Disney princesses that she was physically pained to have not been selected for the date. She was perplexed by why her fellow contestants weren't equally upset—especially when they were being sent on dates where they had to camp in the wilderness and ride tractors in bikinis instead.

"I was like, 'So, you're telling me that you guys don't want this princess-themed date as much as I do? Because this is the best date so far,'" she said now, a couple of years after the whole fiasco. "She had a fairy godmother and was literally wearing $5,000 shoes."

Going on *The Bachelor*, Iaconetti explained, she was expecting to go on fairy-tale dates—the kind "you only see in actual Disney movies." After all, these sorts of extravagant outings are a cornerstone of *The Bachelor*. On Jason Mesnick's season, he let one woman wear $1 million worth of borrowed diamonds and flew her in a private jet to Las Vegas. Brad Womack, meanwhile, took one of his ladies on what he described as a *Pretty Woman*–themed date, letting her select a fancy dress and earrings to wear that she also got to keep, just like Roper. The couple drove to dinner in a Bentley Mulsanne and were later serenaded by the band Train—every woman's dream, amirite? There was even another *Pretty Woman* outing on Sean Lowe's season, this one actually on Rodeo Drive, where his date got to shop at the high-end store Badgley Mischka.

And let us not forget that time the Bachelor was, in fact, an actual prince.

Well, sort of.

In 2006, Lorenzo Borghese was named the Bachelor for the show's ninth season. Borghese was born into an Italian royal family, though he's not technically a prince: His father, Francesco, is the seventeenth prince of Sant'Angelo and San Polo. And when Francesco dies, his title will most likely be inherited by Lorenzo's older brother.

But I mean, close enough, right?

It was for ABC, who decided to set Borghese's entire season in Rome and marketed it with the tagline "This Fall, Your Prince Will Come." Borghese—who owns a luxury pet-product company called Royal Pet Club—knew that the producers "wanted to go after the whole prince angle." He didn't take offense. He never thought he was that good-looking, so when he was offered the Bachelor gig, he was confused as to why a more handsome suitor wasn't selected.

"And then they started talking about doing the show in Italy and talking about the family," he remembered. "And I'm like, 'Yeah, I get it, and I'm OK with it, because you guys need something different. You guys need a storyline. You guys need ratings. If you're talking about a prince meeting his princess, I get it, and I'll help you guys.'"

He knew, however, that he'd likely be lambasted by critics who took issue with his relationship to royalty. He'd grown up in Short Hills, New Jersey, attended college in Florida, and barely knew a word of Italian. His parents tried to teach him both Italian and French when he was a boy, he said, but when he started to stutter in English, a doctor suggested the foreign languages were confusing him.

Nonetheless, the women who came to meet Borghese in an Italian villa bought into the fantasy. "I think they thought that if we were to get married, we'd probably live in a castle and everybody would bow to us and we would do nothing but travel and just be admired by everyone we ran into," he said.

The Bachelor tried to explain to the contestants that his lifestyle on the show was not reflective of his day-to-day back in the States. While the Borgheses do have their own chapel and crypt in Italy—and the family name is all over buildings in Rome—"in the US, I'm lucky to get a free beer," he said.

"I think it was so powerful because when girls are young, they want to be a princess and they want to marry this magical prince," Borghese said. "He's pure as gold and not evil and has the best morals and has a castle and a black horse and has a great life and is the nicest person in the world. And that's a fairy tale. In reality, that's not what we're like."

Growing up, Iaconetti was one of those girls who latched onto those kind of fantastical tropes. She obviously loved Disney princesses, her favorite being Jasmine from *Aladdin*. But she attributes most of her romanticism to chick flicks—films she saw during her teenage years like *The Wedding Planner* that helped shape her vision of the ideal man.

"Watching those movies, I was in awe—like, that's life right there," she recalled. "That's your goal: getting saved by a doctor when your shoe gets stuck, then going to a silent movie in the park, and he throws away all the M&M's that aren't brown. And he looks like Matthew McConaughey."

Dr. Rebecca Hains, author of *The Princess Problem: Guiding Our Girls through the Princess-Obsessed Years*, has spent her career exploring how these media narratives impact girls and women. And the marketing of romance, she said, begins in toddlerhood.

"I think the Disney Princess brand capitalizes on that romance to such an extent that I don't know if girls, at this point, are able to remember a time when they weren't aware of those narratives," she said.

It's all part of what marketers call cradle-to-grave marketing. If you get a woman to love a brand in childhood—let's say, Disney— that brand will go on to play a role during major life milestones. And then, when that woman has children, she wants her kids to enjoy Disney the way she did, experiencing a sense of nostalgia.

Take your adorable little daughter who is obsessed with dressing up as Snow White or Cinderella. She loves wearing her princess costumes so much that she refuses to take them off even during trips to the grocery store or the playground. And during these outings, she's given incessant positive feedback: "Oh, you look so beautiful!" "Are you a little princess?" "Look how beautiful you are!" Getting that kind of external feedback on her appearance reassures your daughter that she's valued by our culture, setting her up "for some pretty unhealthy ideas and behaviors" as she enters adolescence, Hains said.

So when the women on *The Bachelor* say they want to be a princess, or they want their life to play out like a fairy tale, what are they really saying?

Maria Tatar, who chairs the Folklore and Mythology program at Harvard University—and also happens to be my best friend's mom—has taught fairy tales in her courses for decades. She defines them this way: A fairy tale is about persecution. There's a villain, someone who is hunting the protagonist down and torturing her and making her miserable. Then, suddenly, there's a reversal of fortune that typically results in a rise in social station.

And looks and appearances count for a lot in fairy tales, Tatar said. Because the stories focus heavily on plot and action, there's often not much room for interiority. "So if you wanted to express goodness and virtue, you made somebody beautiful," she said. "The minute you said, 'Oh, Cinderella was so beautiful,' or 'Little Red Riding Hood was adorable,' that translates into a kind of goodness. You know she'll triumph in the end."

To recap: A woman in a fairy tale is someone who is living a terrible life. Then—largely due to her beauty—she meets someone who reverses her miserable fate. She becomes wealthy and happy and is in love.

Like Hains, Tatar agreed that after being exposed to so many fairy tales at a young age, most women probably aren't even aware of how powerfully those fantasies are preserved in the brain. "It all corresponds to a very basic, human desire to marry," she said. "To find a partner who is at least your social equal, but preferably above you, who will somehow make you bigger and better and improve your lot."

Money is key to this equation. When a woman on *The Bachelor* says she wants to be a princess, she's not just saying she wants to feel beautiful—she's saying she wants a designer gown and Christian Louboutin glass slippers and Neil Lane teardrop diamond earrings.

"Of course, nobody's really a princess unless you literally marry a prince, so it's all a really over-the-top way of playing dress-up and pretending," said Hains. "It's this really overt consumerism. A celebration of being able to afford all these things."

And what about the whole "happily ever after" thing? What does that even mean? From a literary standpoint, Tatar told me that "happily ever after" was used at the end of stories just to give readers some comfort about situations that were without resolution. But nowadays, the phrase has come to represent far more. In *Marriage, a History: How Love Conquered Marriage*—one of Stephanie Coontz's many books about modern relationships and family life—she wrote about how much expectation is laden upon the couple who wants to live "happily ever after."

First, they must love each other deeply and choose each other unswayed by outside pressure. From then on, each

191

must make the partner the top priority in life, putting that relationship above any and all competing ties. A husband and wife, we believe, owe their highest obligations and deepest loyalties to each other and the children they raise. Parents and in-laws should not be allowed to interfere in the marriage. Married couples should be best friends, sharing their most intimate feelings and secrets. They should express affection openly but can also talk candidly about problems. And of course they should be sexually faithful to each other.

Historically speaking, this type of union—one where emotion is prized over practicality—is still a relatively new concept. Those who go on *The Bachelor* might say they're "desperate" to get married, but as Coontz writes, few modern women truly understand what concessions prior generations of females made when selecting a mate.

"Historically, desperate is agreeing to marry a much older man whom you find physically repulsive," Coontz says in *Marriage, a History.* Desperate is turning a blind eye to prostitutes and mistresses, not being allowed to use birth control and subsequently bearing children, fearing punishment for not completing household tasks. "Women today may be anxious about finding a mate, but most could not even imagine being that desperate," she concludes.

Such desperation started to wane about two hundred years ago, when the concept of what Coontz calls "the love match" first emerged. The love match came about when women were no longer forced to choose a partner for political or economic reasons. As women became increasingly less dependent on men, they were able to pay more attention to their hearts when choosing a mate.

Slowly, the old definition of love started to fade—a love based on the excitement of difference. "The kind of love where the woman loves the man because he's these things that she is not—he's stronger or older or wiser," Coontz told me over the phone, just before she started on her nightly six p.m. glass of wine. When she hung up, she said, she planned to start her evening routine: cooking dinner while her husband read *The New York Times* aloud to her. Ladies: This woman has it all fucking figured out.

As Coontz was seemingly exemplifying in her own marriage, the more modern definition of love is based upon shared interest. "One of the challenges for modern women, I think, is how to make equality erotic," she said. "Because for a hundred and fifty years, we have been trained to see inequality and difference as erotic. Difference as the basis of desire."

Which explains, in part, why women might be drawn to go on *The Bachelor*, where gender roles are more clearly defined—and the man usually has the upper hand. Even on *The Bachelorette*, where a woman is handing out the roses, it's the man who ultimately gets down on his knee at the end of the series.

So why, when women have been fighting for so long for equal rights, would a woman want to put herself in an environment where the man calls the shots?

To understand this, I spoke to a handful of sociologists about how young people today generally feel about marriage. Dr. Helen Fisher, the biological anthropologist who consults for Match.com, conducts a study every year called "Singles in America" to try to get a bead on this. According to her most recent results, singles do still want to get married—but they don't want to get married *yet*. Instead, the majority feel they need to have their career and finances in shape before they tie the knot. Even still, the ultimate prize is a partnership filled with romance, attachment, and commitment—marriage is more or less optional.

It's part of a movement Fisher calls "slow love"—the idea that most singles want to take a *veeeeery looooong* time getting to know each other before walking down the aisle. So there's a one-night hook-up. Then you move into friends-with-benefits territory. Eventually you move in together, learning everything about each other. You live together for maybe five years. Then it's time to get married.

"As it becomes more possible to live a full and happy life and an economically stable life without being married, the standards for what a good marriage is are high, and people generally—I would say overwhelmingly—feel they have the right to leave a marriage or a relationship that doesn't work," agreed Kathleen Gerson, a sociology professor at NYU who studies gender, work, and family life.

But in this setting, Gerson noted, the notion of being "suffused in romantic love" is almost more powerful. If you're not searching for a partner who can bring in a good paycheck or provide for your children, you better be feeling those butterflies *hard*.

"Marriage is no longer compulsory. It is a choice," she said. "And so when people can live autonomously and don't absolutely need marriage to survive, it's a testament to how much we want intimacy and commitment that it remains as powerful and popular as it is."

OK, so now that we know this, it would appear that *The Bachelor* is out of step with what modern-day women want from marriage. As we're well aware, falling in love on the show is about as opposite of "slow love" as you can get. Not only is the courtship process sped up rapidly, but marriage is prized above all else. If you don't get a ring out of the deal, you're essentially considered a failure.

So what's going on here? Are the contestants who go on the

show—and the millions who watch them—really so wildly different from the so-called average young American? I don't think so. Because while the rules of the dating world may be shifting, the media landscape—for better or worse—still propagates the idea that your worth as a woman is cemented when a man loves you enough to marry you.

Just think about the tabloids you see in the checkout aisle at the grocery store. Every single one has to do with relationships, marriage, divorce, and babies. After each season of *The Bachelor* or *The Bachelorette*, the final couple always lands a photo shoot on the cover of *People* magazine by virtue of the fact that they are beautiful, in love, and (usually) engaged.

"It does very much reinforce the notion that if you're not married, you're a loser," said Susan Douglas, a communications professor at the University of Michigan who explores sexism and feminist narratives in the media. "There are so many media texts that traffic in the idea that 'you will find your soul mate, you will find true love, women should have a partner.'

"Then, on the other hand, there's all this single-ladies stuff and a celebration of independent women and not necessarily needing a man," she continued. "I think women are straddling a set of contradictions here that are much greater than [those that] many generations had to navigate."

Jen Schefft knows this contradictory space well. When she and Andrew Firestone called off their engagement after just a few months, she received a ton of backlash—mostly from female fans— who were horrified that she didn't try harder to make it work with the heir of the Firestone Tire and Rubber Company.

"It was like, 'Oh, he's the perfect man and you couldn't keep him,'" said Schefft, who was asked to be a guest on *Oprah* after she ended up with Firestone. "He's the heir to a fortune. He's good-looking. What's wrong with you that you couldn't keep him happy?"

The scrutiny only intensified when she went on *The Bachelorette*. Because at the end of the season, she was the one woman in the history of the show who—gulp!—rejected the marriage proposals of her two final men. At twenty-eight, *Star* magazine branded her a "spinster" for turning down both Jerry Ferris and John Paul Merritt. Elisabeth Hasselbeck, then a co-host on *The View*, said she thought Schefft would be single for the rest of her life.

"It definitely made me feel like, 'Wait a second,'" Schefft said. "All this talk about feminism and girl power and how it's OK to wait for the right guy? *Sex and the City* was still out then. It was supposed to be cool to be single. And I was hearing the complete opposite message. Always from women."

Schefft went on to channel her frustration into a book, 2007's *Better Single Than Sorry: A No-Regrets Guide to Loving Yourself & Never Settling*. In it, she talks about how difficult it was to be labeled "coldhearted, a man hater, a wretched, callous person" for her choices. "I was forced to defend myself for being single when all I was really trying to do was create a situation in which I would be happy," she wrote. "What's wrong with that? We shouldn't feel the need to apologize for depriving *other* people of the fairy tale."

But the whole endgame on *The Bachelor* is the fairy tale. And the first way to convey to viewers that a couple is headed toward happily ever after is by making sure there's a very dramatic declaration of love.

One of the most common refrains I hear from fans of the show is: "Why do they say 'I love you' so quickly?" As the seasons have progressed, it seems the race to drop the L-bomb has only intensified. You've got contestants saying they're falling in love with the

Bachelor in week three, when they've spent no more than a few days with their newfound soul mate.

A lot of that, I think, has to do with the bubble effect. But getting cast to utter those magical three words is also a huge goal for producers. Not only is it a clear indicator of who is "here for the right reasons," but the phrase is promotable. Advertisements can tout that someone said "I love you," leaving viewers to guess who or make fun of the person who said it so soon.

About midway through her journey with Juan Pablo Galavis, producers started pushing Clare Crawley to tell him she loved him. At the time, she hadn't said "I love you" to anyone in ten years.

"The producers were like, 'You have to say it, you have to say it. You might go home.' They would very much encourage it," she said. "It was like, 'Are you going to regret not saying it? This could be the last moment you have with him. Don't you want him to know how you feel? What if this determines if you go home or not?'"

Crawley said she came to a "happy medium" with the team, agreeing to tell Galavis that she was *falling* for him, but never saying "I love you."

Brooks Forester—who eventually left Desiree Siegfried's season because he *wasn't* in love with her—had a similar experience. In the days before he quit the show, he said, nearly all of his ITMs were centered around getting him to say he loved her, and producers were quick to remind him that he was the only one of the three remaining men who hadn't uttered the words.

Still, he refused to give in.

"For me, it was less about saying it on television and more about saying it to Des," he said. "If Des really felt that way about me, and I were to communicate that back to her, how shitty would it be to do that to a person if I didn't actually have those feelings and was just saying it for the show? And I played that scenario out in my head, which is one that probably happened to a lot of people. You'd just be like, 'Fuck it! Yeah, I love her!'"

Producers use a similar tactic when it comes to proposing. Almost every contestant I spoke with who made it to the finals said they felt they had no choice but to get engaged at the end—even though there have been a scant few (Galavis, Schefft, Womack, and Palmer) who dared to defy such pressure.

Even those who do get down on one knee, though, are typically racked with anxiety. The night before he proposed to Catherine Giudici, Sean Lowe started getting cold feet. Part of him felt he was absolutely in love with her—that he couldn't imagine a life without her. But he also felt like things were too good to be true. He was on a television show, after all—and how well did he really know this woman?

In the midst of a freak-out, Lowe was sent to talk to executive producer Martin Hilton. The EP assured him he didn't have to propose to anyone, saying he could always go the Womack route if he so chose. But Hilton also reminded Lowe that this was his only opportunity to give Giudici "the proposal few people on Earth get to have."

Still, the Bachelor was unsure of what to do and begged Hilton for fifteen minutes alone with Giudici. It was late, sometime around midnight, and she was in her hotel room, attempting to brush off her own nerves just hours before a potentially life-changing day. She'd just gotten out of the shower, had no makeup on, and had whitening strips on her teeth when Lowe came knocking.

"He just kind of walked in and talked at me for twenty minutes," Giudici recalled. Lowe told her that he wasn't going to "settle for anything less than a family that will center around Christ," and he wanted to make sure she was on board.

Giudici wasn't particularly religious—she'd grown up Buddhist and Catholic—but she was open to converting to Christianity. (And waiting until marriage to sleep with Lowe, even though she had already lost her virginity.)

Still, Lowe's approach bothered her.

"It frustrated me, because I felt like he'd had nine weeks to talk to me about this," she said. "You choose the eleventh hour to make me feel like this? It kind of cracked my world a little bit."

But Lowe wanted to be certain of his decision—even if that meant asking make-it-or-break-it questions. And frankly, that's more than most of the Bachelors and Bachelorettes on the show do before popping the question. Jesse Csincsak, the snowboarder who got engaged to DeAnna Pappas on *The Bachelorette* in 2008, realizes now that he did not put enough thought into proposing. One day, he just woke up and was told by producers that he was going ring shopping.

"That's when I freaked out. I started throwing up. I was puking on the sidewalk walking down to get the ring and coming back," he said. "It was like, 'Whoa. This is forever.' My parents have been married forty-three years. That was a big freaking deal to me. I didn't take it lightly."

Looking back, he knows the situation seems ridiculous—especially because he's a "bearded man who's around chainsaws all day"—but "you just don't have a choice, kind of."

"There is no 'What if I don't propose' option. It's just 'Here's the ring. Go give it to her.' That's how they make it," he explained. "When you're twenty-five and you're just a baby and you're in a foreign place and are still hungover from the day before, they're in your head. They make you do what they want you to do. They give you a hundred reasons why it's a good idea and they just make it happen."

Schefft also recalls feeling a strange sense of obligation toward the producers. As the Bachelorette, she knew she didn't want to marry either of her final two men, but she still didn't feel she could end the show without picking one of them to at least continue dating.

"The producers basically told me that I was coming across as a horrible person on television—a really cold, bitchy person," she said. "And you're all making a television show and you want people to watch it. I always felt like I wanted to give them what they wanted, without being crazy. I was still true to myself, but I didn't want to disappoint anyone. You're like, 'This is the situation I'm in, and I'll play along, I guess.'"

Ben Flajnik put it almost exactly the same way: This was a game, and he wanted to play. Or, to be more accurate, he was "willing to play" because it was a TV show, and he "liked the producers enough."

"I think maybe I just treated it more as, 'This is a story. Just a fun little chapter. Have fun with it. See where it goes,'" explained the winemaker, who proposed to Ashley Hebert on *The Bachelorette* before getting engaged to Robertson on his season of *The Bachelor*. "I understand engagements and proposals are supposed to be once-in-a-lifetime kind of things, but for me it was all really about seeing it through. I liked Ashley enough. You're not really in love with a person. But Ashley was super cool, and I was like, 'Who knows where this is gonna go?' If she says yes, I'll just do a very long engagement. Maybe I'm just too casual about everything, but it didn't seem like that big of a deal to me at the time. I know it sounds strange. But it wasn't like, 'This is gonna be forever! This is my one and only!' I think I just said, 'Screw it.'"

It's also easier to propose when you're not paying for the ring. Initially, the show's stars were offered free Harry Winston or Tacori rings. Aaron Buerge, the second Bachelor, even opted to pay for an engagement ring himself—and when he and teacher Helene Eksterowicz broke up in 2004, they put it up for sale on eBay. (They got $28,300 for the ring, which they split.)

Meredith Phillips, the second Bachelorette, got less for her diamond, which she was told was valued at $75,000 but only appraised for $5,000.

Nowadays, Bachelors and Bachelorettes have a trickier time selling their rings. That's because in the years since Neil Lane became the show's jeweler of choice in 2008, a contract stipulation has dictated that couples must stay together for two years before they legally own the ring. And if they break up before that two-year mark—which, let's be real, almost all of them do—the ring goes to "ring heaven," Lane is fond of saying.

Producers ask the women who make it to the finals of the show what type of ring they'd be interested in—solitaire, halo, cushion cut—and then Lane brings six diamonds from his Beverly Hills storefront for the men to choose from. The size and value of the rings has increased substantially since the show began. The first one the jeweler provided to Jason Mesnick in 2009 was valued at $65,000: 3.18 carats, with 170 stones surrounding the center diamond. In 2016, however, Lauren Bushnell scored the priciest ring so far from Ben Higgins: a 4.25-carat diamond encircled with 240 round and baguette-cut diamonds. The Art Deco–style ring was supposedly worth $100,000.

The show has been a fantastic marketing ploy for Lane, who has since partnered on collections with midpriced retailers Jared and Kay Jewelers. The most expensive Lane option either of the stores offers is $19,999, but the majority of the designs go for between $3,000 and $4,000. And while he's always catered to high-end clientele, since he started working with the television franchise, his diamonds have become a staple on the red carpet. Angelina Jolie had on two of his diamond brooches when she wore that dress with the thigh-high split to the 2012 Academy Awards, Lorde donned one of his elaborate necklaces at the 2015 Golden Globes to glam up her crop top, and Jennifer Lawrence put her own spin on one of his diamond-chain necklaces at the 2014 Oscars, when she wore the piece backward.

The Bachelor franchise has played a large role in the wedding industrial complex, starting with the televised nuptials between Trista and Ryan Sutter in 2003. ABC spent $4 million to put together the three-part special, much of which focused on the couple selecting the over-the-top touches that would be featured in the wedding. Celebrity wedding planner Mindy Weiss—who has created extravagant bashes for stars like Ellen DeGeneres, Channing Tatum, and Fergie—was assigned to cater to Trista's every whim. (Weiss has gone on to plan the TV weddings of other *Bachelor* couples, including J. P. and Ashley Rosenbaum and Sean and Catherine Lowe.)

No expense was spared, and the pricey details were all over the media: $150,000 on food, $15,000 for the cake, $250,000 for the wedding party's wardrobe. Trista got to walk down the aisle in Badgley Mischka, Stuart Weitzman, and Tacori—all Hollywood-favored designers. The flowers came from Mark's Garden, who provides blooms for the Governors Ball after the Oscars. Trista and Ryan even designed china at Lenox for their reception; Lenox dishware has been seen in the White House.

Stephanie Coontz, the marriage expert, says the modern-day obsession with spending so much on weddings harks back to nineteenth-century visions of marriage as being the highlight of a woman's life.

"And in addition to that, there's a little bit of magical thinking," Coontz said. "People know there's a high chance of divorce. So I think that there's also a sense in which people think, 'Well, if we can make this the most special day that shows our own special, individualized perfection for each other, then this will protect us in some way. It's a sign that we're going to make it.'"

Trista and Ryan's costly affair not only inspired millions of wide-eyed would-be brides but future *Bachelor* contestants too. According to Jesse Csincsak, Mike Fleiss offered him and DeAnna Pappas $750,000 to get married on TV after their engagement. But his fiancée was not pleased with that number, and said, "I want a million dollars, like Trista," Csincsak recalled. (Pappas—now DeAnna Pappas Stagliano—said she would talk to me but then stopped responding to my messages.)

"And at that point, that's when our relationship became a business," Csincsak said. "It was all dollar signs. I was like, 'Seven hundred and fifty thousand dollars? Is there a free option? Because I'll take that.' Mike just responded by saying, 'I'm worth twenty million. I'm offering you seven hundred and fifty thousand. You're going to take it, or I'm going to bury you.'"

Csincsak and Stagliano never made it to the altar, quickly realizing that they weren't as compatible as they'd thought during *The Bachelorette*. Which is obviously a situation that so many Bach contestants find themselves in. So what happens after the cameras stop rolling that makes everything so different? How—just months after a beautiful proposal in the Bahamas where Csincsak and Stagliano declared they were soul mates—did things go so wrong?

At first, Csincsak said, their relationship was great. They spent a few days in the Bahamas, holed up in a hotel room, reveling in their whirlwind courtship. Then they each flew back to their different home states, meeting up every few weeks for the "Happy Couples"—secret rendezvous in L.A. organized by the producers that allow for contestants to get in some face time while the show is still airing. The couples are given code names—Csincsak and Stagliano were Popeye and Olive, the Lowes were Bonnie and Clyde—and sometimes even fly into separate airports to avoid paparazzi.

It's during these Happy Couples meet-ups—and hours spent on the phone—that the couples really get to know each other. And sometimes, they don't like what they uncover.

In her 2012 book, Melissa Rycroft described how unfamiliar she was with Jason Mesnick's day-to-day life outside of *The Bachelor* when they got engaged. They'd never discussed the details of his career, or whether she'd uproot her life and move from Dallas to Seattle. So their telephone calls got awkward, fast.

"The conversations soon grew much shorter, and shallower. We didn't seem to have a whole lot to talk about," she wrote. "And I found myself planning out things to tell him, like I had done [on the show]. I had figured that once we were back in the real world, our relationship would just fall into place. But it just didn't feel as natural as I had hoped."

The couple never ended up in the same city—but even for those who do, the transition can be tough. Catherine Lowe readily agreed to move from her native Seattle to her fiancé's home in Dallas, despite the fact that she'd have to leave her job at Amazon, family, and friends behind. Sean realized what a big deal that was: "I owe her everything because she decided to make that huge sacrifice," he told me.

But Catherine battled unhappiness for months after uprooting her life. Sean went to work every day, leaving her largely alone at home in a city where she knew no one. "I just kept thinking, 'Hold out for your kids, hold out for your kids,'" she remembered. "Because I really didn't like it here, mostly because I didn't have my own life. Now that I've created it, I'm really happy that I stuck it out."

"I'm so glad that she's adjusted so well now, but of course you're going to have some tough moments when you move," said Sean. "I think that's one of the hardest aspects about *The Bachelor*; more times than not, you're going to meet someone who isn't from the same city and if the relationship has any chance of working, you're going to have to live in the same city."

Beyond the obvious struggles of fitting in in a new location, the Lowes also had to navigate the evolving dynamic of their relationship. Catherine had spent three months competing for Sean's attention, and he realized he'd now have to put some effort into making *her* feel pursued. "Like, wait a minute, I've got to make Catherine feel like she's as special as she made me feel for all these weeks," he explained. "I think it's just a matter of absolutely making sure that she knows how much I'm in love with her and what I would do for her and how she's the number one priority in my life."

It's a formula that's seemed to work for the couple, who welcomed their first son, Samuel, in 2016. They're held up as a shining example of what *The Bachelor* can create: an engagement (between a white dude and a half-Filipina, no less), televised marriage, children, and recurring appearances on the franchise (Sean co-hosted a *Bachelor in Paradise* after-show). Given how rare these things are in Bachelor Nation, there's a lot of pressure on the couple to uphold a healthy relationship against the odds. But Catherine, for one, says she relishes that burden.

"I know that sounds weird," she acknowledged. "But a commitment is so much more important than feelings, and that's what Sean and I have really made important to us. We made a commitment to each other, and just because today I don't feel like liking you, that doesn't mean I'm going to be like, 'Bye!' You're never going to find somebody that is always on your side. So the pressure from the public saying 'If you guys break up, you're just another statistic'—I think it's good."

Others, not surprisingly, feel less positive about the public scrutiny. As Ben Flajnik's season of *The Bachelor* aired, he became so bothered by the public's negative reaction to his fiancée, Courtney Robertson, that he briefly called off his engagement to her. Producers had warned him that Robertson might not come off well during the show, but "it was even worse" than Flajnik expected, he said.

"It seemed like I'd proposed to someone who lacked common sense," he said, recalling how the model was painted as the ultimate not-here-to-make-friends villain. "You've gone on this television show and have decided to be a total bitch to these girls. Why couldn't you have kept your mouth shut and flown under the radar? It would have been fine.

"But I was going places and people would be screaming, 'Courtney's a bitch!' I was still engaged to this person, but I couldn't say anything to the person yelling at me. So I'm going, 'Why am I doing this? Why am I defending this woman who is capable of doing some of those things?'"

About a month after the show began airing, Flajnik said, they decided to break up. Of course, fans were unaware of the couple's private dealings. So when paparazzi caught Flajnik cozying up to other women—and the photographs were subsequently published in the tabloids—he felt even worse.

"That shit is really invasive, and gives me anxiety just thinking about it," he said, shuddering. "Having to hit the gas on my car and lose [paparazzi] cars and shit. That was not cool. I'd go to New York for some press tour and there would be cars at the bottom of the hotel and it was like, 'Where can I go? I can't go anywhere.'"

Also working against a burgeoning relationship? The fact that seemingly every single in America now views the Bachelor or Bachelorette as an ideal specimen. After his turn as the star of the show, Italian Bachelor Borghese said gorgeous girls would flock to him anytime he turned up at a bar. Suddenly, overnight, his pool of potential mates had grown exponentially.

"You're like, 'Wow. This is crazy.' It's almost becoming a rock star for a year or two, and you start thinking, 'Do I really want to settle down with this person that I just met, or do I want to keep my options open?'" said Borghese, who—shocker!—broke up with his pick, Jennifer Wilson, only two months after the show started airing.

While added temptation is certainly not helping anybody, there are bigger structural issues at play in the demise of most *Bachelor* relationships. Let's return to our trusty marriage experts for a minute. According to Stephanie Coontz, it's nearly impossible to form a lasting relationship in the time period allotted for filming.

Back in the '50s and '60s, she explained, her research showed that considering your spouse a close friend wasn't of utmost importance to most people.

"The woman would say things like, 'Well, he never really understood my feelings, but he was such a good provider and such a good dad.' Or the guy would say, 'Well, she didn't understand my work, but she was such a good mom and she was so loving,'" Coontz said.

But that's no longer enough for singles looking for partners in the modern world. Coontz has found that most successful relationships these days are not only based on friendship but an understanding between the man and the woman that each will have their desires met equally.

"So you need to negotiate, and some things can't be negotiated," she said. "You have to know each other well enough to know that you're actually going to be marching in the same direction."

And getting to know each other? That takes time, and deeper conversation than "How amazing was our date today?" After you get past the overwhelming "I'm so attracted to you" vibe, you need to know whether or not you share the same values.

"And you don't give each other a quiz to say 'What are your values?'" said Coontz. "You watch TV together instead of being on exciting dates and see if you have the same reaction to the same shows. Those sort of mundane things are very important predictors that get left out of it. You can't figure those things out in ten days—or ten weeks—because they're kind of inappropriate questions. You've got to feel them out and do enough things together so that you've gotten past the, 'Oh, I'm so attracted to you! What a gorgeous date we just had.'"

This explains why Catherine was so pissed when Sean pulled out the Big Serious Religion Question at the very last minute: because it didn't feel appropriate for the setting. But he did ask the question, which is more than most Bachelors do. And maybe that's why he and Catherine are still together.

Why I'm a Fan

DONNIE WAHLBERG

THERE WAS A VIDEO THAT JENNY [McCARTHY, MY wife] posted of me crying while watching *The Bachelor* a couple of seasons back that got a lot of attention. But there's probably 150 videos she has of me watching the show that she's never posted of me crying and commentating at the screen and stuff like that.

Look, I cry at weddings. Then I noticed that I cry at Broadway shows—no matter what the show is, I cry. I thought it was only certain shows—like, obviously *Hamilton* and *Wicked* during the curtain call. But I cried at freakin' *Spider-Man,* so that's a problem. His freakin' web didn't lower him down for the curtain call; he was stuck in the rafters—and I still cried. So when I started watching *Bachelor,* I never expected to cry—I was just enjoying it and getting a laugh out of it. But I started crying. Sometimes I cry at the proposal. I've cried at proposals that I wasn't really happy about—the person I thought shouldn't be the choice. I've also cried at certain people getting dumped. Certain people I feel are sincere in their emotions. It'll affect me, for sure.

I get a lot of head-scratching from my fans when I talk about *Bachelor.* Maybe 80 percent of my fans are female on social media, and even a lot of them are like, "Yeah, not watching. We're watching something else." But I don't care. For the people who are into the show, we really don't care if you judge us for watching *The Bachelor.* I don't even call it a guilty pleasure, I just call it a pleasure.

TV shows—especially something in the vein of *The Bachelor*—are not harmful to anyone. If you can have your psyche damaged by *The Bachelor,* then it's already damaged. I absolutely think reality TV gets a bad rap. If you're talking shit about reality shows, you obviously have some sort of anger issue and need to focus on other things.

Look, there's so much stuff out there that's really intense. There's twenty-four news networks that have all this drama and negative stuff going on. And here you have a TV show that is just fun and silly and shows the best and worst of dating. We're not watching to see whether a nuclear bomb is gonna go off. We're just watching to see if Guy A is gonna make a fool out of himself with Girl A. It's real simple.

I talk about *The Bachelor* a lot. On Mondays, when we're shooting, I'm rushing the director to finish the scenes on *Blue Bloods* so that everyone in the crew who watches *Bachelor* can get home and make it in time to watch it. Around five o'clock, I'm gonna start rushing the director and suggesting other ways to shoot the scenes so we can be done by seven so everyone can make it home at eight to watch. I'm very honest about it. I will literally walk on-set after lunch and say, "OK, it's Monday. *Bachelor in Paradise* tonight. Let's get the hell out of here so everyone can watch it."

—Donnie Wahlberg, musician/actor (New Kids on the Block, *Blue Bloods, Donnie Loves Jenny*)

CHAPTER 10

Basking in the Afterglow

S ean Lowe couldn't wait to Google himself. He'd never experienced fame in his life, and now that he was one of the finalists on *The Bachelorette*, he knew that people would be gossiping about him online.

So while he was still in the midst of competing for Emily Maynard in the Czech Republic, he snuck down to a hotel computer and searched "Sean Lowe Bachelorette." Nothing too revealing popped up, but some sites had posted a few biographical details about him. He had an online footprint, and it was a thrill.

He became even more excited when, after he was sent home, fans began to approach him on the street in his native Texas.

"When people come up to you, especially on this show, they feel like they know you," he said. "So when people would start coming up to me and saying, 'Hey, we're rooting for you, we love you on the show'—it was an exciting feeling. My life flipped upside down in a matter of days."

Since 2003, when Andrew Firestone and Jen Schefft became the first Bachelor couple to appear on the cover of *Us Weekly*, being a part of the franchise has translated into at least a momentary brush with fame. Nowadays, of course, not only do those in Bachelor Nation appear on the cover of tabloids, but they're also constantly interviewed on entertainment programs and are accessible via Twitter and Instagram. It's a lot of attention—and a lot of talking about a relationship that's still being formed.

"In a lot of ways, it's so cool and fun to experience. Of course, going on a photo shoot for a magazine is great," said Schefft, who jumped on Firestone's back like a koala in their first *Us Weekly* cover, whose headline read "Why We Fell in Love." "But people start to treat you like you're an object. I wasn't comfortable having my life exposed that much. I just wanted to go back and be a normal couple, but we could never really be a normal couple."

Firestone, meanwhile, had grown up in the limelight due to his family name. He wasn't as weirded-out by the recognition as Schefft was, because he was "used to people knowing who he was his whole life," she said. Schefft, however, had moved from Chicago to San Francisco, where Firestone had his winery, and had trouble finding her footing after the show. In interviews, she felt like he would always have the perfect sound bite, even if that "wasn't necessarily what was going on between us." She began saying things about her fiancé in interviews that she had yet to even vocalize to him.

"When you're being interviewed, of course you're going to say nice things about the other person," she explained. "We could have had a huge fight that morning, but I'm not going to go and be like, 'Well, he's really pissing me off right now.' So you say, 'He's amazing. We have this amazing relationship.' Meanwhile, we're still trying to get to know each other and talking like we're so in love and know exactly where our relationship is headed when, really, we have no idea."

As a result of all the access, the public starts to feel like they know you—and that attention quickly starts to go to your head. After all, you can sustain the fame from one season of television for only so long. And that kind of attention? You start to get addicted to it. Just ask Chris Bukowski.

When he opened his first sports bar in Arlington, Virginia—the Bracket Room—Bukowski had already been on two seasons of the show. His business partners kept encouraging him to return to television because the more relevant he was, the better the bar did.

"People would be like, 'All right, let's go see Chris at the Bracket Room because we just saw him on TV,'" he said. "We'd host watch parties and marketed it as a female-friendly sports bar. We got national press—*Good Morning America* and Rush Limbaugh talking about my bar. It was crazy."

As a result, every night at the bar, fans wanted to drink with him. He was having fun, and when people were buying him drinks, the bar was making money. He'd gone to school for hospitality and always dreamed of opening a sports bar. Now, he lived above his own. He was at the peak of his popularity. "What I experienced that year was a lot of guys' dream life," he said.

So what exactly did he experience? Girls pursuing him so aggressively, he said, that he even had to get a restraining order against one. Later, when he moved to a condo in Chicago, girls would "blow by security" and sit by his door, just waiting for him to come home.

"Girls would be fighting over me," he said. "It was sweet."

For a while, anyway. Because eventually, Bukowski started to realize that these women really only wanted to hook up with him because he was on TV. Even when he met women in more sober scenarios, he had trouble figuring out if they were interested in him because they were genuinely attracted to him or because he had 90,000 Twitter followers. And when he met the rare girl who wasn't aware he'd been on television, she'd go home and gush to her girlfriends about the date, and one of her pals would say, "Oh, wait, that guy? Wasn't he on *The Bachelorette*?" Once his name was typed into Google, nothing good ever came from it.

So, yes—the show affecting your dating life? Definitely a bummer. But other veterans have experienced far more serious ramifications post-television. Remember Rozlyn Papa, who was kicked off *The Bachelor* after allegedly engaging in an inappropriate relationship with a producer? As you can imagine, that didn't go over well back in Richmond, Virginia, where she was a single mom raising her son.

Papa said that after *The Bachelor* wrapped, she found out that one of the teachers at her son's school had posted nasty comments about her on an online forum.

"She called me a slut. She said that I wasn't a good mom. Really hurtful and untrue things," she recalled. "I went to all of my son's events and was very involved, so reading that was the most hurtful of all."

The teacher, Papa said, used her school email address, making herself clearly identifiable. So Papa went to the principal and the head of the school district, and the teacher was reprimanded and sent on a mandatory hiatus.

The drama didn't stop there. A few months later, Papa got a call from *Entertainment Tonight*, saying one of her former roommates had emailed the television show offering to "talk about personal things from college" in exchange for payment. She wasn't even sure what the roommate was threatening to spill—she'd long had a tumultuous relationship with her parents, and she suffered from depression her whole life—"but just the fact that someone I lived with and thought I'd been friends with felt it was their place to talk about something so personal? It was really unthinkable to me."

Meanwhile, even in Virginia, strangers were taking her photo everywhere she went—Target, the movie theater. She felt like she had no privacy, like everyone was talking shit about her. She started leaving the house less and less, because it was the only place she felt safe.

Finally, about two years after *The Bachelor*, she decided to make a major move: She packed her bags and went to Scotland. She wanted to be somewhere where no one had seen the show. If she just stayed there for a year, she surmised, by the time she returned there would be plenty of new franchise villains.

Now she's back in Richmond, where she does marketing for a real estate company. On her Twitter profile, she once described herself this way: "Survived The Bachelor. Climbed Kilimanjaro. Fought off a rabid raccoon. TWICE. Bring it, world."

"It's a joke, of course, but it's also not," she said of the description. "Some people don't ever get out of that mentality, like 'Oh, I was on *The Bachelor*.' I still get messages on Twitter all the time asking me about it, and I try to embrace it. It's not who I am, but it's something that I've been through."

Fortunately, Papa said, her son never had to deal with as much blowback as she did after her season aired. But Bukowski's family was deeply affected by his television appearances. He said his father became obsessed with reading mean comments about him on the Internet, and he was so bothered by his son's new reputation that they stopped talking for a while.

"I kept telling him, 'Dad, don't read that stuff. If there's a person that saves someone's life, commenters will still talk crap about that guy on the Internet,'" Bukowski said. "But he started to believe what they were saying. And convincing him otherwise was hard to do, because I can't change anything that's already been filmed and aired. That's a big reason why I kept going back on these shows: to try to fix my image and patch everything up."

Clearly, that never worked out the way Bukowski planned—because you can never control how you're going to be portrayed on the Bach. That's why he went on to make a public proclamation in 2015, announcing his retirement from the franchise. He knew if he revealed the plan to the world, he had to hold to it.

Bukowski's story isn't rare. I talked to plenty of show vets who said their time on the franchise caused friction with their family. Craig Robinson, who appeared on Ali Fedotowsky's season of *The Bachelorette*, stopped talking to his parents for four months after the show ended because they didn't approve of his new girlfriend: a single mom who was also a *Playboy* Playmate. He met her because, as a result of the show, he was asked to judge a Playboy Bunny search for *Playboy*'s fiftieth anniversary. His love interest was one of the other judges.

"It was something that never would have happened to me before the show—dating a Playmate. I'd never even had the opportunity to meet someone like that," Robinson said. "I hadn't had any problems with dating, but I'd say before I was looking for a more 'normal' girl with a real career. That changed, because I think at that time I became more interested in how a girl looked instead of how she lived her life."

Once he went official with the relationship on Facebook, his mom called him. She'd Googled his new partner and found her naked all over the Internet. Robinson scoffed, saying it wasn't a big deal.

"She was like, 'Is this really who you want to date?'" he said. "And we got to the point where she said, 'I just don't even think I can talk to you. You're just not yourself.'"

In addition to his new girlfriend, Robinson's lifestyle had changed substantially. He was going to different parties every weekend, doing appearances at clubs for extra cash. He loved the feeling of walking into a club and having everyone ask him for pictures. "There's people who say, 'Oh, I would never do that,' but [when] you're offered that opportunity, it's hard to turn down," he said.

But he was still working full-time as a lawyer, and balancing all his side gigs became increasingly more difficult. His law firm had been reluctant to let him go on *The Bachelorette* in the first place, fearing that he'd never return to his job after the show. And in a way, they were right. Because Robinson's mind-set shifted after being on television. He questioned whether he even wanted to be a lawyer anymore.

"I think everyone on the show kind of goes through that a little bit, because you feel like you've been given this opportunity, and all of a sudden you think you are somebody. To some degree, you're famous now."

Ultimately, his attitude change became such a problem that he was let go from his firm. His boss thought he'd lost his focus at work, which even Robinson admits now was probably accurate.

"I mean, I would have an event in Detroit on a Monday night, then I'd have to be in court on Tuesday morning," he said. "So I'd go out on Monday, hop on a plane and be hungover as shit in court Tuesday morning. It was not a way to have a career, because it was just too much to balance."

In the years since, Robinson has recommitted himself to the legal profession and said he's realized it's really where his passion lies. He's currently working at a firm in Philadelphia.

Robinson's experience speaks to why so many applicants are nervous about going on the show: the likelihood that something they do on television will affect their reputation in their chosen field. So many former participants I emailed said they didn't want to talk to me because they wanted to distance themselves from the franchise in an effort to maintain their careers.

"I'll be honest, I've tried (and sort of accomplished) staying away from all things *Bachelor*-related since my last run," two-time Bachelor Brad Womack very politely responded to me when I reached out to him about an interview. "It's not that I have a bad taste in my mouth about the experience; in fact, in many ways I thoroughly enjoyed it. I just simply want to focus on my career and am desperately wanting anonymity."

Ben Flajnik, who was a winemaker when he became the Bachelor, has also tried to distance himself from the franchise. These days, he's holding down a corporate job at Yelp and has launched his own distilled spirit, Fernet Francisco.

"As many people as there are that love the show, my spirit is a niche bar product, and industry folk that work in bars and restaurants are not watching the show," Flajnik said. "If they get some association that this is the former Bachelor's fernet, most of them will say, 'Fuck that guy. He's probably a douche because he did that thing.'"

But there are plenty of *Bachelor* stars who decide to never return to their old jobs after the show. Andi Dorfman, who was billed as a prominent defense attorney when she was cast as *The Bachelorette*, decided to leave her position after her season ended. She moved from Georgia to New York, where she wrote her first book, *It's Not Okay: Turning Heartbreak into Happily Never After*, in 2016.

In the book, Dorfman acknowledges that a "major reason" she was even selected to be on the show was because of her job, which producers told her provided "great packaging material."

"While some women set themselves apart with tragic stories, dramatic pasts or single mother status, I had my job," she wrote. "Other than that, I was pretty much just your run-of-the-mill single woman."

Because her career was such a big plot point on the show, Dorfman said that fans frequently come up to her on the street and ask why she went on reality television when she had a respectable job— and why she abandoned it when the TV stint ended.

"I find myself feeling incredibly defensive and insecure when these questions get flung my way," she admitted in the book. "What I really want to say in response is: 'Fuck off! Are you still working your first job? Oh, you're not? How dare you make a career change?'"

She goes on to vent about the fact that, in her opinion, no one is above reality television—and that her "status as an attorney" didn't make her "superior." She went on the show, she explained, because she was tired of being so "responsible." She wanted to be "reckless" for once in her life. And she hasn't returned to law because, even though she enjoyed the work, she didn't enjoy the pay—$57,000 for 60 hours of work a week. Apparently, she's making more than that now, though it's not entirely clear how; her second book was just released, however.

Books, television shows, advertising partnerships—these are all the new opportunities that can arise after you are a participant on *The Bachelor*. But choosing which gigs to take can be treacherous. Let's take an obvious example: *Dancing with the Stars*. The ABC show has become home to so many Bach castoffs, including Melissa Rycroft, Trista Sutter, Jake Pavelka, Sean Lowe, and Nick Viall. It's an easy way to make some money immediately following a run on *The Bachelor*—and it keeps the fame train moving for at least a few more months.

But partaking in *DWTS* isn't always the best move for couples in burgeoning relationships. For one thing, it furthers the uneven power dynamic between the star of the show and the person they picked. And it also occupies a lot of time, keeping the newly engaged pair apart during the time when they're supposed to be embarking on a new stage in their relationship.

When Sean did *DWTS*, Catherine Lowe was miserable. She spent most of her time holed up in her temporary apartment, surrounded by all the bags she'd packed to move from Seattle to Dallas. Because Sean didn't want to have sex before marriage, they had to sleep in different units.

"I was alone for ten hours a day," she said. "I pretty much hung out with his dance partner's roommate every day. We didn't really do anything. We kind of toured the city, which was a lot of fun, and went shopping a lot. And when you sit in the audience on *Dancing with the Stars*, you're supposed to look pretty. So I didn't really have anything else to do but look pretty. I didn't really have any sense of—not worth—but I didn't have anything to do, because I'd quit my job."

She kept thinking: "When do I get my time with Sean? When do we get to start our relationship? I've already passed one test, and now I have to take another one."

"I felt kind of gypped, I guess," she said.

Still, she stuck it out, and eventually the couple moved to Dallas. But the reality television opportunities kept chasing them there. First came ABC's *Celebrity Wife Swap*, which also didn't go well. The show finds two families with different lifestyles and asks them to swap wives for a week. The Lowes were partnered with another couple from Bachelor Nation—Jason and Molly Mesnick.

When Molly turned up in Dallas, she seemed bothered by some of the chores Sean had asked her to complete: a to-do list that required her to iron his socks and cook him a bland, low-calorie meal each night. Fans were so disturbed by the way Sean appeared to treat Catherine that he eventually decided to respond on social media, saying he knew he looked like a "jackass" but that editing was to blame for the negative portrayal.

"I guess that's the risk you take when you agree to take part in something like that," he wrote on Instagram.

Despite the negative experience, the Lowes agreed to participate in another reality show the following year: WE tv's *Marriage Boot Camp: Reality Stars.* The idea behind this show is to put a bunch of reality stars with marital woes into a house where they undergo intensive therapy to strengthen their relationships.

"Oh, *Marriage Boot Camp* was my fault," said Catherine, laughing. "Sean usually says no. He's a money guy, so he sees opportunities for what they are. It's like, this is a week of our time and we'll get paid this much money. But he didn't want to do the show, and I kept saying, 'A Christian couple is leading it, and it's about love and working with your relationship. And we should be in counseling anyway! Let's just do it!' And stupid Catherine—the one time I feel OK about it, it goes horribly wrong."

So what happened? Catherine said her fellow castmates—couples from shows like *Here Comes Honey Boo Boo*; *Love & Hip Hop: Atlanta*; and *Basketball Wives LA*—made the show "really raunchy." And their fighting only escalated while they did the show. At one point, Sean lobbed this zinger at Catherine: "My wife is gone. This soulless person who doesn't give a shit about anything is here."

Ouch. Not surprisingly, the couple has largely stayed off TV since—though Sean did co-host the *Bachelor in Paradise* after-show on ABC in 2016. Catherine has since launched her own high-end stationery business, LoweCo., and the couple makes additional money by posting advertisements on their Instagram accounts.

"As much as I don't want to do the ads, it's like, 'Well, I have a beautiful home and a child that I have to pay for, and I don't have to go to an office every day,'" Catherine said. "If that security goes away, then I have to get a nine-to-five, which I would be happy to do. But it's kind of that inner monologue of: 'Shoot, do I do it and look stupid, get paid a lot of money, and hope people forget about it the next day? Or do I keep my pride?'"

Pride? I think that went out the window the second you went on *Marriage Boot Camp*, babe.

Why I'm a Fan

JASON RITTER

I'M NOT THAT BOTHERED THAT I'M A GUY THAT watches *The Bachelor*, but it would be amazing if dudes talked about it the way they talk about a crazy football game: "Oh, wow, did you see that play?" And I'm like, "Oh yeah, man, wow," and I name one of the three stats that I looked up to get through a conversation like this. I think *The Bachelor* does accomplish the same exact thing that any sport does, where you have the playoffs and the semifinals and the finals. The way that it's set up is very much like any kind of sports game.

There should be signs so you can suss out other *Bachelor* fans. I feel like I should wear a rose on my lapel or something. It's not the same thing as coming into work and asking, "Everyone watch *Game of Thrones* last night?" Because I don't watch *Game of Thrones,* so it's doubly embarrassing. "I didn't see that, but Alex was being a little aggressive on *The Bachelorette!*"

I go back and forth on how I feel about the show. Sometimes, I feel like: "This show is a very hopeful show about the power of love." And other times, it feels like a scientific study: "Look! We put two twenty-year-olds in a magical place and give them alcohol and they think they're in love! It's so not true! Love is not real and it's chemicals."

I feel like it becomes a reflection on your own issues surrounding romance. [My fiancée] Melanie [Lynskey] and I have gotten into little fights about the show. I'll be using Nick Viall as a punching bag but actually be talking about myself and how I feel. I'm like, "He's just trying to be honest! It's complicated!"

I feel like the most confident, cocky people get rewarded on the show, even if they're lying. Those dudes who are super smooth and say all the right things. The people who are like, "I'm a little bit more complicated and am not 100 percent sure, but I'm at least being honest with my feelings"—they don't get rewarded. I get all worked up about this, because I identify with those people more. I would much rather be honest about what I really feel than be like, "I'm all in and I can't wait to start our lives."

As a person who has come to feel like the ugly truth is better than the pretty lie, I can never stop thinking: "Are you guys still going to be in love when you're going on dates that don't have helicopters and boats and fireworks going off and when you're the only person in the castle?" That's a lot of money to rent out an entire castle or wine cellar.

But I do enjoy watching that, because it's a nice reminder of how big and crazy the world is. Every once in a while, I'm like, "That's a good idea!" Some things you can't do, like ride a horse down Rodeo Drive. But this is also what we've been trained to think of as romantic and incredible. It's that weird thing where you think: "This is reinforcing gender roles. . . . But, aw, what if someone said that to me?"

—Jason Ritter, actor (*Kevin [Probably] Saves the World, Parenthood*)

CHAPTER 11

Riding the Coattails

FabFitFun. SugarBearHair. DIFF Eyewear. MVMT watches. If these brands sound familiar, it's probably because you've scrolled past advertisements for them roughly a gazillion times on your Instagram feed. They're just some of the companies who have sought out high-profile *Bachelor* contestants to shill their products on social media, where #SponCon—sponsored content—has become unavoidable.

Yes, SponCon has become so prevalent that it's seriously possible for Bach alumni to make a living off Instagram these days. Contestants going on the show can almost guarantee their social media followings will increase dramatically as a result of their newfound fame. And those numbers translate into big bucks.

During Rachel Lindsay's season of *The Bachelorette*, one of the members of my Bach Discush crew made a point of noting how many followers the male suitors gained while the show was airing. Dean Unglert, for example, started off with 24,000 followers and ended up with roughly 500,000 by the finale.

How much can you actually make off Instagram? For the answer to this all-important quandary, I turned to Ashley Iaconetti, who appeared on Chris Soules's season of *The Bachelor* and then went on *Bachelor in Paradise* twice. As a result, she has accumulated more than 600,000 Instagram followers—and she hasn't had to get a day job since.

The first company to approach Iaconetti about posting an advertisement on her Instagram account was FabFitFun, a seasonal gift box that arrives in your mailbox with beauty and lifestyle products four times a year. At first, they weren't offering her much: $250 to post a picture. But as her following continued to grow, more companies reached out to her, and she got an agent to help her sift through the offers—DJ turned talent manager Paul Desisto, who has somewhat of a monopoly on representing those from Bachelor Nation.

Nowadays, Iaconetti would never post an ad for $250. She's figured out, roughly, how many followers translate into how many dollars. 250,000 followers = $1,000/ad. 500,000 = $2,000/ad. And if you have 1 million followers? You're probably getting at least $10,000 per ad.

Each company gives her different instructions on how to post its ads on Instagram. Some want specific captions and hashtags, while others are open to the creative ways in which she decides to feature their products. She doesn't get too much backlash from her followers over the posts anymore, though fans were unhappy when she partnered with a med spa in LA called DoctorFatOff.

"People gave me a lot of shit for not promoting a healthy body image," she said. "I'm like, That's kind of silly. Everything is to help us feel better about ourselves. I feel like that's the same as saying, 'Don't buy mascara.' It's all the same."

At this point, Iaconetti said she feels comfortable posting about two ads per week. "And I know people are going to read this and say, 'Oh, this is so ridiculous that these people are making money and don't have to work,' but that's not how I look at it," she said. "Yes, I get money from ads, but I'm also working every day on jobs that don't pay anything."

The kind of jobs she's talking about are usually media appearances—she'll turn up on *Access Hollywood* to recap *Bachelor* episodes, or write about the show for Cosmopolitan.com. Even if the gigs don't pay, she feels like they're helping her forge a broadcasting career, which is what she was hoping for when she got her master's degree in broadcasting from Syracuse University. Slowly, she's gaining traction—she recently covered the *Fifty Shades Darker* premiere and the *Snatched* film junket for *Access Hollywood*. She also hosts two podcasts, including one with former Bachelor Ben Higgins for iHeartRadio, and she is paid for those because they feature advertisements.

Another source of income comes from club appearances, which Desisto also helps her book. These tend to be less lucrative than Iaconetti's Instagram gigs. For instance, she recently flew to Mohegan Sun, a casino in Connecticut, to party with fans. She was paid $3,000 for the appearance, about $500 of which went toward her flight. Part of the reason she takes those jobs, though, is to hang out with her friends from Bachelor Nation, at least a few of whom typically share the billing with her at nightclubs.

"And guys from *The Bachelor* get more money through appearances, because guys are what girls want if they're going out for a night," she said. "Girls get more through ads, because obviously females are our demographic, and females follow us on Instagram and are more apt to buy what we're selling."

Meanwhile, Iaconetti has become adept at figuring out how to get free trips. She'll often reach out to different hotels to see if they'd be interested in hosting her and her friends in exchange for social media posts. Last year, the Atlantis resort in the Bahamas agreed to put her and four others from Bachelor Nation up after she sent their marketing team an email.

"They responded so quickly and were like, 'Yes, of course! What time? When do you want to be here?'" she said, noting she still had to pay for her flight and a certain amount of food. The group agreed to post one Instagram, tweet, and Snapchat per day, tag the resort, and the deal was done.

Iaconetti will also attend charity events thrown by Bach alumni, but she's not paid to go to those. Even though her hotel and travel are provided, the incentive there is almost entirely to chill with others from the franchise.

"And I really enjoy talking to the fans at those events," she said. "The word 'relatable' comes up with me all the time. People share stories of heartbreak or tell me how they found The One to give me hope that I might find The One too. I think it's awesome that people feel like they can talk to me so openly because I've been so open and expressive on the show."

I wanted to see Iaconetti and the rest of the crew in action, so I started keeping my eyes peeled for various Bach-related events. Fortunately, there's usually at least one happening per month. I decided to kick things off with a bang, so for my first event, I flew to Kansas City, Missouri, for a charity event being thrown by Jade Tolbert. Jade is married to Tanner Tolbert, and the two met on the second season of *Bachelor in Paradise*. They're another one of the rare couples in Bachelor Nation held up as an example of what the franchise can create—they got married on TV and welcomed their first child in 2017.

Jade seemed stoked that I wanted to attend: "I am actually really excited my event will be getting covered by you for your book!" she emailed. "I've been scraping this together on my own, so hopefully it will turn out all right!"

What she'd been planning was an event with about a dozen former Bach contestants, all of whom had agreed to come to Missouri for an evening to benefit Project Future Light, which is rebuilding an orphanage in Thailand. General admission tickets went for $48, but those who shelled out an extra $20 got to pose with the entire group for a photo.

But it seemed that even those who didn't spring for the VIP tickets ended up with pictures, because the Bach alumni all spent nearly the entire night posing for selfies. By the time I arrived at the One Light Luxury Apartments—a high-rise in downtown Kansas City's Power & Light District—little lines of camera-toting fans were forming in front of each contestant. Because the event was being held in the building's rooftop pool and bar space, most of the reality stars were holding court in their own cabanas.

The crowd, primarily comprised of young women, had arrived as instructed: in attire one might wear to a cocktail party at the Bachelor mansion.

I sat down in some very modern chairs with some ladies who were waiting for the official group photos to begin. Two twenty-one-year-olds, Victoria Jaskiewicz and Bella Villaca, told me they'd driven about an hour from nearby Kansas in the hopes of getting to know some of the contestants better.

"Hopefully, I could be best friends with some of them," said Jaskiewicz, who was wearing a form-fitting minidress and some booties. "I definitely could vibe with some of them."

"Going shopping with some of the girls would be nice," chimed in Sheena Keuhn, a thirty-one-year-old sitting nearby who had trekked nearly three hours from Milan, Missouri, for the event. She was wearing a black dress with cutouts that she had purchased specifically for the night from Simply Dresses—a company she found after twins and former contestants Emily and Haley Ferguson promoted it on their Instagram accounts.

"Amanda's here!" Jaskiewicz said, pointing toward Amanda Stanton, who had just arrived with her then fiancé, Josh Murray. "Everyone's, like, swarming! She's the sweetest person *ever*. Who doesn't love Amanda?"

I asked the ladies if they felt like the contestants were as famous as popular celebrities like Kim Kardashian, Leonardo DiCaprio, or Lady Gaga.

"I feel like they're just as famous to me," said Jaskiewicz. "They're idolized by a lot of people—millions of people around the world. So that makes you famous."

"Do you feel like they feel awkward too?" Villaca said, observing fans bombarding Stanton and Murray. "I don't want to be like, 'Hey, I'm a huge fan of yours! I watch every movie that you've done.'"

Before anyone could answer, Jade's voice came over the speaker system: "If I could get everyone's attention, I need everyone to be really quiet," she instructed. "I know all of you are VIP and the reason you're VIP is because you want a picture with the whole group at the step-and-repeat. So I need all of you just to make a line and we're just gonna go quick, quick, quick! And it's all gonna be available for you online."

Nearly the entire room made a beeline for the photo area—a kitchen surrounded by walls of wine racks. Before each attendee got their turn, they were handed a red rose to show off in their picture.

Four girlfriends who'd met as roommates at Southern Illinois

University Edwardsville—roughly a four-hour drive from Kansas City—queued up immediately.

"We saw the Instagram post about this on Jade's account and then we were like, 'Guys, we *have* to go,'" explained Abby Bridges, twenty-one.

"I got out of class at eleven fifty this morning and then we came right from there," added Ashley Mason, also twenty-one. "I just want to have, like, short conversations with them all and take some pictures. Just to see how they're doing in real life, now that they're not on the shows."

"Yeah, just seeing them in real life—when I first saw them walking in, I was like, 'This is crazy,'" Bridges said.

By the following morning, when I looked the roomies up on Facebook, Mason had already made a photo of herself with Ashley Iaconetti her profile picture.

"You got to meet Ashley I!!!!! So cool!" one of her friends commented below the shot.

"How was she in person?" asked another.

"She was really cool!" Mason responded. "I'm glad we went :)"

Plenty of fans got pictures like this, but the biggest bragging rights of the night went to those who ponied up during the auction. That's right: Jade had organized for the single Bach contestants to go on thirty-minute "mini dates" in the cabanas with whoever paid the most for the honor.

James Taylor—the singer-songwriter from JoJo Fletcher's season who was, unfortunately, far less musically talented than James Taylor of "Sweet Baby James" fame—brought out his guitar case in an effort to secure the highest bidder.

"I can't wait to sing for one of you," he promised. "I've got something pretty cool prepared."

As it turned out, his mini date went for the most by far—a whopping $2,500. Iaconetti, who was serving as the emcee, had a more difficult time drumming up support for Wells Adams and JJ Lane.

"You never know how far you're gonna get with JJ. He is looking for a girlfriend tonight!" she teased. "You guys, JJ is gonna treat you like a princess, and he's gonna let you vent to him no matter what state you're in. . . . He is a mush ball. He is always there for you. And he gives the best massages eeeever! You guys, it's for orphans. *Orphans!*"

Lane eventually secured $700; Adams went for $650.

Around eleven p.m., when the fans had dispersed, Jade told the Bach alums that she'd planned for them to get a table at a nearby nightclub and invited me to tag along. At age thirty, I had been to maybe one nightclub in my entire life, but obviously I felt I had to attend for the experience. So we all piled into the elevator and walked over to Mosaic, a so-called ultra lounge that describes itself on its website as "downtown Kansas City's premier destination for cocktails after work" with "soft seating, Champagne by the glass, and an outdoor balcony."

We bypassed the line and were led to a small booth covered with bottles of Belvedere Vodka. Nelly's "Ride Wit Me" blasted overhead. The group smushed into the booth except for Taylor, who had brought along a gaggle of women all eager to buy him drinks. It was too loud to hear anyone, and Stanton, looking tired, rested her head on Murray's shoulder. I knew I should stick it out for the cause—the cause being you, dear readers—but after thirty minutes, I ducked out and went to get a slice of pizza. I'm just not meant for that club life, y'all.

I proceeded to take a few months off from the event circuit, but I dove back in last January, when Iaconetti told me about a charity event she herself was putting together in L.A. with Sarah Herron. This one was to benefit ovarian cancer research and SheLift, Herron's organization that seeks to empower girls through outdoor activities—and the tickets were far pricier. I paid $126 just to get in, and if you wanted a reserved table with a *Bachelor* shirt, roses, and three bottles of wine from the *Bachelor* collection—yes, that's a real thing—you had to pony up even more dough.

The event coincided with the premiere of Nick Viall's *Bachelor* season, and sixteen show alums were scheduled to appear. The night took place at Sycamore Tavern, a sports bar on Sunset Boulevard that isn't particularly trendy, but had agreed to donate its space for the evening. Iaconetti and Herron had also rounded up a fair number of other sponsors: Sprinkles cupcakes, FabFitFun, and Match .com.

Most of the fans who showed up at the Hollywood bar seemed to have the same aim as those in Kansas City: selfies. But this L.A. crowd was *way* more aggressive. Instead of mingling with the plebes, most of the Bach crowd started off the evening upstairs in a private green room. Subsequently, the fans had gathered en masse around the door leading to this VIP area, and every time a contestant would emerge, total pandemonium ensued. It was almost impossible to move anywhere, and I was reminded of how I felt when I attended my first Hanson concert in 1997: hot, anxious, and generally overstimulated. Nearly every young woman was dressed in sequins and had heavy, filled-in eyebrows. There were so many LuMee cases.

The most disturbing incident I witnessed occurred when one twenty-year-old from Manhattan, Vera Antebi, approached Chase McNary—another veteran of JoJo Fletcher's season. After taking a photo with him, she proceeded to grab his hand, tousle his hair, and pinch his cheeks—all while filming herself doing so on Snapchat.

This would have been less weird if McNary had been aware of it, but he was surrounded by so many other selfie-seekers that in the midst of taking photos, he barely seemed to notice a girl was filming herself touching him.

"Look at all of these comments. My friends are bugging out," Antebi said, showing me her phone. She had come to L.A. with her friends on her winter break from Monmouth University.

"We asked Jade how long the rose ceremony is on average, and she said *eight hours*," Antebi continued. "They're all so genuinely nice, and that's what I really like about them. They want to keep the conversation going, you know? None of them are like, 'OK, done with the pictures.' They're just so nice, you know?"

Indeed.

Because the Sycamore Tavern was far closer to my house than One Light Luxury Apartments, I departed after only an hour at the bar. I mean, seen one *Bachelor* event, you've seen 'em all, no?

Well, not quite. A month later, with Valentine's Day approaching, an invite showed up in my work email inbox alerting me to a Bach-related event at the Hotel Bel-Air. Yes, you read that right: Mindy Weiss—the celeb wedding planner who has designed all the televised *Bachelor* nuptials—was co-hosting a "Galentine's Day Party" with Bachelorette Kaitlyn Bristowe and a stationery company called Wedding Paper Divas. Bristowe was one of my favorite Bachelorettes, and the Bel-Air is one of the nicest hotels in town, so this felt like a definite "yes."

I rounded up a few of my *gals,* and we drove over to the five-star hotel, where actual white swans greet you upon arrival. Immediately, this felt different from the previous Bach events. A concierge led us to the Herb Garden Suite, an 1,800-square-foot room with vaulted wood ceilings and French windows, which goes for around $5,000 a night.

Inside, Weiss had set up a truly Instagram-worthy scene. Pillows on the couch, created by Shutterfly, read YAASSS QUEEN and FIERCE. One young woman sat in a pink club chair, having her caricature drawn by artist James Malia. There was an entire table set up filled with stamps, stickers, and notecards where someone named Calligraphy Katrina would write whatever you wanted in beautiful lettering on a DIY valentine. Liz Castellanos, who said she did the makeup for all the hosts on *E!*, was on hand to apply fake lashes and lip touch-ups. And of course, no party would be complete without a photo-booth room: This one was filled entirely with balloons shaped like flowers.

There were also no outright fans in attendance—only fashion types and magazine editors who planned to cover the event. Bristowe was dressed casually, sporting a black choker and tank top with a skull on it. "I feel so underdressed," she admitted when Weiss called her up in front of the room. The pair thanked everyone for coming, and Weiss encouraged guests to check out the "beautiful moments" throughout the room. My friends and I noshed on french fries that came in "fries before guys" holders and gossiped about what Bristowe got out of doing the event. It was clearly a classy affair, and she probably got a free trip to L.A.—but was there something more at stake? Maybe a connection with Weiss, should she want to get married to Shawn Booth down the line?

I wasn't able to ask her directly, because every time I tried to approach her, she magically disappeared into some other corner of the huge suite. My friends agreed that it seemed like she was dodging me. (She had, sadly, already declined an initial interview request.) This was disappointing, but I cheered up when, upon departing, we were handed very pretty miniature bouquets designed by Mark's Garden and a box filled with candy and Champagne.

Had I seen all the post-*Bachelor* event world had to offer? It felt like something was missing. And like clockwork, that very something soon popped up on my Instagram feed: a dating boot camp with one of the "top matchmakers in the nation" co-hosted by Iowa farmer and former Bachelor Chris Soules.

Mind you, this was a couple of months before Soules was involved in a tragic accident in April 2017. While driving his pickup truck near his home in Iowa, he rear-ended a tractor trailer and the person in the trailer—one of his neighbors—was killed. When the 911 call was eventually released, it became apparent that Soules had stayed at the scene until emergency vehicles arrived—but he then fled to his home, where he was later arrested. His trial was set to begin in January 2018.

Since, Soules has all but vanished from social media. But back in March 2017, he was busy promoting this dating boot camp on his Instagram. And it didn't take long for the trolls to emerge. Was the former Bachelor—whose 2015 engagement to Whitney Bischoff ended just six months after he put a 4-carat diamond on her finger—really qualified to be offering romance tips?

"No disrespect," Instagram user @kaciereed commented below Soules's advertisement, "but obviously you are still single and were not able to make it work with 25 or 30 or however many girls it was . . . you are not giving dating advice at this thing, right?"

"Do you have to be married to help others find soul mates?" Soules responded to the commenter. "Last time I checked Chris Harrison is even single. . . ."

Clearly, tensions were already running high. And this dating boot camp, to be held at a country club in suburban Maryland, was unique. But was it worth flying across the country for? I decided to check out the matchmaker's website before making a final decision.

The event was being put on by Susan Trombetti, whose company Exclusive Matchmaking will revamp your online dating profile, give you a makeover, and even perform a background check on your potential suitor. For $2,000, she'll spend half a day with you—plus lunch!—to give you a full "dating analysis."

Fortunately, the cheapest ticket at the dating boot camp with Soules was an affordable $89. (Actually, it eventually got knocked down to $35—a ticket sans lunch—but that option was unavailable when I bought my pass.) There were more expensive packages, for those so inclined. For $550, you'd get a picture with Soules, forty-five minutes alone with Trombetti, and a group wingman session. For $3,000, you'd get all that *plus* a makeover and many more hours of Trombetti's coveted guidance.

It felt like the $89 ticket was the right move. But what would I get for my $89?

"When you think about the qualities you want in a man, does someone like Chris Soules factor in?" the boot-camp invite asked. "Do you want a man who is intelligent, successful, devoted to his family, beloved by his friends, funny, sensitive, athletic, hardworking, playful . . . shall I go on?

"Chris is all of this and more, and we get the exclusive opportunity to ask him what he's looking for from a woman. The Bachelor didn't share ALL of his secrets on TV. He's bringing a few special insights to my exclusive boot camp to help you understand what a successful man REALLY wants from a woman. Don't you want to know?"

I *did* want to know! Also, I may or may not have had a soft spot for Soules, and may or may not have harbored a secret fantasy in which we lived on his farm and I worked on a memoir about living on a farm and he tended to the corn on that farm. Whatever, guys. I'm not totally immune to the power of *The Bachelor*. Sue me.

After I informed my Bach Discush crew about my impending weekend adventure, I was able to rope one of my friends, Molly, into coming along for the journey. I knew she would be the perfect partner in crime. She's a hilarious writer and podcaster who co-founded the website HelloGiggles, and she's always down for anything out-there.

So with Molls's ten-year-old Chihuahua, Wags, in tow—she won't travel anywhere without him—we departed for Baltimore. We landed at ten p.m. on Friday and the learning began at nine thirty a.m. on Saturday, so we went straight to bed to assure we'd be in the right state of mind for the boot camp.

As soon as we woke up, Molls ran her outfit by me. She'd decided to go with her Tory Burch "lemonade" sweater—a bold teal number with a small lemon emblazoned on the right breast. I selected a Pendleton cape, bell bottoms, and clogs, because I like to pretend I'm the daughter Stevie Nicks never had.

I wouldn't say the looks were subtle, per se, so when we walked in twenty minutes late to the boot camp, all eyes were on us. There were about fifteen ladies in attendance, ranging in age from roughly twenty-five to fifty-five. The average age looked to be thirty-nine.

The event was being held in a country club conference room that overlooked a golf course. Each small table was decorated with a bottle of fake tulips that had been glued to the tablecloth. There was a metal water bottle at every chair accompanied by a bottle opener; both read EXCLUSIVE MATCHMAKING.

Soules was nowhere to be found. Instead, Trombetti stood at the front of the room, running through a PowerPoint presentation. A plump blonde in her early fifties, she was wearing a clingy blue dress and looked like she'd gotten her hair and makeup professionally done. She gave me a Paula Deen vibe, even dropping into a Southern accent every few minutes despite the fact that she'd ostensibly lived in Maryland her entire life.

We were here, she said, to create a dating action plan. We would make a list of the nonnegotiables we were looking for in a man—but this couldn't contain anything superficial. Height, weight, education, career—none of those could go on the list.

"You've paid me for the truth," she said. "Your friends, they don't tell you the truth. And listen, it's hard for me to hurt people's feelings."

As hard as it was for her, she said, she would tell us if we had too much weight on us. She would tell us if we were being bitchy. She would tell us if we slept with guys too soon—or if we made them wait too long for sex.

"I'm sorry if you're religious, but you've gotta have sex," she insisted. "Stop denying that you want sex as much as he does. I'm telling you, there's a problem if you're not gonna have sex."

Good thing I have no religious convictions, I guess?

She then launched into a speech about how to tell if a man isn't the committal type. Is he always late for dates? Does he fail to call you when he says he will? Does he miss your birthday or dinner with your family? These are the kind of men who are telling you, point-blank, that they are not ready for commitment. And we need to be listening to them.

"Can you blame them when they keep coming back? After all, you are lovable," Trombetti continued. "You have the strength to say no! They will call and come back as many times as you let them! You don't need this drama! It doesn't feel good because it isn't good!"

I was starting to feel pretty #TeamSusan. We need and deserve to be loved and cherished, she said. We need to make ourselves important so that others follow that direction. And if a man doesn't treat us well, we need to kick him to the curb. "I am giving you permission to put you first," she almost shouted.

YES, GIRL!

Now that we felt good about asking for the kind of commitment we needed, Susan began to talk about how to find an eligible man. She said she had a "big background in liquidating frauds" and warned us that you never know just how dangerous someone you're dating might be. "It takes four seasons for crazy to come out," she said. "He could be mentally ill. He could be an alcoholic. . . . I'm not concerned over a DUI. I'm concerned over three DUIs."

Oh, OK. So three DUIs is where you draw the line. Good to know.

"It's OK if he's had financial issues," she went on. "It's OK if he's had a DUI. If he was dealing coke out of his dorm, I don't know if I'd like that, but you've gotta set your own boundaries."

And where does one find this non-coke-dealing potential husband? Online, probably, since it's 2018. Fortunately, Susan was ready to arm us with plentiful tips about how to create an alluring online dating profile. Our profile photo, she said, was 95 percent of what men paid attention to, so we needed to wear bright colors in it.

"Something like that," she said, pointing to Molls's lemonade sweater, a compliment Molls was exceptionally proud of and did not let me forget for the rest of our weekend. Whatever, Susan, get on board with the Southwestern vibes.

Other tips for our online dating profile: No bikinis! If we show too much cleavage, we will be attracting the wrong guy. No negatives or absolutes, like, "Don't contact me if you have baby-mama drama." No photos in which you're wearing sunglasses. No photos with your hot friends. No photos with children. No photos with other people's children. No photos with animals. No professional work photos.

"You want to invoke romance—not visions of arguments over the boardroom table!" she said. Because a professional headshot totally screams bossy, mean work lady instead of accomplished career woman.

My confidence in Susan was waning. And then this:

In order to expand our dating pool, she said, we had to get up off the couch and start exploring new social circles. And where is the best place to do that? Not in suburban Maryland!

"You need to move where the men are that you want to date," Susan advised. "I don't care if it's a hole-in-the-wall in Beverly Hills."

As someone who lives just a few miles from 90210, I can tell you that I don't come across too many holes-in-the-wall on Craigslist. Nonetheless, Susan continued to advise the room to get out of town and join high-end concierge services that would allow for access to exclusive movie premieres and gallery openings.

"I'm telling you, after a few of these things, you're going to start saying to yourself, 'How many goddamn pictures can I take with Brad Pitt?'" she said. (Quite a few, according to a "Susan Trombetti Brad Pitt" Google Images search.)

"I was at one premiere and I saw Orlando Bloom. I think he'd just broken up with Katy Perry, because he was looking [to date] when I met him. These guys? They're just people. They're these incredible people you never thought you would meet—but you could," said Trombetti.

Other places to find single, rich dudes? The Four Seasons in Lanai, Hawaii, or any Ritz-Carlton.

"One of the biggest things Chris Soules can teach you about finding love? Put your ass out there in the most unorthodox ways and get out there," she said.

Oh, right. Chris Soules. Remember him? Nearly four hours into the day, there was still no sign of him. But finally, after a lovely lunch of cold cuts and egg salad—and after some drama involving his car service—he arrived. We quickly learned that Chris would not be delivering any sort of prepared remarks—instead, he was sitting for a question-and-answer session with Susan.

"I'm going to start by asking you something you've probably never been asked," she began. "Who is your favorite Disney character?"

SUSAN IS THE NEXT DIANE SAWYER, Y'ALL.

His answer, by the way, was Ariel. He said he would most like to marry Ariel, the Little Mermaid, who most definitely would be sporting a bikini in her dating profile pic.

Now, mind you, up until Chris's arrival, I had been typing away on my laptop, jotting down all of Susan's pearls of wisdom. And no one batted an eye. But when Chris began talking, Susan's hired security quickly approached me and told me I couldn't type anything that they were saying during their conversation. Because Chris Soules was relaying state secrets to us, apparently. I slammed my laptop closed in a huff and just began taking notes with good ol' paper and pen, which Mr. Security Man didn't seem to mind.

Nonetheless, Molls was rattled. She was worried that Susan's team would Google us and uncover that I was a journalist and Molls was a comedian who had been trolling the event all day on Twitter. In other words, that we were not there for the right reasons.

Molls kept whispering, "Should we just go? Should we just go?" over and over again under her breath. As she later told me, she was paranoid that we'd be found out, escorted into the women's locker room, and "given the shaming of a lifetime." Then we'd have to go outside, hang our heads woefully, and wait eleven minutes for an Uber in the suburbs.

Fortunately, I was able to convince Molls to stay and turned my attention back to Chris and Susan. She had moved on from Disney characters to his dating preferences.

"What do you find most appealing in a woman?" she inquired.

"Looks is important, obviously," he answered.

"Listen, ladies! *LOOKS!*" she said, nodding toward the faux-eyelash station that had been set up for later in the day.

"Um, but really it's about personality and how you hold yourself," he continued. "If they have an aura of strength about them, I think that's something that's important to me. Someone who has been raised well, and you can just tell that they have a background of having a good heart."

He went on to contradict nearly everything Susan had been talking about all morning, saying how he wanted a woman who had a career and was able to put him in his place. He said he hated text messaging and preferred making telephone calls.

Susan gasped. "Amazing! A guy who actually calls!"

"You don't fall in love through texts. If a guy's throwing texts, you need to hold him accountable and move on or don't respond until you get a phone call," Chris advised.

"This is a *man's* opinion," Susan said.

After about fifteen minutes, Chris's time with us had already come to a close, so Susan proposed a toast: "Here's to all the bastards you're never gonna miss, and the hot guys you're gonna kiss!" We toasted with Champagne. I don't drink, but Molls said it tasted cheap.

At this point, Susan disappeared with Chris, and we were subjected to a series of increasingly dark presentations. With no explanation, representatives from local charities came forward to talk about the work their organizations do. In theory, this was to encourage the seminar participants to embrace charity work, because

Susan had said earlier that men are attracted to philanthropic women.

But I felt bad for the charity reps, who could sense that their presence wasn't entirely welcome by the guests. To make matters worse, those who had paid extra to take photos with Chris kept getting called out of the room in the middle of the presentations.

Then came a young lady from a local beauty salon to tell us about how important proper brow shape was—that brows frame our face and are the "window to our soul." We learned all about eyelash extensions, microblading, and permanent makeup.

Oh, and then there was the doctor from the Laser Center of Maryland. He was brought in to tell us all about the services he can provide to women: facial rejuvenation, laser-assisted liposuction, Botox, lip fillers.

By this point, Molls and I were sinking into a deep depression. Susan returned, her cheeks red, as she told us she'd been taking shots upstairs with Chris. We decided to skip the rest of the plastic surgery presentation and duck out early. I requested an Uber. It took eleven minutes to arrive.

Why I'm a Fan

PATTI STANGER

IT'S VERY UNUSUAL FOR A SHOW TO LAST THAT long on the air at network level in the love space. And we still fall apart when we see the people cry in the car. The producers and I know why they're doing it: They haven't eaten. They've only drank alcohol. They haven't talked to their loved ones on the telephone. They haven't seen TV or read a book. They're sequestered. And you get ruthless.

Some of them are there for the right reasons. It's not an absolute. Some of the girls say, "I've tried everything—online dating, mixers, traveling, nothing has worked, this is my last resort. Who is better to fix me up than *The Bachelor*?" But people need to remember that this is a TV show. Part of it's not real life. They cast for reasons. They're gonna put [in] four or five people that the main person is attracted to and the rest is gonna be for drama and excitement, like the Corinnes of the world.

People can meet on television, but it's in the execution. Chemistry rules the street, and that cannot be changed. Can a girl look at a guy who is an 8 and he becomes a 10 in her eyes? Yes, by the personality. He might be shorter, he might be not as rich, but there's something there. It's not that way for a guy. When the Bachelor comes along, he sees twenty-five women and he knows right away who he's interested in. Men are like, "Oh, I could do her," and that's it. "The rest I'm not gonna touch."

In the last generation, there have been more women graduating from college than men. When the market crashed, a lot of men who were super successful over thirty lost their money. If they didn't invest wisely and didn't buy real estate, they basically were crying in their soup. So with that being the case, the new generation of millennials are saying to themselves, "I watched my parents suffer to make money to put me through college. They're miserable, they get divorced at fifty. Quality of life is way more important to me. So maybe I won't make as much money, but I'll live a better life." Your generation is less materialistic. You don't really need the expensive car. With Elon Musk coming out with a $32,000 Tesla, you'll be fine. A Prius is an ambiguous car. Is he rich and environmental, or just poor? This generation doesn't see the fairy tale of the men rescuing them, because they don't have poster people. In my day, it was still Cinderella. But now, the Prince is dead and Cinderella knows she's gotta make it on her own.

I think on the show, people want that because it's a fame game. It's a competition to win the crown, like Miss America. And you're drunk. You're not eating because you're afraid you're gonna look fat on-camera. Then there's Champagne throughout the entire day. Now you're in a room with twenty-five women and one fucking guy. And everyone's talking nonstop about who's gonna get him and how they're gonna get him.

Because viewers love it when the guy gets on the knee and proposes. That's the money shot. The ratings prove you love it. We're talking Nielsen, here. And you're still watching. Even cord cutters are watching. So they're doing something right.

—Patti Stanger, matchmaker (*The Millionaire Matchmaker, Million Dollar Matchmaker*)

CHAPTER 12

Intoxicated by Happily
Ever After

The moment I began considering writing a book about *The Bachelor*, I was hosting one of my weekly viewing parties. Nearly every Monday during Bach season (read: January through September), a bunch of young women congregate in my living room with bottles of rosé and a plethora of Trader Joe's snacks. Friends have long stopped inviting me to events on Monday nights, and my roommates gird themselves for a couple of hours of raucous discussion.

It's almost always the highlight of my week. When the gatherings began, I barely knew most of the girls who came—in fact, some I'd communicated with only via Twitter. (I'm sure that sounds sketchy, but you're talking to someone who thought her best friend in 1998 was a girl she met in an AOL chat room.)

In the years since, we've helped one another through breakups, sweat it out at the gym together, and even gone on road trips across California. Sure, my colleagues still love to mock my "Bach niiiiights!"—imagine that shrieked with a Valley Girl inflection—and plenty of people tell me they mute my Twitter feed while the show is on. But this seemingly trivial reality show has actually been responsible for some of the best moments in my young-adult life.

Which brings me back to that fateful Bach Night. It was a special one. We were welcoming our first guest from the show, JJ Lane, a contestant from Kaitlyn Bristowe's season of *The Bachelorette*. He'd started following me on Twitter—a lot of Bach folks do this, I think because they want proximity to someone in the media?—and before long, he'd agreed to be our guest of honor at a viewing party. These days, we're quick to welcome members of Bachelor Nation into the fray, and we've also watched alongside notable fans like Allison Williams, Melanie Lynskey, and Lorene Scafaria. (Living in L.A. and interviewing celebrities for a living doesn't hurt.)

When Lane showed up, he was totally awesome. Even though he'd been painted as the villain of the season, he was gracious and dishy, spilling lots of fun behind-the-scenes info with a group of ladies he'd just met. I remember sitting on my couch, thinking about how judgmental I'd been while watching him on the show. I started to wonder if most of the people on the show were as wildly different in real life—and if they had the kind of war stories Lane did.

This was also, coincidentally, around the time that Lifetime was debuting a new show called *UnREAL*. Created by Marti Noxon and Sarah Gertrude Shapiro—the latter of whom had worked as an actual producer on *The Bachelor* for many years—*UnREAL* was a fictionalized version of *The Bachelor*. It depicted life behind the scenes on a reality dating show called *Everlasting*, where producers treated contestants like total shit in order to make juicy television. Because of Shapiro's background, the show got a lot of attention when it debuted—and strong critical reviews.

"Judging from the first four episodes of *UnREAL* . . . the job of a reality producer is, however the participants may justify it, a grifter's game," read *New Yorker* critic Emily Nussbaum's 2015 review of the first season. "It's a profession for people whose personality disorders make them adept at exploiting the personality disorders of others, who possess the compartmentalization skills of those shrinks who rubber-stamp torture techniques for the CIA (Eating disorders? Daddy's death? An on-set date rape? It's all fodder for the story—or something to be covered up.) Like a slaughterhouse exposé, *UnREAL* is designed as an audience intervention, forcing viewers to taste the cruelty in their reality-TV bacon. The fact that the show itself also tastes like bacon—at once sweet and salty, greasy and irresistible—is no accident."

In his review in *The New York Times*, Jon Caramanica echoed a similar sentiment: "The acerbic and unrelentingly sad *UnREAL* doesn't exist just to send up reality television, or to pick at its scabs," he said. "Rather, *UnREAL* uses that access as a tool to ask questions about these sorts of programs: not just about how they operate—savagely, if its stories are to be believed—but also why participants on both sides of the camera subject themselves to them."

I reached out to Shapiro numerous times for an interview for this book, but she never responded; I heard through the grapevine that she's "done talking about *The Bachelor*." Alas, when I interviewed her for the *LA Times* prior to *UnREAL*'s debut in 2015, it was clear that her time on the Bach was anything but positive.

A native of Santa Barbara, where her father taught at the nearby UCSB, Shapiro began dreaming of a directing career when she was a teenager. She went to college at Sarah Lawrence, where she hoped to study under the poet Mary Oliver. She was rejected from the poet's workshop but went on to major in fiction writing and filmmaking. During her senior year, she began interning for indie-film powerhouse Christine Vachon and later got a job managing the studio of fashion photographer David LaChapelle.

At age twenty-two, she migrated from New York to Los Angeles in the hopes of pursuing her directing dream. Instead, she landed on one of Fleiss's shows: *High School Reunion.* While there, she said, she signed some sort of contract that committed her to "unlimited renewable options for perpetuity"—meaning she was obligated to work on other Next Entertainment productions too.

When she was asked to start on *The Bachelor,* though, she was horrified.

"I said, 'Oh my God, I'm a feminist!'" she recalled, describing her horror at the proposition. "It was like the apocalypse to me. Like, the worst thing that had ever happened. It was like asking a vegan activist to work in a slaughterhouse."

Still, she went, and under Levenson, she climbed the ranks from associate producer to field producer, where she was responsible for coming up with romantic dates and storylines. She told me that she didn't remember all the seasons she worked on during her three-year tenure with the show, but she was certain she was around for Andrew Firestone's and Bob Guiney's.

After a few years, she was miserable, but she was "such a good Jewish kid that I could not make myself get fired." Instead, she told her boss she was going to kill herself if she didn't leave. It was 2005, and she put all her stuff into her car, drove to Portland, Oregon, and considered becoming a kale farmer.

"I was so damaged," she said. "I couldn't be near recording devices or talk on the phone for months."

So what did she witness that was so traumatizing? Mainly, she said, it was realizing that what was happening on the show was having a real-life impact on the contestants. She wondered whether the participants were aware of what they were signing up for, because "truly, they can't know what they're signing up for. You can't really understand the power of editing, and there are a lot of really smart people making these shows. It's a chess game you can't win."

During her time on the show, she kept thinking back to her days in college, sitting in feminist seminars that would pose the question: "How much would it cost you to sell your soul?" She'd always thought the answer would be millions of dollars, but at *The Bachelor*, she realized it "was just a fucking paycheck. After eighteen years of your parents building your morality, the desperation of staying alive sinks in so quickly."

Michael Carroll, who became one of Shapiro's closest friends at the show, said everyone knew how unhappy she was. She was a "smart New York chick" who was constantly complaining: "Why am I doing this? I'm a feminist, and I hate this shit."

So why didn't Carroll have a problem with the job? "I'm from Jacksonville, Florida. I didn't grow up in a feminist environment," he said with a shrug. "But Sarah was a Jewish New York girl, who went to a great college and wanted to do things and wanted to make films. And she was a big schlub. Like one of those, like, East Village girls. Dirty T-shirt, hair in a fucking ponytail, hated everything. Jeans showing her fucking butt crack. Fucking dirty tennis shoes. She was always grumpy."

There were, of course, moments on *The Bachelor* that Shapiro enjoyed. She admitted that she wasn't immune to the princess fantasy the show was selling and even got a thrill out of eyeing the pricey diamond rings that were used during the proposals.

"Diamonds can hypnotize anyone," she said. "Sometimes, I'd have to transport them to the show, and I politically don't believe in diamonds. I think the whole thing is bullshit. I know it's not right. And I still would get weird around diamonds, trying them on with my dirty, baggy jeans and down jacket. That idea that some girls are pretty, pretty princesses that deserve to be taken care of and rescued and saved and cared for? That sets us up for a lot of heartbreak."

To Shapiro's mind, so much of the appeal of *The Bachelor* is related to its sentimentality—that the show creates a world where everyone knows what their role is. The guy is chivalrous and the girl is a princess. "To be a perfect contestant, you should be a lawyer that gives really awesome blow jobs and doesn't really care about being a lawyer," she said with a laugh. "Like, 'I just passed the bar for fun!' You're really professionally successful, demure, and submissive— sexy, but not slutty."

And yet with *UnREAL*, Shapiro's intention wasn't to pass judgment on fans of the franchise. "Our aim was to have compassion for why we fall into these fantasies," she explained. "I'm not above it. I love being wooed, and I totally want someone to get me a helicopter ride. Who doesn't?"

It wasn't long before those in Bachelor Nation started responding to the show. While many former contestants were quick to say they related to *UnREAL*—and recognized numerous producing tactics portrayed on it—others were displeased with the depiction. Chris Harrison, for one, was decidedly not a fan, saying the main difference between the fictional show and the reality show was that "people watch *The Bachelor*." Oooh! Sick ratings burn!

"It's complete fiction," he went on to say in an interview with *Variety*. "As much as they would love to jump on our coattails—they were begging for us to talk about it and for people to write about it—at the end of the day, no one is watching. I mean, absolutely nobody is watching that show. Why? It is terrible. It is really terrible."

Lifetime will air the third season of *UnREAL* in 2018, so obviously someone is watching. In any event, it certainly rattled plenty of people affiliated with the show—even Scott Jeffress, who worked with Shapiro during the early days of *The Bachelor*.

"It's a little frustrating for me. They're kind of lifting the skirt and showing behind the scenes," Jeffress said. "I don't have any animosity about it, but it's a shame for our industry that this has to happen—that we have to tell those tales. . . . It bothers me a little bit that it kind of softens what the viewer is seeing. It was inevitable it was gonna happen. And God bless [Shapiro] that she's the one that did it. She'll make the money for it. But it kind of blows the cover on the whole *Bachelor* thing."

Yes, *UnREAL* did raise questions about the way in which reality producers manipulate contestants—and just how ethical it may or may not be to do so. But I think it also started to force fans to examine the way we consume the show. Right around the time the program began airing, I started noticing a glut of similarly themed essays popping up on female-centric publications:

Elle: "9 Reasons Strong, Intelligent, Feminist Women Watch *The Bachelor(ette)*"
HuffPost: "*The Bachelor*: Why Smart Women Watch (and Love) It"
The Washington Post: "10 Times *The Bachelor* Shows Made Feminists Proud"

The Guardian: "Does Bingeing on *The Bachelor* Make
Me a Bad Feminist?"
Vogue: "Why Feminists Are Unabashedly Obsessed with
The Bachelor"

This was obviously a topic female viewers were struggling with. Something about loving *The Bachelor* made many women feel ashamed—like they were, in some way, betraying their gender. So I returned to feminist scholar Andi Zeisler to get her thoughts on the flood of think pieces exploring the connection between the show and feminism.

"It almost seems to be less about *The Bachelor* and more about this idea in the past few years that if you identify as a feminist, you have to somehow justify everything that you consume," Zeisler theorized. "Every piece of pop culture or media, you have to kind of justify watching it as a feminist act, which I find a little bit assbackward. But people really feel like their consumption patterns have to be explained as part of a larger identity."

After reading some of the essays just mentioned, Zeisler told me she felt like women were "twisting themselves into pretzels" to explain why watching the show was actually a feminist act. To her mind, none of the arguments were convincing—and that's OK.

"Establishing feminism as a purity test is just a losing proposition, because we do things all the time in our daily lives that contradict a feminist world view," she said. "It could be as simple as being married or shopping at Target. There's kind of no way to win once you start thinking about it like that. If you're actively working toward feminism, watching *The Bachelor* or shopping at Target or wearing leather shoes or whatever—that's not going to cancel out that part of your life."

When she starts seeing men "writing tortured essays about how watching *Sunday Night Football* is really shaking their faith in themselves as left-leaning progressives"—that's when, she joked, she'll give these feminist arguments more credence.

But Susan Douglas, the UMichigan communications professor who authored *Enlightened Sexism: The Seductive Message That Feminism's Work Is Done*, told me she understood why so many women were troubled by their fandom. Young women in the twenty-first century who are college educated and have managerial positions—in other words, the main *Bachelor* demographic—have been told for years they can do anything they want. And yet these same women still face pressure to be thin, beautiful, and stylish.

"They are pinioned between wanting the fruits of feminism without sacrificing the femininity that's going to help them advance, not just in relationships, but at work," Douglas said. "So on the one hand, you're like, 'Oh my God, this is the dumbest show ever. The dates are stupid. It is reinforcing the most retrograde standards around female beauty and performance.' In the other ear, it is a tale of courtship and romance in this age of 'How do you even meet men?'"

The show, she argued, also appeals to women on a more basic level. Let's say you're watching the nightly news. Will Donald Trump's economic policy really produce deficits? Who knows? Here, on *The Bachelor*, you can be a completely authoritative judge about which kinds of women are performing a kind of womanhood you, as a woman, admire—and that you think men might admire.

"Sometimes, *The Bachelor* does show that a man and woman with their own careers can fall in love, and she doesn't have to give up the world for him, and what's so bad about that?" Douglas said. "On the other hand, it's historically been very white. It's very heteronormative. It's very, very middle class. And all of the women have to be a size zero, look great in a bikini, and be very conventionally pretty. So there are very narrow corporate standards of thinness and beauty—stereotypes of female behavior—that the show incessantly reinforces."

That, of course, is what is troubling to feminists about watching *The Bachelor*. But like Zeisler, Douglas agrees that just because you watch the show, it doesn't mean, for example, that you wouldn't support equal pay for women, go to bat for Planned Parenthood, or condemn sexual harassment.

The fact that these discussions are happening within Bachelor Nation is a relatively new phenomenon, fueled largely by fan engagement on social media. According to Twitter, *The Bachelor* was one of the top five most-tweeted-about reality shows on TV in the United States between 2015 and July 2017. On average, the tech company said, *The Bachelor* gets roughly 260,000 tweets per episode; *The Bachelorette* generates about 180,000.

There are also about a dozen prominent podcasts about the franchise, where fans not only recap weekly episodes but dive into the social dynamics at play on the program. *The Ringer*'s Juliet Litman hosts *Bachelorette Party*, Bustle has *Will You Accept This Podcast?*, and *HuffPost* is behind *Here to Make Friends*. In the past year, even Bach alums have gotten in on the podcast game, with Kaitlyn Bristowe, Ben Higgins, Ashley Iaconetti, Becca Tilley, Dean Unglert, and Olivia Caridi all offering up their insights on the franchise.

"I think pop culture has really started to engage with the show because it has a universally appealing premise," said Emma Gray, who co-hosts *Here to Make Friends* with her *HuffPost* colleague Claire Fallon. "It taps into these really basic notions of love and weirdness around sex and dating and fulfillment. And then Twitter popped up at the right time, making it so everyone wanted to watch live and go on Twitter and make fun of it so they could be in on the conversation in real time. They've created this loop where people feel like they need to be a part of this community online in order to watch it."

Young women are the primary demographic for Gray's show, which goes up once a week while *The Bachelor* is on the air. Roughly 50,000 listeners tune in to each podcast, she said.

Even Reality Steve has a *Bachelor* podcast now. Reality Steve—whose real name, sadly, is not Reality Steve—is Steve Carbone, a forty-two-year-old blogger who lives in Dallas, Texas. And to ABC's dismay, his moniker has become synonymous with the Bachelor franchise.

For the better part of a decade, Carbone has made a living reporting spoilers about *The Bachelor*. Which wasn't his intention when he started recapping television shows in 2003, sharing his thoughts on *Joe Millionaire* with a list of email subscribers. When that show came to a close, his followers asked if he had plans to recap any other shows—and the next dating program on the television schedule was *The Bachelorette*. At the time, writing was just Carbone's hobby. He did it for fun and was hopeful that someday, a professional TV site might hire him to do some freelance work.

But in 2009, everything changed. A tipster contacted him with this note: "Hey. I know you write about the show and you've got a following. Well, I've found something out about the ending of this season of *The Bachelor*." The season currently on the air was Jason Mesnick's—and the ending of that season went down in the Bach history books when Mesnick, infamously, spurned fiancée Melissa Rycroft on the "After the Final Rose" special and told her he was still in love with his runner-up, Molly Malaney.

Carbone's source had the dirt before the special aired, and "based on who it was and what they knew, I was like, 'OK, this is legit,'" the blogger recalled. So he ran with it, publishing the information on his site roughly two weeks before the finale aired.

There were doubters, of course, but when the prediction turned out to be true, Carbone instantly became the *Bachelor* authority. Suddenly, anonymous sources started turning up left and right, willing to give him dirt on the show.

Carbone said his sources vary every season, and when one begins anew, he has no idea where his information will be coming from. By now, though, he said he's confident good scoops will come his way—"it's just a matter of how detailed, and when."

"It's become easier now, because of the popularity of the site," Carbone explained. "I don't need to solicit anything anymore."

So how does he tell good tips from the bad ones? "The best example I can give," he said, "is if I get an email that's one sentence long, misspelled, and has no punctuation, saying, 'I no who wins.' It's like, 'OK, but how do you know?' When they tell me how they know, that's when I know if it's legit or not."

If someone says they're a friend or a cousin of the contestant in question, Carbone's ears perk up—people on the show often spill to those around them, even though they're not supposed to. Once he has a tip, he'll follow up by doing some good old-fashioned social-media stalking—tracking down biographical details, double checking locations, and digging up photos to piece everything together.

The show has also gotten more lax about filming in public. Early dates often take place in very visible settings, and oftentimes, fans are invited to witness the dates. They're not supposed to say what they see during filming, but they do—and within hours, Carbone's inbox is flooded with pictures, tweets, and Instagram postings.

Sometimes, all he has to do is a quick search of the word "bachelor" or "bachelorette" on Instagram, and information he wasn't expecting will pop up. Even if it's stuff from early on in the season, it helps Carbone to narrow down the field.

And what, exactly, are these anonymous sources getting out of sharing information with Carbone? Zip. Nada. Zilch. "I think people just like feeling they're part of it," Carbone surmised.

He certainly can't pay his sources—he tried that once and almost got into some serious legal trouble. During Ben Flajnik's time as the Bachelor, Carbone attempted to contact three women who had competed on the 2012 season, searching for information about Flajnik's final pick. Two of the women responded but told Carbone they couldn't help him for fear they'd get in trouble if they did. That's when he offered to pay the ladies in exchange for information, but they both declined.

Just a few weeks later, Carbone received an email from a lawyer at Warner Bros., alerting him to the fact that the company was aware of his exchanges with the female contestants. It wasn't long before he was served with a lawsuit on his doorstep.

"ABC had their smoking gun of 'Oh shit, this guy is now offering our contestants money and sooner or later, someone's going to take it because we don't pay them,'" Carbone said. "If they can make money on the side by doing this, they're going to take it. So that's probably why they didn't want me doing that anymore, is my guess."

Eventually, Carbone reached a settlement with the show, the gist of which reads, "Stay away from our contestants," he said. Essentially, he's chilled out on soliciting information, but no one can stop him from publishing information that comes to him.

While he had to pay his own legal fees, he was not required to pay anything to anyone involved with the show, Carbone said. To this day, he has never had any interaction with Mike Fleiss or any of the producers—only the legal team at Warner Bros.

"It was a little bit empowering to know that they were really bothered by me," he said, a hint of pride in his voice. "But I've never done the spoilers so people won't watch. I've done them so they'll watch the show differently. You can see storylines; you can see editing."

Indeed, Carbone's spoilers don't seem to have had any major impact on the show's ratings. Since the couple at the end almost always breaks up anyway, knowing who "ends up together" isn't that big of a deal.

In the meantime, Carbone is able to make a living off his site. He started putting advertisements up in 2010, and he was able to make the blog his full-time job by August 2011. Roughly 65 percent of his traffic comes from mobile devices, which isn't great, since desktop ads are more lucrative than mobile ones. Still, his traffic is strong. When any one of the Bachelor shows is on, he said he gets between 6 to 8 million page views a month. Off-season, that number drops precipitously to around 2 million per month.

It might seem like easy work, he said, but it's all-consuming. "I'm almost like a doctor in that I'm constantly on-call," he said. "At any point during the day, I can get an email, a text, a direct message, an Instagram message, a Snapchat message—something that says, 'Hey, here's what I've heard, you might want to look into this.' My phone is my job."

With outsiders trying to capitalize on the lucrative Bachelor market, it only makes sense that Warner Bros.—which produces the show—would do the same. In 2016, the company announced its consumer products line would start releasing the Bachelor Wines: "a collection of wines inspired by the award-winning television series," according to a press release. The line offers three varietals. There's the Fantasy Suite, a Cabernet Sauvignon; the One on One, a Chardonnay; and the Final Rosé, a Zinfandel and Petite Sirah blend. The wines are manufactured by winemakers in California's Central Coast and Central Valley and retail for $16.96 a bottle.

You probably won't be surprised to learn that I purchased all three bottles for my Bach Discush group to sample, and let me tell you: They were *not* a hit. Iaconetti brought an extra bottle of the Fantasy Suite one week—I hope one that she was gifted for free—and one year later, I still have it. I put that damn bottle of wine out on the table Every. Single. Week. No one wants to drink that shit.

Bachelor candy, on the other hand? That went more quickly. In 2016, Sugarfina created an official collaboration with ABC called the "Will You Accept This Rose?" Bento Box. It was filled with the Final Rose and the First Impression Rose (made with Whispering Angel rosé).

"Our core demographic is young women—kind of that eighteen to late thirties age range. They are also a big fan of *The Bachelor*, so from an audience perspective it was just perfectly aligned," Rosie O'Neill, Sugarfina's founder, told me. "This is a young woman who loves to post on social media, loves to have something new and fresh and cute to share on her feed, and the candies are so cute and they connect directly with *The Bachelor*. So we think during the viewing season that people will get excited about it and have something cute to post."

In a way, watching *The Bachelor* has become a badge of honor, as something that was once considered gauche now carries an odd sense of cultural cachet. Huge celebrities like Jennifer Aniston, Sean Penn, and John Mayer go on talk shows hosted by Jimmy Kimmel and Ellen DeGeneres and spend their entire interview segments discussing their love of *The Bachelor*. Even the snarky Howard Stern admits he's a fan and sometimes spends large portions of his Sirius XM radio show talking about it—though he's often just complaining about the vocal fry the female contestants speak with.

Still, even though many high-profile stars now openly discuss their love of *The Bachelor*, there's always a hint of irony that comes along with the admission. Like, "Yes, I love this show, but I don't *really* love it—I just love to make fun of it. It's a train wreck! Hahahahaha!" And after spending all this time reporting on the show? I have to say: I think that's bullshit.

I think we watch *The Bachelor* because we're anxious about our own love lives, and the show gives us an outlet to express our fears about the modern dating world. It allows us to see a world filled with courtship, chivalry, and romance—and while we may scoff at the helicopters and hot tubs, deep down I think many of us still long for those kinds of things while we're spending hours swiping left on Tinder.

Helen Fisher, the cultural anthropologist, thinks the show serves as a modern-day campfire of sorts, allowing us to discuss mating rituals in a communal setting—even if that community is Twitter.

"For millions of years, we lived in these little hunting and gathering bands. We sat around the fire at night, gossiping about who did what to whom and 'Oh, she was mean to him, so he's leaving her,' and 'Oh, I would have done it differently,'" Fisher said. "In other words, they were getting dating tips. They were sharing these experiences of watching other people around them and other people's romantic lives. We've been doing this forever. But now we're also sharing an experience in a society where we don't know much about each other."

Love, of course, is something we've all experienced—but not in the way *The Bachelor* depicts it. And that's why Scott Jeffress—the executive producer from the show's early days—thinks it fills a certain void for us. It gives us hope that a frothy, beautiful love story is just out of reach.

"*The Bachelor* was the perfect thing after 9/11," he said. "Disaster movies were down at the box office. People did not want to be depressed or sad. They wanted to have a fantasy. They wanted to imagine what could be and be happy. I truly think that's why *The Bachelor* hit at the perfect time."

Sure, maybe that's the purpose *The Bachelor* served initially, before we knew that every couple coming out of the show stood little chance of actually making it to the altar. Beyond the inevitable breakups, how are we supposed to buy into the fantasy when we now understand so much about how the sausage is made? There are so many things that taint the illusion: The contestants who now go on the show to become social-media influencers. The bubble effect that convinces the cast they're head-over-heels with the Bachelor or Bachelorette. The producers who masterfully persuade participants to drop the L-bomb and get down on one knee. The editing that makes everything seem far more dramatic than it actually was. The life-altering effect the experience can have on individuals' reputations and careers after their fifteen minutes fade away.

How do we watch *The Bachelor* now, knowing what we know?

This is something I've spent a lot of time thinking about in the course of writing this book. Now more than ever I understand how incredibly problematic the show can be. And yet, first and foremost, I'm a fan. When I'm sitting in front of my television every Monday, surrounded by a group of my best friends, there's no place I'd rather be. And should that make me feel bad? Even if I'm watching the show with a critical eye, just by turning it on every week and giving ABC ratings, aren't I propagating some of the very things I find so troublesome to see?

Perhaps. But I actually don't think these issues would be solved if we all just stopped watching. There are bigger, more fundamental questions that we need to be grappling with: Why are so many of us desperate for the type of fame that television can bring? Why is it so easy—and so fun—to judge others from the privacy of our own homes? And why do so many of us depend on romantic love to validate our worth?

Frankly, these are all ideas I'm still contending with in my own life—especially when it comes to marriage. At thirty-two, I've now lived in Los Angeles for more than a decade. I moved across the country at eighteen and managed to form a life of my own. I have a great group of friends, many of whom dutifully show up at my home each week with veggie platters and tortilla chips just to watch reality TV with me. I have a fun career that I'm proud of. Joan Rivers once told me I was a "smart cookie." And I have a dog who's really fucking cute.

And yet, I'd be lying if I said I didn't feel like somewhat of a failure of a woman because I haven't found a man to spend my life with. And sometimes, those very feelings are exacerbated by watching *The Bachelor*. Those sad women who leave in the limos, questioning why they're not good enough to attract a special man? I've been that woman. On many a Saturday night, in fact.

So many critics are quick to say that *The Bachelor* has screwed up an entire generation of women—created unrealistic expectations for so many of us who will never get to fly in a helicopter or wear a $100,000 ring on our finger. But I would argue that that kind of hope isn't entirely damaging.

More often than not, somehow the show manages to make me feel good about still being single. I watch men being so open and communicative with their emotions and I'm reminded of why I'm waiting for the kind of man who will be that way with me. I watch how fun and exciting it can be to fall in love and remember how good those feelings are—how they're worth fighting for, and how the instant they overtake you, the lonely Saturday nights quickly fade from memory.

So, yes: I will continue to watch *The Bachelor*. I'm hopeful that the show will continue to evolve, tweaking its tried-and-true formulas so that the contrast between the supposed fairy tale unfolding on-screen and the reality of dating off-camera isn't quite so stark. But in the meantime, I'll be planted in front of my TV, watching alongside a group of women as we all try to understand the inscrutable, wicked, brilliant thing that is love.

Acknowledgments

Even after I sold the book proposal for *Bachelor Nation*, I wasn't sure I actually had it in me to write an entire book. I looked at my contract with Dutton over and over again, my eyes always settling on one daunting figure: 75,000 words.

The idea that I would be able to write that much while keeping up with my assignments at the *LA Times* was so overwhelming that I asked my former colleague Rebecca to lunch to discuss my anxiety. Rebeks, who now writes for *Vanity Fair*, had written a book already and made it look easy. "You can totally do this," she said encouragingly. "Think about how many stories you write in a year. How many words is that?"

She was right. On average, I wrote far more than 75,000 words per year at the newspaper. This small bit of reassurance gave me the boost I needed at a moment when I was feeling paralyzed. Thank you, my OG work wife, for giving me the perspective I needed to get started on this journey.

While balancing my day job and writing a book hasn't been easy, I owe endless gratitude to my editors at the *LA Times*—especially

Laurie—for giving me the flexibility to work on this project. They allowed me to take some time off to head back to Massachusetts to write—freedom I know some staff writers at other publications would not have been as fortunate to have.

When I told my friends that I was moving in with my parents for a couple of months to work on this book, I got more than a few perplexed looks. And frankly, even I wasn't sure it was a great idea. Yes, my mom and dad live in an idyllic New England town by the sea— and room and board would be taken care of—but I wasn't positive the environment would, uh, fuel my creativity.

I couldn't have been more wrong. Mom and Dad, thank you so much for welcoming me back home with open arms and for sitting through endless conversations with me about a show you don't even like that much. Mom, it was so generous of you to allow me to work in your beautiful art studio. I remember one day, when I felt completely distraught and trapped by writer's block, you found me in tears on the couch and asked: "How can I help you?" That support was exactly what I needed. Dad, I can't explain how much it means to me that you are always my number one cheerleader. Even though it's embarrassing when you awkwardly boast about me to your friends who definitely don't want to hear about my myriad accomplishments, I know you only do it because you love me. I love both of you so much.

And, Kim, thank goodness you came home just when our parents were starting to drive me a bit crazy. It's been so special watching you mature over the past few years and start off your law career with such a bang. I know that we'll always have each other's backs when Valentine's Day rolls around again and we're still single— though hopefully we won't be for too much longer.

To Bach Discush: Tierney (my most loyal VP), Katie, Lindsey, Meredith, Annie, Molls, Marissa, Gillian, Sasha, Kara, Saba, Lauren,

Acknowledgments

Baker, and Kat. You are truly the heart and soul of this book. Many would say we're crazy for spending a good portion of our day emailing about a reality show, but we know better than that. We know that this show has provided us with meaningful friendships and provoked important discussions about love and identity. Thank you all for supporting me along the ride and for showing up with legit snacks each and every Monday. And I'm sorry that I get mad when you say you can't make it. I JUST WANT TO SEE YOU BECAUSE I LOVE YOU, OK?

Margaux—but Meg, because I can't—I really have you to thank for getting the ball rolling on this book. When I was completely in the dark about the publishing world, you generously offered to lend your valuable expertise. You connected me with Nicole, who has proven to be an incredible agent. And, Nicole, you believed in this book when it was nothing but an idea that still needed a whole lot of reporting to back it up. Thank you for taking a chance on me, fighting on my behalf, and always looking out for my best interests.

Jess, you were such a supportive editor. Even when I missed deadlines and procrastinated to the max—and we both know I really do mean the MAX—you kept your cool. You were always willing to listen when I needed to vent my frustrations and calmed me down when I was spiraling. I so appreciate your guidance in pushing me toward the finish line.

Lauren, you are the warmest, most supportive best friend. Not only did you allow me access to your office whenever I needed it—thanks to Jason for that too!—but letting me hide out in your apartment during a tough deadline was invaluable. How lucky I am to have such a smart, thoughtful writer in my life to bounce ideas off of. From our A1 on my literal day one at *The Wall Street Journal*, I knew you were a kindred spirit.

Jeffers, I was terrified to have you as my first reader on a draft of this book. You're such an accomplished reporter who has written about things far more important than *The Bachelor*. And yet you treated this subject with an open mind and came back to me with incredibly thoughtful advice. Thank you for serving as a mentor on this book and every day at work. I kind of want to be you.

To my roommates—Allison and Max—for letting me dominate the dining table with my laptop and stacks of transcripts. Also for ordering pizza with me every Sunday. And maybe other days.

Chloe, what can I say? You tried out for *The Bachelor* for me. Is there a greater gift? While I still don't understand how it's possible that you didn't get past the first round—obviously, they realized you were too sane and stable for this process—you really went out on a limb for me. I shall keep your headshot affixed to my fridge for the rest of time.

Riggins, you curled up by my feet every single time I was at work on my laptop. That was so nice. You have taught me more about love than *The Bachelor* ever could. And you are way cuter than Copper.

Finally, to all the cast and crew members who were willing to open themselves up to me for this book: I owe my biggest thanks to you. I judged some of you unfairly when I watched you on TV. Since then, I've come to respect the bravery it takes to bare yourself in front of the world in the way you all have. I hope that this book will help others to understand you better too.

List of Bachelors and Bachelorettes

The Bachelor

Season 1, spring 2002: ALEX MICHEL

Winner: Amanda Marsh
Proposal: No
Current status: Not together

Season 2, fall 2002: AARON BUERGE

Winner: Helene Eksterowicz
Proposal: Yes
Current status: Not together

Season 3, spring 2003: ANDREW FIRESTONE

Winner: Jen Schefft
Proposal: Yes
Current status: Not together

Season 4, fall 2003: BOB GUINEY

Winner: Estella Gardinier
Proposal: No
Current status: Not together

Season 5, spring 2004: JESSE PALMER

Winner: Jessica Bowlin
Proposal: No
Current status: Not together

Season 6, fall 2004: BYRON VELVICK

Winner: Mary Delgado
Proposal: Yes
Current status: Not together

Season 7, 2005: CHARLIE O'CONNELL

Winner: Sarah Brice
Proposal: No
Current status: Not together

Season 8, winter 2006: TRAVIS LANE STORK

Winner: Sarah Stone
Proposal: No
Current status: Not together

Season 9, fall 2006: LORENZO BORGHESE

Winner: Jennifer Wilson
Proposal: No
Current status: Not together

List of Bachelors and Bachelorettes

Season 10, spring 2007: ANDREW BALDWIN

Winner: Tessa Horst
Proposal: Yes
Current status: Not together

Season 11, fall 2007: BRAD WOMACK

Winner: None
Proposal: N/A
Current status: N/A

Season 12, 2008: MATT GRANT

Winner: Shayne Lamas
Proposal: Yes
Current status: Not together

Season 13, 2009: JASON MESNICK

Winner: Melissa Rycroft
Proposal: Yes
Current status: Not together

Season 14, 2010: JAKE PAVELKA

Winner: Vienna Girardi
Proposal: Yes
Current status: Not together

Season 15, 2011: BRAD WOMACK

Winner: Emily Maynard
Proposal: Yes
Current status: Not together

Season 16, 2012: BEN FLAJNIK

Winner: Courtney Robertson
Proposal: Yes
Current status: Not together

Season 17, 2013: SEAN LOWE

Winner: Catherine Giudici
Proposal: Yes
Current status: Married

Season 18, 2014: JUAN PABLO GALAVIS

Winner: Nikki Ferrell
Proposal: No
Current status: Not together

Season 19, 2015: CHRIS SOULES

Winner: Whitney Bischoff
Proposal: Yes
Current status: Not together

Season 20, 2016: BEN HIGGINS

Winner: Lauren Bushnell
Proposal: Yes
Current status: Not together

Season 21, 2017: NICK VIALL

Winner: Vanessa Grimaldi
Proposal: Yes
Current status: Not together

THE BACHELORETTE

Season 1, 2003: TRISTA REHN

Winner: Ryan Sutter
Proposal: Yes
Current status: Married

Season 2, 2004: MEREDITH PHILLIPS

Winner: Ian McKee
Proposal: Yes
Current status: Not together

Season 3, 2005: JEN SCHEFFT

Winner: Jerry Ferris
Proposal: Yes
Current status: Not together

Season 4, 2008: DeANNA PAPPAS

Winner: Jesse Csincsak
Proposal: Yes
Current status: Not together

Season 5, 2009: JILLIAN HARRIS

Winner: Ed Swiderski
Proposal: Yes
Current status: Not together

Season 6, 2010: ALI FEDOTOWSKY

Winner: Roberto Martinez

Proposal: Yes
Current status: Not together

Season 7, 2011: ASHLEY HEBERT

Winner: J. P. Rosenbaum
Proposal: Yes
Current status: Married

Season 8, 2012: EMILY MAYNARD

Winner: Jef Holm
Proposal: Yes
Current status: Not together

Season 9, 2013: DESIREE HARTSOCK

Winner: Chris Siegfried
Proposal: Yes
Current status: Married

Season 10, 2014: ANDI DORFMAN

Winner: Josh Murray
Proposal: Yes
Current status: Not together

Season 11, 2015: KAITLYN BRISTOWE

Winner: Shawn Booth
Proposal: Yes
Current status: Engaged

Season 12, 2016: JOJO FLETCHER

Winner: Jordan Rodgers

Proposal: Yes
Current status: Engaged

Season 13, 2017: RACHEL LINDSAY

Winner: Bryan Abasolo
Proposal: Yes
Current status: Engaged

A Note on Sources

This book is a work of nonfiction. I have made every effort to verify all facts through articles, books, and interviews, nearly all of which are listed on the following pages. In select cases, when a source requested anonymity, I granted it—typically because the source still worked in the television industry and feared retribution.

Whenever possible, I met sources in person. If this was not an option, I completed interviews via telephone or video call. The only interview conducted via email was with Allison Williams.

I reached out to every Bachelor or Bachelorette who ever appeared on the show via email to request interviews. I found contact information via LexisNexis and public records. If no contact information was available for an individual, I searched for the information of the individual's publicity or management representative.

Interview List

Auerbach, Gary, via phone, November 22, 2016.

Bigger, Eric, via phone, August 16, 2017.

Borghese, Lorenzo, via phone, June 7, 2016.

Bukowski, Chris, via phone, December 14, 2016.

Carbone, Steve, via phone, August 17, 2016.

Carroll, Michael, Los Angeles, May 2, 2016.

Cody, Diablo, via phone, January 26, 2017.

Coontz, Stephanie, via phone, August 6, 2016.

Crawley, Clare, via phone, July 27, 2016.

Crescenti, Tim, via phone, December 13, 2016.

Crevier, Glen, via phone, November 18, 2016.

Csincsak, Jesse, via phone, October 6, 2016.

Douglas, Susan, via phone, August 10, 2016.

Dries, Kate, via phone, February 14, 2017.

Ferriter, John, Los Angeles, November 3, 2016.

Fisher, Helen, via phone, August 9, 2016.

Flajnik, Ben, via phone, September 30, 2015.

Forester, Brooks, Los Angeles, May 10, 2016.

Garofola, Michael, New York City, May 17, 2016.

Gerson, Kathleen, via phone, September 16, 2016.

Glaser, Nikki, via phone, July 23, 2017.

Gray, Emma, via phone, May 8, 2017.

Greenfield, David, Los Angeles, July 31, 2016.

Hains, Rebecca, via phone, December 9, 2016.

Hatta, Ben, via phone, October 3, 2015.

Iaconetti, Ashley, via phone, February 13, 2017.

Isenberg, Brad, via phone, May 3, 2016.

Iyengar, Sheena, via phone, October 4, 2016.

Jeffress, Scott, Los Angeles, September 30, 2015.

Johnson, Chad, via phone, June 12, 2017.

Johnson, Sandi, Los Angeles, January 13, 2017.

Joynt, Sharleen, via video call, September 23, 2015.

Lowe, Catherine, via phone, October 7, 2016.

Lowe, Sean, via phone, September 28, 2016.

Lynskey, Melanie, via phone, August 1, 2017.

Maguire, Daniel, Los Angeles, August 17, 2017.

Majors, Evan, via video call, December 9, 2016.

Malina, Joshua, via phone, August 30, 2017.

Miller, Kallissa, Los Angeles, September 19, 2016.

O'Neill, Rosie, via phone, December 19, 2016.

Papa, Rozlyn, via phone, August 18, 2016.

Perrin, Duan, via phone, May 4, 2016.

Phillips, Meredith, Portland, Oregon, June 12, 2016.

Pratt, Heidi and Spencer, via phone, August 30, 2017.

Price, Dave, via phone, May 2, 2016.

Rego, Justin, via video call, July 10, 2016.

Renfroe, Jay, Los Angeles, August 25, 2016.

Ritter, Jason, via phone, August 23, 2017.

Robinson, Craig, via phone, June 13, 2017.

Rose, Erica, Los Angeles, July 6, 2016.

Scheer, Paul, via phone, January 26, 2017.

Schumer, Amy, via phone, January 12, 2017.

Siegfried, Desiree, via phone, August 8, 2016.

Stanger, Patti, via phone, August 25, 2017.

Tatar, Maria, via phone, December 13, 2016.

Ventiera, Vinny, Los Angeles, August 17, 2017.

Viall, Nick, Los Angeles, October 5, 2015.

Wahlberg, Donnie, via phone, August 28, 2017.

Waterman, Jen Schefft, via phone, July 6, 2016.

Williams, Allison, via email, July 11, 2017.

Zeisler, Andi, via phone, December 5, 2016.

Selected Bibliography

BOOKS

Ackerman, Diane. *A Natural History of Love.* New York: Vintage, 1994.

Ansari, Aziz, with Eric Klinenberg. *Modern Romance.* New York: Penguin Books, 2015.

Cherlin, Andrew J. *The Marriage-Go-Round: The State of Marriage and the Family in America Today.* New York: Vintage, 2010.

Coontz, Stephanie. *Marriage, a History: How Love Conquered Marriage.* New York: Viking Penguin, 2005.

Dorfman, Andi. *It's Not Okay: Turning Heartbreak into Happily Never After.* New York: Gallery Books, 2016.

Fisher, Helen. *Anatomy of Love: A Natural History of Mating, Marriage, and Why We Stray.* New York: W. W. Norton & Company, 2016.

———. *Why We Love: The Nature and Chemistry of Romantic Love.* New York: Henry Holt and Company, 2004.

Fleiss, Mike, and Michael Silver. *Sports with an Attitude: The World's Most Irreverent Sports Quiz Book.* New York: Price Stern Sloan, 1993.

Guiney, Bob. *What a Difference a Year Makes: How Life's Unexpected Setbacks Can Lead to Unexpected Joy.* New York: Tarcher, 2003.

Harrison, Chris. *The Perfect Letter.* New York: Dey Street Books, 2015.

Iyengar, Sheena. *The Art of Choosing.* New York: Twelve, 2010.

Johnson, Emily Maynard. *I Said Yes: My Story of Heartbreak, Redemption, and True Love.* Nashville, TN: Nelson Books, 2016.

Klein, Jessi. *You'll Grow Out of It.* New York: Grand Central Publishing, 2016.

Leo, Richard A. *Police Interrogation and American Justice.* Boston: Harvard University Press, 2008.

Lowe, Sean, with Nancy French. *For the Right Reasons: America's Favorite Bachelor on Faith, Love, Marriage, and Why Nice Guys Finish First.* Nashville, TN: Nelson Books, 2015.

Pozner, Jennifer L. *Reality Bites Back: The Troubling Truth about Guilty Pleasure TV.* Berkeley, CA: Seal Press, 2010.

Robertson, Courtney, with Deb Baer. *I Didn't Come Here to Make Friends: Confessions of a Reality Show Villain.* New York: It Books, 2014.

Rycroft, Melissa. *My Reality.* New York: Gallery Books, 2012.

Schefft, Jen. *Better Single Than Sorry: A No-Regrets Guide to Loving Yourself and Never Settling.* New York: William Morrow, 2007.

Sutter, Trista. *Happily Ever After: The Life-Changing Power of a Grateful Heart.* Boston: Da Capo Lifelong Books, 2013.

ARTICLES

"ABC Enters into Multi-Year, Wide-Ranging Deal with Producer Mike Fleiss and Telepictures Productions." PR Newswire, October 10, 2002.

"ABC: Former Bachelor Contestants Mull Class Action." *Class Action Reporter,* February 28, 2012.

Adalian, Josef. "Reality Vet Signs Eye's Dotted Line." *Daily Variety,* April 22, 2003.

——, and Michael Schneider. "WB Ramps Up Reality Skeins." *Daily Variety,* October 15, 2001.

Angelo, Megan. "The Roses! The Romance! The Roasts!" *New York Times,* February 12, 2012.

Aurthur, Kate. "'Bachelor' Faces Up to the Harsh Reality." *Los Angeles Times,* May 15, 2002.

——. "Reality Stars Keep on Going and Going." *New York Times,* October 10, 2004.

——. "'The Bachelorette' Ratings Are Falling Hard." *BuzzFeed,* July 11, 2017.

Babb, Christina Hughes. "Hello, Chris Harrison." *Advocate: Lake Highlands Edition,* October 2015.

"Bachelor Contestant Gia Allemand Dies After Apparent Suicide Attempt." CNN Wire, August 14, 2013.

Barney, Chuck. "Reality-TV Impresario Has Finger on Viewers' Hot and Sordid Pulse." *Contra Costa Times,* February 18, 2003.

Bellafante, Ginia. "One Small Step for Man, 25 Backward for Women." *New York Times,* April 14, 2002.

Belloni, Matthew, and James Hibberd. "Unscripted Win Is Dose of Reality." *Hollywood Reporter,* January 22, 2009.

Boedeker, Hal. "The Guy Who Saved ABC." *Orlando Sentinel,* January 15, 2003.

Braxton, Greg. "'Bachelor' Casting at Issue." *Los Angeles Times,* March 18, 2011.

Brodesser, Claude. "Feuds." *Variety,* June 7, 2004–June 13, 2004.

Brownfield, Paul. "Fox Has Own 'Bachelor' Idea." *Los Angeles Times,* December 3, 2002.

———. "In a War of Bad Taste, There Are No Winners." *Los Angeles Times,* January 5, 2005.

———. "TV's Big Noisemaker—and Proud of It." *Los Angeles Times,* November 20, 2002.

Byrne, Alanna. "ABC's 'The Bachelor' Sued for Racial Bias." *Inside Counsel,* April 2012.

"Calling All Brides . . . A Nationwide Search Begins for Potential Brides Willing to Marry a Millionaire Live from Las Vegas on Network Television." Business Wire, December 7, 1999.

Carlson, Erin. "It's the Women, Not the Bachelor, That Keeps 'The Bachelor' Going." Associated Press, April 17, 2007.

———. "Producer: 'Bachelor' Finale Wasn't Fixed." Associated Press, March 4, 2009.

Carr, David. "Casting Reality TV, No Longer a Hunch, Becomes a Science." *New York Times,* March 28, 2004.

———. "Viewers Don't Want Conventional." *New York Times,* August 27, 2012.

Carter, Bill. "Even as Executives Scorn the Genre, TV Networks Still Rely on Reality." *New York Times,* May 19, 2003.

———. "TV's Millionaire Groom Has a Past in Entertainment." *New York Times,* February 18, 2000.

Chocano, Carina. "Just Call It America's Funniest Prostitutes." *Salon,* February 21, 2000.

———. "Who Wants to Marry a Multimillionaire?" *Salon,* February 16, 2000.

Collins, Scott. "It's a New Reality for ABC, WB." *Los Angeles Times,* May 19, 2004.

De Moraes, Lisa. "He May Make $19,000, But 'Joe' Brings In 19 Million—Viewers." *Washington Post,* January 8, 2003.

Farhi, Paul. "On Fox, Making Reality a Reality." *Washington Post,* February 10, 2003.

———. "Popping the Question." *Washington Post,* November 20, 2002.

Fernandez, Maria Elena. "Bighearted." *Los Angeles Times,* July 19, 2009.

Flahardy, Cathleen. "Racial Discrimination Case Against 'The Bachelor' Dismissed." *Inside Counsel,* October 2012.

"'Frankenbiting' Scares Up Reality Controversy." *Newsday,* July 21, 2005.

Freydkin, Donna. "Reality-Show Contestants Raise Glasses, Concerns." *USA Today,* February 18, 2003.

———. "Will Viewers Find 'Bachelorette' as Engaging as 'The Bachelor'?" *USA Today,* November 25, 2002.

———. "Young and Voyeuristic." *USA Today,* January 15, 2003.

Gajewski, Ryan. "The 'Bachelor' Mansion's Owner Tells All." *Us Weekly,* January 2, 2017.

Gardner, Chris. "Hitched, Hatched, Hired." *Hollywood Reporter,* May 22, 2015.

Gay, Verne. "Will Viewers Tune In to Feel the Pain?" *Newsday,* January 8, 2003.

Gerhart, Ann, and Jennifer Frey. "Runners-Up in the Bridal Sweepstakes." *Washington Post,* February 19, 2000.

"Ghoulish New US TV Game Show Concept Pits Relatives in Battle of Wills." *Agence France Presse*, October 25, 2002.

Goldstein, Patrick. "Reality Moves Up to the Big Time." *Los Angeles Times*, April 22, 2003.

Gordon, Julie. "'Bachelor' Secrets Spilled." *amNewYork*, March 5, 2009.

Grego, Melissa. "'Bachelor' Boss Weds." *Daily Variety*, October 10, 2002.

Hibberd, James. "'Bachelor' Cleans Up." *Hollywood Reporter*, March 3, 2009.

"Inside *The Bachelor*; A Human Behavior Lab." ABC News Transcript, March 15, 2010.

"Inside *The Bachelor*; Stories Behind the Rose." ABC News Transcript, July 26, 2010.

James, Caryn. "It's Her Turn, but Don't Call Her Heartbreaker." *New York Times*, January 8, 2003.

Lang, Derrik J. "As the Writers' Strike Winds Down, Reality TV Continues to Grow Up." Associated Press, February 12, 2008.

Leitereg, Neal J. "Hot Property: A Change of Genre in Calabasas." *Los Angeles Times*, May 21, 2016.

Lisotta, Christopher. "Is Honeymoon Over for ABC's 'Bachelor'?" *Television Week*, April 18, 2005.

Littlejohn, Janice Rhoshalle. "'Bachelor': A Little Sweet, A Little Bitter." *Los Angeles Times*, April 22, 2002.

Longwell, Todd. "What Price Reality?" *Hollywood Reporter*, June 5, 2009.

Lowry, Brian. "Cold Reality Is Setting In." *Los Angeles Times*, March 1, 2000.

———. "Fox Hands Rivals a 'Wedding' Present." *Los Angeles Times*, February 24, 2000.

———. "In Reality, There's Really No Such Thing as Bad Buzz." *Los Angeles Times,* January 20, 2003.

———. "Probe Absolves 'Multi-Millionaire,' Fox Says." *Los Angeles Times,* April 13, 2000.

"Mel Gibson Sells California Home to the 'Bachelor' Creator." WENN Entertainment News Wire Service, October 8, 2012.

"Mike Fleiss Marries Laura Kaeppeler." *Yerepouni Daily News,* April 10, 2014.

Mongillo, Peter. "What Does Guy from Texas Know About 'Jersey Shore'?" *Austin-American Statesman,* January 6, 2011.

"Multimillionaire Groom Was In Fact a Stand-Up Comic Linked to Fox TV." *Edmonton Journal,* February 18, 2000.

"New 'Bachelor' Says He Liked Anonymity." Associated Press Online, April 19, 2004.

"Nominate Your Favorite Candidate for America's Most Eligible Bachelor." PR Newswire, October 8, 2001.

Peyser, Marc. "Spinsterhood Is Powerful." *Newsweek,* January 13, 2003.

Poggi, Jeanine. "The Business of 'The Bachelor.'" *Advertising Age,* October 12, 2015.

Quinn, Steve. "The Natural." *Dallas Morning News,* May 18, 2003.

"Rick Rockwell Talks About His 'Multimillionaire' Marriage." *Larry King Live,* February 29, 2000.

Rosenthal, Phil. "Looking for Love in All the Wrong Places." *Chicago Sun-Times,* January 6, 2003.

Rubin, Daniel. "A Spurned Husband's Altered State for Millionaire, 'A Rough Couple of Days.'" *Philadelphia Inquirer,* February 27, 2000.

Satzman, Darrell. "Home of the Week: A Modern Take on a Stately Classic." *Los Angeles Times,* March 6, 2011.

Seal, Mark. "Reality Kings." *Vanity Fair,* July 2003.

"Sean Lowe and Catherine Giudici Exchanged Vows and Neil Lane Wedding Bands During the Much-Anticipated ABC Special 'The Bachelor: Sean and Catherine's Wedding.'" PR Newswire, January 29, 2014.

Seibel, Deborah Starr. "Reality As They Know It: One Hectic Day in the Lives of Four Power Brokers." *Broadcasting & Cable,* August 30, 2004.

Sigesmund, B. J. "Behind 'The Bachelor.'" *Newsweek,* April 11, 2002.

Smith, Emily. "Now He's 'Bachelor' Himself." *New York Post,* March 7, 2012.

Speier, Michael. "The Bachelor." *Daily Variety,* March 25, 2002.

Stanley, Alessandra. "Blurring Reality with Soap Suds." *New York Times,* February 22, 2003.

———. "It's All About Hottitude and Tweaking 'Reality.'" *New York Times,* February 13, 2003.

———. "When in Rome, Bachelorettes, Just Pretend It's Las Vegas, with More Convincing Props." *New York Times,* October 2, 2006.

Starr, Michael. "'Bachelor' Looks for a Tough Guy . . . Any Ideas, Fellas?" *New York Post,* May 29, 2002.

Steinberg, Brian. "How ABC Keeps Fans in Love with 'The Bachelor.'" *Advertising Age,* February 11, 2011.

Tomashoff, Craig. "A Barnum of Reality Chases the Relateable Concept." *New York Times,* February 23, 2003.

———. "Casting Reality TV? It's Now Difficult to Find Real People." *New York Times,* August 28, 2011.

Triplett, Ward. "He's Got Game." *Kansas City Star,* April 28, 2004.

"TV Mogul Mike Fleiss' Disturbing the Peace Charge to Be Dismissed." WENN Entertainment News Wire Service, March 9, 2015.

Volmers, Eric. "The Bachelor King, Mike Fleiss, Shares His Secrets in Banff." *Calgary Herald*, June 13, 2012.

Wilson, Craig. "Why People Will Do Almost Anything to Get on TV." *USA Today*, February 25, 2000.

Wong, Tony. "A Night at the Bachelor Mansion." *Toronto Star*, February 16, 2013.

Wyatt, Edward. "The Reality of Hollywood's Sweatshop: Low Pay, Few Breaks." *International Herald Tribune*, August 3, 2009.

Yahr, Emily. "Days of Whine and Roses." *Washington Post*, December 16, 2012.

Youn, Soo. "'Bachelor' Creator Charged in Malibu Dispute with David Charvet, Brooke Burke." *Hollywood Reporter*, November 20, 2014.

LAWSUITS

Claybrooks v. American Broadcasting Companies: https://www.leagle.com/decision/infdco20121016b40

Sharp v. Next Entertainment: https://casetext.com/case/sharp-v-next-entertainment

Index

Aaron, Hank, 18
Abasolo, Bryan, 107, 277
ABC, 1, 2, 3, 19, 28, 41, 42, 44, 46, 47,
    49, 52, 56, 58, 59, 77, 84, 93, 94,
    98, 99, 100, 103, 104, 105, 107,
    115, 116, 123, 129, 140, 151, 186,
    188, 202, 219, 220, 221, 257, 259,
    261, 264
Academy Awards, 202
Access Hollywood (TV show), 227
acts, episodes broken into, 161
Adams, Wells, 182, 232
adrenaline dates, 133–34
advertisement opportunities,
    225–27, 256
advertisers and moral standard, 167
affairs with producers, 157–61, 214–15
African Americans, 103, 104, 105, 106
after cameras stop rolling, 203–7
"After the Final Rose" (specials), 32, 54,
    89, 90, 257
Aladdin (movie), 189
alcohol (drinking). *See also* Bachelor
    franchise
  under the covers (sex), 181, 182
  Inside the Bubble strategy, 117,
    121–26, 130, 132, 133
  key element, 3, 35, 111, 223, 246

method to the madness, 154, 155, 157,
    158, 164
producer manipulation using, 4, 245
Allison (talent agency worker), 10
All the Hate Mail! (Gale), 151
Allure, 101
Ally McBeal (TV show), 47
"Almost Paradise" (Reno and Wilson), 123
American Idol (TV show), 18
American Pie (movies), 6
"America's Most Eligible Bachelor,"
    28–29
Aniston, Jennifer, 261
Antebi, Vera, 233–34
AOL, 72, 247
applications for *Bachelor,* 77–81
Archive of American Television, 57
Are You the One? (TV show), 166
Aron, Arthur, 134
Atlantis, 228
@midnight (TV show), 68
Auerbach, Gary (producer), 67

Bach Discuss (e-mail group), 3, 9, 10, 11,
    225, 238, 261
"*Bachelor, The:* Why Smart Women Watch
    (and Love) It" *(HuffPost),* 253

Index

Bachelor, The (TV show). *See also*
Bachelor franchise; Fleiss, Mike;
*Who Wants to Marry a Multi-
Millionaire?* (special); *specific
contestants*
affairs with producers, 158–61, 214–15
budding idea for, 15, 27–32
budget for, 32
Cinderella date, 185–86
dates on, 128–34
demographics, 227, 255, 257, 261
editing, 163–64
engagements broken, 24
falling for the fairy tale, 185–89, 190,
191, 193, 195, 196, 204–5, 206
"I liked fucking you" (Galavis), 136–37
intoxicated by happily ever after,
191–95, 247–65
late-night swim, 171–73
lawsuit by *Bachelor* employees, 42–43
list of bachelors, 271–74
make-it-or-break-it discussion,
198–99, 208
marriages from, 3
racial discrimination lawsuit against,
103–4
ratings success, 41, 44, 45–46, 47, 49,
52, 130, 225, 246, 256
reality of creating the fantasy, 35–49
reviews/criticisms of, 44–45, 46, 49, 103
riding the coattails (income from), 227
sex pre-Fantasy Suite, 171–73
trade-outs, 129–31
Virgin Bachelor (Lowe), 177, 178
Bachelor candy, 261
Bachelorette, The (TV show). *See also*
Bachelor franchise; Fleiss, Mike;
specific contestants
crying, 39
falling for the fairy tale, 193, 195,
203–4
idea for, 49–50
list of bachelorettes, 275–77
ratings success, 105, 225, 256
reality of creating the fantasy, 50–52
rejecting proposals, 195–96, 198, 200

reviews/criticisms of, 51–52
sex pre-Fantasy Suite, 174–76, 177, 180
villain, 165–66
Bachelorette Party (podcast), 256
Bachelor franchise. *See also* alcohol;
Bachelor Nation; fairy-tale
romance; Fleiss, Mike; Kaufman,
Amy; love; marriage; producer
manipulation; reality television;
roses; why I'm a fan; *specific
Bachelor shows and specials;
specific contestants*
after cameras stop rolling, 203–7
applications, 77–81
background checks, 23, 25, 62, 79,
85, 237
basking in afterglow (fame),
211–22, 264
budding idea for, 15–32
contracts for contestants, 12, 86–89, 113
under the covers (sex), 171–82
crying, 39, 86, 99, 102, 109, 124,
145–46, 152, 154, 156, 163, 172,
173, 245
diversity on, 103–7
drafting a game plan, 97–111
Fantasy Suite, 12, 51, 140–41, 146,
173–74, 176, 177, 178–80, 181
golden ticket (husband plus luxury),
10–11, 19–21, 34, 45, 76, 79, 130,
191, 252
ideal date, 9, 28, 29, 30, 66, 79, 130,
189–90, 207
Inside the Bubble strategy, 115–39,
197, 263
intoxicated by happily ever after,
191–95, 247–65
limos, 3, 28, 35, 102, 109–11, 127,
143, 264
mansion, 27, 28, 37, 49, 102, 109, 111,
115–22, 128, 143, 154, 164, 165,
185, 186
method to the madness, 143–67, 251
money negotiations, 99
princess dream, 112–13, 118–19,
185–91, 246, 252

Index

ratings success, 41, 44, 45–46, 47, 49, 52, 105, 130, 225, 246, 256
reasons for being on, 89–92, 93, 97, 125, 171, 192
reviews/criticisms of, 44–45, 46, 49, 51–52, 103, 124–25, 188, 264
riding the coattails (income from), 225–44
road to the mansion (casting), 77–93
roots of television romance, 55–74
Bachelor in Paradise (TV show). *See also* Bachelor franchise; *specific contestants*
basking in afterglow, 221
drunken incidents, 125–26
falling for the fairy tale, 205
marriages from, 3
method to the madness, 154–56
pool encounter, 123–24, 181, 182
raccoon, Crawley confiding in a, 162–63
riding the coattails (income from), 226, 228
spin-off, 93, 123
Bachelor Nation (rose lovers), 1, 2, 105, 150, 177, 184, 205, 212, 220, 221, 226, 227, 228, 248, 252, 256. *See also* Bachelor franchise; Kaufman, Amy; why I'm a fan
"Bachelor pad," crashing at, 42
Bachelor Pad (TV show), 154, 155, 157–58
Bachelor Wines, The, 233, 260–61
background checks, 23, 25, 62, 79, 85, 237
Badgley Mischka, 52, 187, 202
Baldwin, Andrew, 12–13, 273
Banff World Media Festival, 85
Barris, Chuck, 55–57, 58, 59–60
Basketball Wives LA (TV show), 221
basking in afterglow (fame), 211–22, 264
BBC, 183
Beatles, The, 57
Beat the Clock (TV show), 61
beauty and fairy tales, 190, 191
bedrooms in the mansion, 117

Better Single Than Sorry: A No-Regrets Guide to Loving Yourself & Never Settling (Schefft), 196
Big Bang Theory, The (TV show), 21
Big Brother (TV show), 27, 29
Bigger, Eric, 3, 106–7
Big Lebowski, The (movie), 27
biographical info on contestants, 84, 107–8
Bischoff, Whitney, 236, 274
Bitch Media, 176
Black Sabbath, 26
Blind Date (TV show), 69–72
blogs, 257–60
Bloom, Orlando, 241
Blue Bloods (TV show), 210
Bochco, Steven (producer), 47
body types, 4, 5, 33–34, 44, 78, 80, 81, 141, 256
"boink date," 64, 66
Booth, Shawn, 176, 235, 276
Borghese, Lorenzo, 101, 173–74, 187–89, 207, 272
Boston Consulting Group, 29
Boteach, Rabbi Shmuley, 24
Bowlin, Jessica, 272
Bracket Room, 213
brain and love, 134–36, 138
Bravo, 33, 140
Breaking the Magician's Code (special), 18
Brice, Sarah, 272
Bridges, Abby, 231
Bristowe, Kaitlyn, 93, 141, 174–76, 177, 234, 235, 248, 256, 276
Bubble (Inside the) strategy, 115–39, 197, 263
budding idea, 15–32
Buerge, Aaron, 46, 200–201, 271
Bukowski, Chris, 102, 126, 138, 148, 154–56, 213–14, 215–16
bullying of contestants, 176
bus dating show, 73
Bushnell, Lauren, 201, 274
Bustle (podcast), 256
BuzzFeed, 105

Index

Callahan, Ryan (producer), 159, 160, 161
Calligraphy Katrina, 235
campfire, Bachelor franchise as, 262
candles, 36–37, 83, 117
Canseco, Jose, 17
Caramanica, Jon, 249
Carbone, Steve (Reality Steve), 257–60
careers post-television, 90–92, 217–19, 220, 263
Caridi, Olivia, 100–101, 256
Carroll, Michael (producer), 35–36, 41, 42, 85–86, 102, 105, 120, 122, 129, 143–45, 149, 174, 179, 251
cash incentives for producing team, 38
Castellanos, Liz, 235
casting (road to the mansion), 77–93
Castle (TV show), 150
CBS, 23, 27, 30, 44
celebrities on talk shows about *Bachelor,* 261–62
Celebrity Big Brother (TV show), 94, 95
Celebrity Wife Swap (TV show), 158, 220
Champagne, 12, 35, 111, 122, 235, 243, 246
charity dates, 133
charity events post-television, 228–34
chemistry and love, 245
Chicago Sun-Times, 47, 65
Chicago Tribune, 58
children's lessons from watching, 183–84
Chocano, Carina, 21–22
Chrisleys, The, 94
Christianity, 177, 199, 221
Christian Louboutin, 186, 191
Cinderella (movie), 186
Clark, Dick (producer), 19, 56
Claybrooks, Nathaniel, 103, 104
clothing, 100, 101
club appearances, 227
CNN, 23–24
code names used by production, 131–32
Cody, Diablo, 140–41
Cohen, Andy, 65
Comedy Central, 68
Conger (Rockwell), Darva, 20–21, 22, 24. *See also* Rockwell, Rick
consensual sex, 124

consent discussion, 181–82
consumerism and princess dream, 191
Contra Costa Times, 16, 48
contracts for contestants, 12, 86–89, 113
control room, 37–38, 41, 117, 144
Coontz, Stephanie, 191–92, 193, 202–3, 207–8
Cosby Show, The (TV show), 104
Cosmopolitan.com, 227
Cougar, The (TV show), 47
cradle-to-grave marketing, 189–90
Crawley, Clare, 119, 136–37, 138, 162–63, 171–73, 174, 179, 197
Creative Artists Agency, 25
Crescenti, Tim (producer), 61, 63, 64–65
Crevier, Glen, 16–17
crying, 39, 86, 99, 102, 109, 124, 145–46, 152, 154, 156, 163, 172, 173, 245
Csincsak, Jesse, 122, 199, 203–4, 275
cultlike obsession, 140
cultural dates, 133
Curb Your Enthusiasm (TV show), 33
cynicism, 184

Daily Cal, The, 16
Dallas Morning News, The, 31
Dance Moms (TV show), 94
Dancing with the Stars (TV show), 93, 219–20
Darnell, Mike, 18, 19, 20, 22, 27–28, 47
Date My Mom (TV show), 73
dates on *Bachelor,* 128–34
dating boot camp, 236–44
Dating Game, The (TV show), 55, 56–58, 59, 60–61
dating life post-televison, 214, 216–17
dating-show genre. *See* Bachelor franchise; roots of television romance; *specific shows*
David (teenage relationship), 6–7
Deen, Paula, 238
DeGeneres, Ellen, 202, 261–62
Delgado, Mary, 272
demographics, 227, 255, 257, 261
Designers' Challenge (TV show), 31

Index

Desisto, Paul, 226, 227
desperation and marriage, 192
diamonds, hypnotizing by, 252
"Diane in 7A" hoax (Gale), 150
DiCaprio, Leonardo, 230
DiDomenico, David, 30
difference, basis of desire, 193
DIFF Eyewear, 225
diversity, 103–7
DoctorFatOff, 226
"Does Bingeing on *The Bachelor* Make
    Me a Bad Feminist?" *(The
    Guardian),* 254
Donnie Loves Jenny (TV show), 210
dopamine, 135–36
Dorfman, Andi, 92, 93, 127, 174–75, 177,
    180, 218–19, 276
Douglas, Susan, 195, 255–56
Downs, Hugh, 24
Downton Abbey (TV show), 183
drafting a game plan, 97–111
drama post-television, 214–15
drinking. *See* alcohol
drunken incidents, 125–26
Dunham, Lena, 11
Dutton, Donald, 134
Dynasty (TV show), 48

eBay, 201
editing process, 94, 161–64, 221, 251, 263
Eksterowicz, Helene, 201, 271
Electra, Carmen, 68
"elements of surprise," 87
Elle, 253
Elle Decor, 117
Elon Musk, 246
"emotional and mental distress," 88
"emotional leveraging," 145–46
E! News, 124
*Enlightened Sexism: The Seductive
    Message That Feminism's Work Is
    Done* (Douglas), 255
Entertainment Tonight (TV show), 214
Entertainment Weekly, 68, 104
E! (TV show), 235

Everlasting (fictional TV show), 248
Exclusive Matchmaking, 237, 238
Exposed (TV show), 73

FabFitFun, 225, 226, 233
Facebook, 78, 216, 231
Faddoul, Lacy, 3
fairy-tale romance (falling for the fairy
    tale). *See also* Bachelor franchise;
    golden ticket; love; marriage;
    princess dream
  falling for the fairy tale, 185–208
  fantasies about, 9–10, 11, 12, 24, 75
  happily ever after, 191–92, 247–65
  Kaufman and, 5–6, 6–7
  love, 191–93, 196–98
  reality of creating the fantasy,
    36–37, 47
  roots of television romance, 55–74
Fallon, Claire, 256
fame, basking in afterglow, 211–22, 264
fame whore, 79
Family Feud (TV show), 61
family friction post-television, 215–17
Family Guy (TV show), 18
fans. *See* Bachelor Nation; why I'm a fan
Fantasy Suite, 12, 51, 140–41, 146,
    173–74, 176, 177, 178–80, 181
Fantasy Suite (wine), 261
Fastlane (TV show), 48
fear and adrenaline dates, 133–34
Fedotowsky, Ali, 103, 110, 157, 165, 216,
    275–76
feminism, 11, 44–45, 46, 49, 53–54,
    75–76, 176, 195, 196, 250, 251,
    253–56
Fergie (Stacy Ferguson), 68–69, 202
Ferguson, Emily and Haley, 230
Fernet Francisco, 218
Ferrell, Nikki, 136, 274
Ferris, Jerry, 196, 275
Ferriter, John, 19, 21, 25
Fetman, Cary, 100
Fifty Shades Darker (movie), 227
Final Rosé (wine), 261

Index

Firestone, Andrew, 139, 168, 195–96, 212, 250, 271
First Amendment, 104
"first-impression rose," 127–28, 160
first out of the limos, 110
Fisher, Helen, 134, 135, 138, 193, 262
Flajnik, Ben, 99, 103, 150, 151–52, 153, 163–64, 168, 180, 200, 206–7, 218, 259, 274
Flashdance (movie), 64
Flavor of Love (TV show), 104
Fleiss, Aaron, 18, 48
Fleiss, Heidi ("Hollywood Madam"), 15, 30
Fleiss, Mike (creator and producer), 15–27. *See also* Bachelor franchise; *specific other programs by*
  affairs with producers reported to, 158
  Alexandra Vorbeck (wife), 16, 40, 43, 48
  Bachelorette, The (TV show) and, 49–51
  background checks, 85
  Barris and, 55–56
  budding idea for *The Bachelor*, 27–32
  diversity view of, 104
  Flajnik and, 164
  Kaufman and, 13
  Laura Kaeppeler (wife), 48
  Levenson and, 36, 43–44
  mansion and, 116
  partying and, 41–42
  reality of creating the fantasy, 41, 45, 47–48, 49
  salesmanship of, 49
  sex appeal, 48–49
  stipend from wife, 40
  wedding offer to Csincsak, 203
  weed and, 15, 16, 27, 36, 40–41
Fletcher, JoJo, 105, 231, 233, 276–77
food, 118, 119, 130, 132
Footloose (movie), 123
Forester, Brooks, 127, 146, 147, 197–98
Fox, 17, 18, 19, 20, 22, 23, 24, 25, 26, 28, 39, 46, 47, 48, 65
"Frankenbiting," 161–62

friendship, successful relationships, 7, 192, 207–8
Friends (TV show), 75
"fun packet," casting process, 84

Galavis, Juan Pablo, 83, 119, 120, 133, 136–38, 147, 148, 149, 153, 171, 172, 173, 174, 179, 197, 198, 274
Gale, Elan (producer), 13, 150–51, 152–56, 158, 165
"Galentine's Day Party," 234–35
Game of Thrones (TV show), 95, 223
Game Show King, The (Barris), 58
Gardinier, Estella, 272
Garfinkle, David (producer), 70
Garofola, Michael, 91–92
Garrett, Lee, 105
General Hospital (TV show), 35
Gerson, Kathleen, 194
Get Out (movie), 54
getting in shape, contestants, 100, 101, 102
Gibbons, Leeza, 24
gifts to coworkers from Levenson, 40
Girardi, Vienna, 273
"girl chats," 120–21
Girls (TV show), 54
Giudici (Lowe), Catherine, 97, 100, 198–99, 202, 204–6, 208, 220, 221–22, 274. *See also* Lowe, Sean
Glaser, Nikki, 75–76
Golden Globes, 202
golden ticket (husband plus luxury), 10–11, 19–21, 34, 45, 76, 79, 130, 191, 252. *See also* fairy-tale romance; love
Gong Show, The (TV show), 55, 58, 59
Good Morning America (TV show), 108, 213
Goodson-Todman, 61
Google, 138, 211, 214, 216, 241, 242
Gosling, Ryan, 81
Graden, Brian, 73
Grant, Matt, 13, 273
Grateful Dead, 26, 27, 57

Index

Gray, Emma, 256–57
Greatest Sports Moments of All Time (special), 18
Greenfield, David (producer), 59–61
Grimaldi, Vanessa, 93, 274
Grodd, Marcus, 3
group dates, 183
Grushow, Sandy, 23
Guardian, The, 254
Guardians of the Galaxy Vol. 2 (movie), 150
Guiney, Bob, 51, 128, 250, 272
Guinness Book of Records, The, 23
Gunn, James, 150

Hains, Rebecca, 189, 190, 191
Hamilton (Broadway show), 209
handlers, 82, 83, 84, 98, 109
Hanson, 233
happily ever after, 191–95, 247–65
"Happy Couples" rendezvous, 204
Haraden, Marshall, 115–16
Hardwick, Chris, 66, 67, 68
Harris, Jillian, 98, 103, 275
Harrison, Chris (host), 1, 30–31, 44, 50, 117, 125, 151, 152, 160, 164, 165, 175–76, 181, 236, 252–53
Harry Winston, 200
Hartsock (Siegfried), Desiree, 90–91, 98–99, 127, 177–78, 197, 276. *See also* Siegfried, Chris
Hasselbeck, Elisabeth, 196
Hatta, Ben (Fleiss's assistant and producer), 26, 27, 29, 40, 41, 43, 85, 118–19, 145–46, 156–57
Hayes, Robby, 3
Heavenly Creatures (movie), 113
Hebert (Rosenbaum), Ashley, 103, 200, 202, 276. *See also* Rosenbaum, J. P.
heights, fear of, 4–5, 6, 78
helicopters, 4, 8, 9, 78, 88, 128–29, 136, 146, 224, 252, 262, 264
HelloGiggles, 238
Hendrix, Jimi, 26
Here Comes Honey Boo Boo (TV show), 221

Here on Earth (movie), 5
Here to Make Friends (podcast), 256
herpes, 85
Herron, Sarah, 125, 126, 233
Hewitt, Jennifer Love, 68
HGTV, 31
hidden cameras and microphones, 87
Higgins, Ben, 100, 156, 201, 227, 256, 274
High School Reunion (TV show), 47, 250
Hills, The (TV show), 95
Hilton, Martin (producer), 98, 198
Holder, Eric, 92
Hollywood Reporter, 26
Holm, Jeff, 276
hometown dates, 106, 138, 173
Horst, Tessa, 273
host. *See* Harrison, Chris
Hotel Bel-Air, 234–35
Howard Stern Show (TV show), 17
HuffPost, 253, 256
human desire for love, 15, 24, 75, 94, 95, 97, 223
husband plus luxury. *See* golden ticket

Iaconetti, Ashley, 3, 101, 186–87, 189, 226–27, 228, 231, 232–33, 256, 261
ideal date, 9, 28, 29, 30, 66, 79, 130, 189–90, 207
I Didn't Come Here to Make Friends: Confessions of a Reality Show Villain (Robertson), 164
iHeartRadio, 227
"I liked fucking you" (Galavis), 136–37
Inside Amy Schumer (TV show), 34
Inside the Bubble strategy, 115–39, 197, 263
Instagram, 78, 79, 90, 94, 101, 156, 212, 221, 222, 225–26, 227, 228, 230, 231, 235, 236, 258, 259, 260
Internet, 72, 138, 150
"in-the-moment" (ITM) interviews, 82–83, 107, 117, 121, 143–50, 165, 175, 178, 185, 197

Index

In Touch, 100
intoxicated by happily ever after, 191–95, 247–65
introductions (limo entrances), 109–11, 127
Isenberg, Brad, 41, 119
isolation of contestants, 88, 109, 118, 149, 245
Italian Americans, 104
It's Not Okay: Turning Heartbreak into Happily Never After (Dorfman), 218–19

Jackass (TV show), 46
Jackson, DeMario, 123, 124, 181, 182
Jackson, Michael, 64
James, Caryn, 46, 52
Jared, 201
Jaskiewicz, Victoria, 229, 230
Jeffress, Scott (producer), 25–26, 28, 30, 36–37, 37–38, 39, 41–42, 49, 51, 103, 122–23, 166–67, 174, 253, 263
Jenny McCarthy Show, The (TV show), 68
Jeopardy! (TV show), 57
Jerry Springer (TV show), 35
Jersey Shore (TV show), 104
Jezebel (blog), 2
Joe Millionaire (TV show), 46–47, 257
Johnson, Chad, 125–26
Johnson, Christopher, 103, 104
Johnson, Sandi (producer), 40, 48–49
Jolie, Angelina, 202
Journal of Personality and Social Psychology, 134
Joynt, Sharleen, 83–84, 120–21, 137–38, 147–48, 149, 153–54
judging others, 209, 248, 255, 264, 270
Jumbo Jet Crash: The Ultimate Safety Test, 19
Juno (movie), 141

Kaeppeler, Laura (Fleiss's second wife), 48
Kardashians, 11, 76, 90, 94, 115, 230
Katie (film critic), 10

Kaufman, Amy, 1–13. *See also* Bachelor franchise; Bachelor Nation
 application for *Bachelor,* 78–81
 banned from *Bachelor* events, 1–3, 4, 77, 78, 152
 fairy-tale romance, 5–6, 6–7
 Fleiss and, 13
 Gale and, 150–51, 152–53
 "in-the-moment" (ITM) interview, 143–45
 marriage and, 8, 9, 79
 reasons for watching, 263–65
Kay Jewelers, 4, 201
Kelley, David E. (producer), 47
Kendrick, Anna, 95
Keuhn, Sheena, 230
Kevin (Probably) Saves the World (TV show), 224
kids and marriage, 76
Kimmel, Jimmy, 261–62
King, Kenny, 105
King, Larry, 23–24
Klein, Chris, 5, 6
Kraus, Peter, 107
KWTV, 30

L.A. Weekly, 62
LaChapelle, David, 250
Lady Gaga, 230
Lamas, Shayne, 273
Lane, JJ, 3, 232, 248
Lane, Neil, 4, 54, 89, 154, 155, 186, 191, 201–2
Lange, Jim, 56, 58
Larry King Live (TV show), 23–24
last out of the limos, 110
late-night swim (Crawley and Galavis), 171–73
Late Show, The (TV show), 70
LATimes, 2, 249
laughing at other people, 3, 141, 184
Lawrence, Jennifer, 202
lawsuit by *Bachelor* employees, 42–43
League, The (TV show), 169
Leave It to Lamas (TV show), 47

Index

Lenox, 202

Leo, Richard A., 148–49

Let's Make a Deal (TV show), 57

Letterman, David, 70

Levenson, Lisa (producer), 32, 35–37, 38–40, 41, 43–44, 45, 104, 250

LGBTQ, 73

Lieber, Eric (producer), 61, 64, 65

lie detectors, 73

Lifetime, 36, 248

Limbaugh, Rush, 213

limos, 3, 28, 35, 102, 109–11, 127, 143, 264

Lindsay, Rachel, 103, 104, 105, 106–7, 225, 277

lion reunions, 184

Litman, Juliet, 256

LiveJournal (blog), 72

loggers, 161

Lorde, 202

Los Angeles Times, 25, 45

Louis Vuitton, 32

love. *See also* Bachelor franchise; fairy-tale romance; golden ticket; marriage; princess dream

    brain and, 134–36, 138

    fairy-tale romance, 191–93, 196–98

    happily ever after, 262–63, 264–65

    human desire, 15, 24, 75, 94, 95, 97, 223

    Inside the Bubble strategy, 119, 134–36, 138–39

    shifting views of, 11

Love Connection (TV show), 61–65, 66, 67

Love & Hip Hop (TV shows), 94, 221

"love match," 192

Lowe, Sean, 91, 97–98, 99, 102, 110, 127, 177, 178, 179–80, 187, 198–99, 202, 204–6, 208, 211, 219, 220, 221, 274. *See also* Giudici (Lowe), Catherine

LoweCo., 222

LuMee, 233

lust vs. love, 135

Luyendyk, Arie, Jr., 107

Lyne, Susan, 47

Lynskey, Melanie, 112–13, 223–24, 248

Maguire, Daniel, 182

Maitland, Tommy, 58

Majors, Evan, 36, 40, 43, 104

make-it-or-break-it discussion (Lowe and Giudici), 198–99, 208

makeup artist, 100–101

Making a Murderer (TV show), 148

Malaney (Mesnick), Molly, 220–21, 257. *See also* Mesnick, Jason

Malia, James, 235

Malina, Joshua, 183–84

Mall Masters (TV show), 31

"man chats," 120

mansion, 27, 28, 37, 49, 102, 109, 111, 115–22, 128, 143, 154, 164, 165, 185, 186

Mark's Garden, 202, 235

marriage, 3. *See also* Bachelor franchise; fairy-tale romance; love

    budding idea, 19, 21, 22, 24

    happily ever after, 191–95, 247–65

    Kaufman and, 8, 9, 79

    producers owning rights to, 89

    proposals, 3, 8, 10, 20, 28, 37, 45, 46, 50–51, 113, 155, 156, 198–200, 246, 252

    rings, 4, 20, 45, 51, 76, 89, 113, 154, 155, 194, 199, 200–202, 252

    roots of television romance, 63, 71

    shifting views of, 11

    successful relationships, 207–8

    wedding industry, 202–3, 234

Marriage, A History: How Love Conquered Marriage (Coontz), 191–92

Marriage Boot Camp: Reality Stars (TV show), 95, 221, 222

Married . . . with Children (TV show), 17

Marriott, Evan, 47

Marsh, Amanda, 45, 271

Martinez, Roberto, 275–76

Mason, Ashley, 231

Mastrangelo, Karri-Leigh (producer), 157–58
Match.com, 134, 193, 233
Match Game (TV show), 57
Mayer, John, 261
Maynard, Emily, 97, 100, 102, 110, 138, 211, 273, 276
McCarthy, Jenny, 66, 67–68, 209
McConaughey, Matthew, 189
McKee, Ian, 275
McNary, Chase, 233–34
medical examination, casting process, 84
menstruation and ITMs, 145
"Men Tell All" (specials), 176, 180
Meredith (newspaper editor), 9, 10, 11
Merritt, John Paul, 196
Mesnick, Jason, 90, 103, 187, 201, 204, 220, 257, 273. *See also* Malaney (Mesnick), Molly
method to the madness, 143–67, 251
Michel, Alex, 29–30, 31, 32, 37, 38, 44, 45, 46, 50, 271
midget on *Dating Game,* 60–61
Miller, Kallissa, 67–68, 69, 73–74
"Millionaire Groom's Dirty Secret" (*The Smoking Gun*), 22
Millionaire Matchmaker, The (TV show), 246
Million Dollar Matchmaker (TV show), 246
"mini dates" auction, 231–32
Mixer Room in the mansion, 117, 120
Models and Mutts date, 133
Mohegan Sun, 227
Molly (podcaster), 11, 238, 240, 242–43
Moonves, Leslie, 23
moral standard and advertisers, 167
Moretz, Chloë Grace, 150
Mosaic nightclub, 232
Mosca, Elise, 154, 155–56
MTV, 46, 67, 68, 69, 73, 104, 166
Murray, Josh, 180, 230, 232, 276
MVMT, 225
Myers, Mike, 58
My Reality (Rycroft), 90

Naked and Afraid (TV show), 70
Nash, Bruce (producer), 18, 25
National Organization for Women (NOW), 44–45
NBC, 21, 28, 56, 68, 130
NCIS (TV show), 21
negotiation, successful relationships, 208
Nelly, 232
Netflix, 79, 148
New Kids on the Block, 210
Newlywed Game, The (TV show), 58, 59
Newsday, 49, 50
New Yorker, 249
New York Post, 46
New York Times, The, 23, 30, 44–45, 46, 51–52, 193, 249
Next Entertainment, 23, 25, 42, 250
Next (TV show), 73
Nicks, Stevie, 238
Nielsen ratings, 105, 246
night-vision cameras, 182
"9 Reasons Strong, Intelligent, Feminist Women Watch *The Bachelor(ette)*" (*Elle*), 253
nipples and *Dating Game,* 60, 61
Nolan, Taylor, 181
notes on each contestant, 107–9
Not Safe with Nikki Glaser (TV show), 76
Noxon, Marti, 248
Nussbaum, Emily, 249
NYPD Blue (TV show), 47

O'Connell, Charlie, 272
Octopussy (movie), 64
Oliver, Mary, 250
Olympios, Corinne, 34, 123, 124, 181, 182, 245
O'Neill, Rosie, 261
One Light Luxury Apartments, 229, 234
One on One (wine), 261
online dating profiles tips, 240–41
opportunities post-television, 219–22
Oprah (TV Show), 195
Orlando Sentinel, 47

Index

Osbourne, Ozzy, 26
Oxford, Kelly, 150

Paisley, Brad, 78
PALIO scale (Personality, Appearance,
    Lifestyle, Intelligence,
    Occupation), 62
Palmer, Jesse, 107–8, 129–30, 131, 132,
    198, 272
Papa, Rozlyn, 86, 89, 90, 128, 158–61,
    214–15
Pappas (Stagliano), DeAnna, 122, 199,
    203–4, 275
Parenthood (TV show), 224
parties on sets, 41–42, 43
Paskin, Willa, 174
Password (TV show), 57
Pavelka, Jake, 79, 86, 103, 128, 158, 159,
    160, 219, 273
Pemberton, Lacey, 46
Penn, Sean, 261
People, 116, 195
Perrin, Duan (producer), 104
Perry, Katy, 241
persecution, fairy tales about, 190–91
personality disorders, reality
    producers, 249
personality tests, casting process, 82, 84
Phillips, Meredith, 39, 43–44, 99,
    201, 275
"physical or verbal aggression," 88
"picker," 66, 67, 69
Pitt, Brad, 241
Playboy, 66, 67, 68, 186, 216
podcasts, 11, 227, 238, 256, 257
Police Interrogation and American Justice
    (Leo), 148–49
pool encounter (Olympios and Jackson),
    123–24, 181, 182
pop-up text bubbles, 69–70
positive delusions, 138
power balance in a relationship, 80
Pozner, Jennifer, 124–25
Pratt, Heidi and Spencer, 94–95
prefrontal cortex, 138

prenuptial agreement, 20–21
Press Democrat, 16–17, 18
Pretty Woman-themed dates, 187
princess dream, 112–13, 118–19, 185–91,
    246, 252. *See also* fairy-tale
    romance; love
Princess Problem, The: Guiding Our Girls
    through the Princess-Obsessed
    Years (Hains), 189–90
private investigator, casting process, 84
producer manipulation. *See also* Bachelor
    franchise
  alcohol and, 4, 245
  contract for contestants, 87
  under the covers (sex), 172, 178–79
  drafting a game plan, 102–3, 109–10
  editing process, 94, 161–64, 221,
    251, 263
  falling for the fairy tale, 197, 198, 200
  happily ever after, 249, 252, 253, 263
  Inside the Bubble strategy, 115–39,
    197, 263
  "in-the-moment" (ITM) interviews,
    82–83, 107, 117, 121, 143–50, 165,
    175, 178, 185, 197
  method to the madness, 143–50,
    152–57, 161–64, 164–67
  reality of creating the fantasy, 37–38,
    48–49
  roles for contestants, 102–3, 123,
    164, 165
  roots of television romance, 60,
    63–64, 65
Project Future Light, 229
proposals, 3, 8, 10, 20, 28, 37, 45, 46,
    50–51, 113, 155, 156, 198–200,
    246, 252
provocateur, 48. *See also* Fleiss, Mike
psychological tests, casting process,
    85–86
publicity requirements, 88–89

quality of life, importance of, 246
Quinn, Molly, 150
Quinn (fictional character), 36

Index

raccoon, confiding in a (Crawley), 162–63
racism, 103–6
ratings success, 41, 44, 45–46, 47, 49, 52, 105, 130, 225, 246, 256
Real Housewives, 65, 90, 94
Reality Bites Back: The Troubling Truth About Guilty Pleasure TV (Pozner), 124–25
Reality Steve (Steve Carbone), 257–60
reality television. *See also* Bachelor franchise; why I'm a fan; *specific reality shows*
  basking in afterglow, 219, 220
  budding idea, 15, 24, 28, 29
  under the covers (sex), 181
  drafting a game plan, 100
  fans of, 12, 76, 94–95, 112, 168, 183, 210
  happily ever after, 248, 249, 256
  reality of creating the fantasy, 35, 44, 46
  road to the mansion (casting), 81, 87, 90, 92
  roots of television romance, 55
reasons for being on *Bachelor,* 89–92, 93, 97, 125, 171, 192
reasons for watching *Bachelor,* 253–54, 263–65
recognition from *Bachelor,* 79, 93, 94, 246
recontextualizing scenes, 162
Rego, Justin ("Rated R"), 110, 165–66
Rehn (Sutter), Trista, 33, 37, 41, 45, 50–51, 52, 202, 203, 219, 275. *See also* Sutter, Ryan
rejecting proposals (Schefft), 195–96, 198, 200
relatability and trust, 146–47
Renfroe, Jay (producer), 70, 71, 72
Reno, Mike, 123
rescue dogs date, 133
Resort at Squaw Creek, 130–31
reunions requirements, 89
reviews/criticisms, 44–45, 46, 49, 51–52, 103, 124–25, 188, 264

"Ride Wit Me" (Nelly), 232
riding the coattails (income from), 225–44
Riggins (dog), 79, 264
Ringer, The (podcast), 256
rings, 4, 20, 45, 51, 76, 89, 113, 154, 155, 194, 199, 200–202, 252
Ritter, Jason, 223–24
Rivers, Joan, 264
road to the mansion (casting), 77–93
Robbie, Margot, 78
Roberts, Julia, 48
Robertson, Courtney, 151–52, 163–64, 206, 274
Robinson, Craig, 157–58, 216–18
Rockwell, Rick, 20, 21, 22, 23–24, 25, 85. *See also* Conger (Rockwell), Darva
Rodgers, Jordan, 276–77
role-reversal. *See Bachelorette, The*
roles defined by producers, 102–3, 123, 164, 165
Rolling Stone, 79
romance. *See* fairy-tale romance
Room Raiders (TV show), 73
roots of television romance, 55–74
Roper (Tolbert), Jade, 184, 185–86, 187, 228–29, 231, 232, 234. *See also* Tolbert, Tanner
Rose, Erica, 43, 101, 164
Rosenbaum, J. P., 202, 276. *See also* Hebert (Rosenbaum), Ashley
roses. *See also* Bachelor franchise
  "After the Final Rose" (specials), 32, 54, 89, 90, 257
  budding idea, 27
  "first-impression rose," 127–28, 160
  Inside the Bubble strategy, 119, 127–28, 129
  reality of creating the fantasy, 35, 37
  rose ceremonies, 43, 44, 100, 110, 117, 128, 159, 161, 162, 234
Royal Pet Club, 188
Rutherford, Angelic, 117
Rycroft, Melissa, 90, 204, 219, 257, 273

Index

Sacramento Union, 16
salary for star, 99
Salesforce, 92
Salon, 21
Sarah Lawrence, 250
Sasha (television host), 9, 10
Sawyer, Diane, 242
"Say Yes to the Dress" parties, 8
Scafaria, Lorene, 248
Scandal (TV show), 184
Scheer, Paul, 168–69
Schefft, Jen, 99, 139, 179, 195–96, 198,
    200, 212–13, 271, 275
Schumer, Amy, 33–34
Seal, Mark, 48
Selden, Catherine (therapist), 83–84, 86
selfies, 11, 151, 229, 233–34
Selleck, Tom, 26
September 11 terrorist attacks, 263
"severe mental stress," 88
Sex and the City (TV show), 196
sex pre-Fantasy Suite (Bristowe and
    Viall), 174–76, 177, 180
sexual exploitation, 44
sexually transmitted diseases (STDs), 84,
    85, 88, 157
sex (under the covers), 171–82
Shapiro, Sarah Gertrude (producer), 248,
    249–52, 253
shared interest, love based on, 193
Sheen, Charlie, 15, 124
SheLift, 233
shirtless Bachelor (Lowe), 102
Shocking Behavior Caught on Tape
    (special), 18–19
Shot of Love with Tila Tequila, A (TV
    show), 104
Shteamer, Casey, 150
Shutterfly, 235
Sideshow Bob (character), 150
Siegfried, Chris, 276. *See also* Hartsock
    (Siegfried), Desiree
Simply Dresses, 230
Simpsons, The (TV show), 150
Singer, Marty, 124
Singled Out (TV show), 66–69

"Singles in America" study (Fisher),
    193–94
single vs. married, 264–65
Sirius XM radio, 68, 262
60 Minutes (TV show), 59
Slate, 174
"slow love," 194
slut-shaming, 11, 180–81
Smoking Gun, The, 22
Snapchat, 228, 233, 260
Snatched (movie), 34, 227
social media, 87, 209, 221, 225, 228, 236,
    256, 261, 263. *See also specific
    social media*
*"Some Evidence for Heightened Sexual
    Attraction Under Conditions of High
    Anxiety"* (Dutton and Aron), 134
Soules, Chris, 101, 140, 186, 226, 236,
    237, 238, 241–42, 243, 244, 274
Spears, Britney, 76
Spelling, Aaron (producer), 18, 48
Spelling, Tori, 90
Spider-Man (Broadway show), 209
Splash (spa), 72
SponCon, 94, 225
sports and Bachelor franchise, 223
Sports Night (TV show), 183
Sprinkles, 233
Stanger, Patti, 245–46
Stanley, Alessandra, 46
Stanton, Amanda, 230, 232
Star, 196
Stern, Howard, 168, 262
Stone, Sarah, 272
Storify, 150
Stork, Travis Lane, 272
"strenuous physical activity," 88
Stuart Weitzman, 52, 202
stylists, 100, 185, 186
successful relationships, 207–8
"suffused in romantic love," 194
SugarBearHair, 225
Sugarfina, 261
Sunday Night Football (TV show),
    21, 255
Survivor (TV shows), 30, 168

Index

"Suspension Bridge Experiment," 134
Sutter, Ryan, 33, 37, 41, 51, 52, 202, 203, 275. *See also* Rehn (Sutter), Trista
Swiderski, Ed, 275
Swingers (movie), 33
Sycamore Tavern, L.A., 233, 234

tabloid stories, 84
Tacori, 52, 200, 202
Tatar, Maria, 190, 191
Tatum, Channing, 202
Taylor, James, 231, 232
tea lights, 12, 37
Telepictures Productions, 26, 27
Temptation Island (TV show), 28
"10 Times *The Bachelor* Shows Made Feminists Proud" *(The Washington Post)*, 253
therapist. *See* Selden, Catherine
Thiessen, Tiffani, 48
Thompson, Mark, 22
Tierney (TV news editor), 9, 11
Tilley, Becca, 256
Tinder, 69, 262
"Tink-Tink Spot," 117
Togetherness (TV show), 113
Tolbert, Tanner, 184, 228. *See also* Roper (Tolbert), Jade
Toronto Sun, 116
Total Divas (TV show), 94
Totally Hidden Video (TV show), 17–18
trade-outs, 129–31
Train, 187
Trainwreck (movie), 34
Trauger, Aleta, 104
Travolta, John, 124
trips (free) post-television, 228, 235
Trombetti, Susan, 237, 238–42, 243, 244
truth vs. lies, 224
Tumblr, 151
TVG, 30–31
Twitter/Tweets, 2, 3, 95, 105, 150, 151, 184, 212, 214, 215, 228, 242, 247, 248, 256–57, 258, 262
Two and a Half Men (TV show), 113

Uber, 242, 244
ultraviolet wands, 73
under the covers (sex), 171–82
"under-the-stars thing," 10
Unglert, Dean, 225, 256
UnREAL (TV show), 36, 248–49, 252–53
UPN, 25
US Department of Justice, 91–92
Us Weekly, 116, 177, 212

Vachon, Christine, 250
validation from romance, 5, 34, 89–90, 195, 264
values, successful relationships, 208
Vanity Fair, 16, 17, 19, 20, 22, 27, 47, 48
Variety, 44, 253
Vaughn, Vince, 33
Veep (TV show), 169
Velvick, Byron, 272
Ventiera, Vinny, 182
ventral tegmental area of brain, 135
VH1, 104
Viall, Nick, 32, 34, 92–93, 127–28, 140, 174–75, 176, 180, 181, 219, 223–24, 233, 274
Vietnam, 57, 171
View, The (TV show), 196
Viewers for Quality Television, 21
viewing parties, 1, 53, 151, 247–48, 263, 264
Villaca, Bella, 229, 230
Villa de la Vina. *See* mansion
VIRGIN Bachelor. *See* Lowe, Sean
virgins and sex, 76
Vogue, 83, 254
Vorbeck, Alexandra (Fleiss's first wife), 16, 40, 43, 48
voyeuristic quality, 112, 168, 169

WAGS (TV show), 94
Wahlberg, Donnie, 209–10
Wall, The (TV show), 68
Wallace, Mike, 59

Index

Walt Disney Company, The, 186, 187, 189, 190, 242, 243
Warner Bros., 12, 26, 98, 124, 182, 259, 260
Washington Post, The, 45, 253
Watch What Happens Live (TV show), 65
wedding industry, 202–3, 234
Wedding Paper Divas, 234
Wedding Planner, The (movie), 189
weekly viewing parties, 1, 53, 151, 247–48, 263, 264
Weiss, Mindy, 202, 234, 235
West Wing, The (TV show), 130, 184
WE tv, 221
We Were Feminists Once (Zeisler), 176
Who Wants to Be a Millionaire? (TV show), 19, 183
Who Wants to Marry a Multi-Millionaire?: A Television Phenomenon (special), 22, 23
Who Wants to Marry a Multi-Millionaire? (special), 19–25, 26, 27, 31, 47. *See also Bachelor, The* (TV show)
"Why Feminists Are Unabashedly Obsessed with *The Bachelor*" *(Vogue),* 254
why I'm a fan. *See also* Bachelor franchise; Bachelor Nation; reality television
  Allison Williams, 53–54
  Amy Schumer, 33–34
  Diablo Cody, 140–41
  Donnie Wahlberg, 209–10
  Heidi and Spencer Pratt, 94–95
  Jason Ritter, 223–24
  Joshua Malina, 183–84
  Melanie Lynskey, 112–13
  Nikki Glaser, 75–76

Patti Stanger, 245–46
Paul Scheer, 168–69
"Why We Fell in Love" *(Us Weekly),* 212
Wicked (Broadway show), 209
Wild Orchid, 69
William Morris, 19
Williams, Allison, 53–54, 248
Will You Accept This Podcast?, 256
"Will You Accept This Rose" Bento Box, 261
Wilson, Ann, 123
Wilson, Jennifer, 207, 272
Wire, The (TV show), 183
Witherspoon, Reese, 11
Womack, Brad, 53, 103, 115, 187, 198, 218, 273
"Women Tell All" (specials), 1, 32, 151–52
Wong, Andrea, 28
Woodstock, 57
Woolery, Chuck, 61–62, 64
World's Deadliest Volcanoes (special), 18
World Series, 130
World's Meanest People Caught on Tape, The (special), 18–19
World's Scariest Police Shootouts (special), 18

Xanax, 171

Young Adult (movie), 141

Zeisler, Andi, 176, 254–55, 256
"zhuzh," 36
Zimmer, Constance, 36
Zorn, Ben, 181
Zucker, Jeff, 28

About the Author

Amy Kaufman is a staff writer at the *Los Angeles Times*, where she has covered film, celebrity, and pop culture since 2009. On the beat, she reports from industry events like the Academy Awards, the Sundance Film Festival, and the Grammys. In addition to profiling hundreds of stars—Lady Gaga, Julia Roberts, Stevie Nicks, Jane Goodall—she has broken major investigative stories on sexual harassment in Hollywood. Amy currently lives in Los Angeles with her Australian shepherd, Riggins, and dreams of living in a Laurel Canyon tree house.